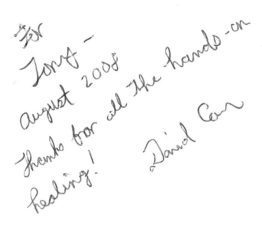

For
Tony –
August 2008
Thanks for all the hands-on
healing! David Carr

D0758891

FULL·TIME

FULL.

A SOCCER STORY

ALAN TWIGG

TIME

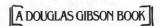
A DOUGLAS GIBSON BOOK

McClelland & Stewart

LIBRARY AND ARCHIVES CANADA CATALOGUING IN PUBLICATION

Twigg, Alan, 1952–
Full-time : a soccer story / Alan Twigg.

ISBN 978-0-7710-8645-8

1. Soccer teams – Canada.   2. Soccer players – Canada – Biography.
3. Older athletes – Canada – Biography. 4. Twigg, Alan, 1952–. 5. Soccer.
I. Title.

GV944.C3T95 2008   796.334092'271   C2007-906295-4

We acknowledge the financial support of the Government of Canada through
the Book Publishing Industry Development Program and that of the
Government of Ontario through the Ontario Media Development
Corporation's Ontario Book Initiative. We further acknowledge the support of
the Canada Council for the Arts and the Ontario Arts Council for our
publishing program.

Typeset in Scala by M&S, Toronto
Printed and bound in Canada

A Douglas Gibson Book

This book is printed on acid-free paper that is 100% recycled,
ancient-forest friendly (100% post-consumer recycled).

McClelland & Stewart Ltd.
75 Sherbourne Street
Toronto, Ontario
M5A 2P9
www.mcclelland.com

1 2 3 4 5   12 11 10 09 08

To Tara

instead of a novel

ALSO BY ALAN TWIGG

Thompson's Highway: British Columbia's Fur Trade, 1800–1850
Understanding Belize: A Historical Guide
Aboriginality: The Literary Origins of British Columbia, Vol. 2
Cuba: A Concise History for Travellers
First Invaders: The Literary Origins of British Columbia
Cuba: 101 Top Historical Sites
Intensive Care: A Memoir
Twigg's Directory of 1,001 B.C. Writers
Strong Voices: Conversations with 50 Canadian Authors
Vander Zalm: From Immigrant to Premier
Vancouver and Its Writers
Hubert Evans: The First Ninety-Three Years
For Openers: Conversations With 24 Canadian Writers

You don't stop playing football because you get old,
you get old because you stop playing football.
– Sir Stanley Matthews

I will write my life as if it were a love story, for who shall say it is not?
It began with my great love of football and it will end the same.
– Ferenc Puskas

ETERNAL COMBAT:
THE LURE OF LUBAANTUM

The roots of our Soccer Tribe lie deep in our primeval past.
– Desmond Morris

Two years ago, I didn't have any idea I would write a book about soccer. I was in the mountains of southern Belize, at the ruins of Lubaantum, standing at the centre of a Mayan ball court. There were stone grandstands on both sides, surrounded by the jungle.

The grass at midfield was lush, birds were singing, and I wanted to run. It was easy to imagine the ebb and flow of a soccer-like game, played with a rubber ball, that was invented by Q'eqchí natives before Christ was born. That odd sensation of feeling at home in a foreign setting was a form of time travelling.

Little has changed at Lubaantum since the days when the Franciscan monk Fray de Benavente accompanied the conquistador Cortez on his journey to Honduras from Mexico City, passing through present-day Guatemala and the southern edge of present-day Belize in 1525. "The Indians run and jump so much that it is as if the balls have quicksilver within," wrote the Spanish friar, perhaps the continent's first soccer journalist. "I don't understand how, when the balls hit the ground, they are sent into the air with such incredible bounce."

The setting is postcard perfect. Should Hollywood ever make a movie about the game's first two superstars – the mythological ballplaying twins Xbalanque and Hunahpu – Lubaantum would be ideal. All they would have to do is decide whether David Beckham would play Xbalanque or Hunahpu.

As I stood there, itching to run for a ball, imagining those heroic twins – the forerunners of Ferenc Puskas and Alfredo Di Stéfano, soccer's most dynamic duo in the flesh – outwitting their opponents and winning favour with the gods, it first dawned on me that I should try to write about how soccer connects us. Obviously I would not be approaching the subject from the vantage point of a famous player or an accredited sports journalist. Instead I would undertake a private investigation from my perspective as a Canadian who still plays enthusiastically – and relatively well – in his mid-fifties.

At least I had a uniquely unpublished viewpoint. Canadian men have appeared in the World Cup precisely once. Canada is one of the few so-called developed nations never to have scored a World Cup goal in men's competition. We drift on the outskirts of the soccer universe, like Uranus and discredited Pluto (no longer a planet), always ranked near the bottom of the world's top one hundred teams. Canadians are mostly beneath the underdogs, so who would care? And who would even take a chance on publishing such a book?

A game plan was needed.

First, to get his attention, I told my agent that if soccer skills and writing talents could be combined and somehow measured mathematically, I'd probably have a higher score than Pelé or Maradona (both of whom were close to being illiterate). Secondly, I pointed out that Canada doesn't have any serious soccer books other than instructional guides, even though more Canadians play soccer than hockey – and it's been that way for years. Thirdly, my Vancouver team had an international match set up against former professionals from Spain's First Division.

The Cinderella angle won the day. We were told our big game in Spain would be played in a converted bullring in Granada, home to the Alhambra. Already our opponents were taunting us, saying they would humiliate us like matadors. Being Canadians, we naturally assumed this remark was made in jest.

The whole world might not be watching, but some of our wives would be there, reminding us to wear sunscreen.

⚽

At Lubaantum, on clear days, you can see the Caribbean Sea, thirty kilometres away. I arrived in the late afternoon, when there was a slight chill in the air, and clouds were threatening to burst. My driver, Pablo Bouchub, an herbalist from Punta Gorda, parked on an embankment that was greasy with mud. Ours was the only vehicle.

We picked our way down into a green ravine, about two hundred metres wide at the base – it must have once been a riverbed – then ascended the slippery slope on the far side.

The most impressive Mayan ruins, in terms of size and grandeur, can be found at Tikal, in northeastern Guatemala, and the world's largest Mayan ball court is at Chichén Itzá, in the Yucatán, but neither can match the eeriness of Lubaantum in the mist, where, magically, it is still possible to wander the grounds as the sole visitor.

Although Lubaantum is one of seventeen major Mayan archaeological sites in Belize open to the public, there is no designated walkway into the place. There isn't any signage, just a small administration office. Five Mayan women, traditionally dressed, were seated patiently on the cement veranda of the park office, like human gargoyles, waiting for a gringo tourist to finally appear. None of them made eye contact as I approached. Nobody spoke.

From reading guidebooks and writing my own history of Belize, I knew there were still about 5 million Mayans in northern Central America. The continuity of the past was severely disrupted in the 1980s when Ronald and Nancy Reagan decided to export their Just Say No message. To stifle the cultivation of marijuana called Belize Breeze, CIA-hired planes sprayed Belizean fields with paraquat, preventing farmers around Lubaantum from placing their plastic garbage bags full of marijuana on the back roads to find a few dollars left in exchange.

Belizeans responded by turning their coastal paradise into one of the world's major transshipment points for cocaine. Ever since then, poorly policed powerboaters have used the hundreds of islands along the Northern Hemisphere's longest barrier reef to evade capture, mimicking the nautical manoeuvres of pirates such as Henry Morgan and Blackbeard, and Belize City, said to be built atop rum bottles, has reverted into being one of the most dangerous cities on the planet. The Q'eqchí Maya around Lubaantum have reverted to being a forgotten people.

"The Maya gave the world the concept of zero," their leader, Gregorio Ch'oc, told me, "and in return for it, they got zero." So I could hardly ignore the five women who had been waiting patiently for a tourist to finally appear. Yet how could I buy trinkets from just one of the five women? I was charmed by their eyes-averted timidity, and I felt sorry for them. I imagined them walking home to their families without anything to show for their long day of waiting on the cement. Pablo understood my dilemma, but he stood aside.

Impatient to see the ball court, I decided to give each of them the same amount of money, but not to buy anything. As soon as I walked away, I worried that I might have insulted them, as if they were beggars.

I barely heard Pablo lecturing about plants and trees as he led the way into Lubaantum. The further he went with his spiel, explaining how Mayans had excelled as astronomers and mathematicians, the more I wished he would shut up. "I wrote a history of Belize," I wanted to blurt out, but I refrained from making that mistake.

I've learned that an historian is someone who regurgitates other people's words, and takes longer to do it than a journalist does. I have also learned that local knowledge should always count more than book knowledge. So when Pablo insisted that a team of archaeologists from Ontario had got it all wrong, and that Lubaantum's largest plaza was really a ball court, I took him seriously. Thanks to Pablo's vociferous arguments, the park authorities had relented and removed a sign designating the field as a plaza. There were two other indisputable ball courts at Lubaantum, but the largest open area had the grandeur of a Roman theatre. Whether Pablo was right or not, here I could *feel* the atmosphere of a violent athletic contest. Here Pablo could point to slanted stones, offset from the bleachers, where he believed players had bounced the ball to make it airborne. I didn't fully appreciate all of Pablo's theory, but I admired his passion.

Few British-based books on football – or soccer – bother to mention in any detail how the Mayans of Meso-America developed their highly physical and long-lasting game in which players from two opposing teams tried to move a rubber ball without touching it with their hands. The object of Mayan soccer was to propel the ball – with their feet, hips, chests, and, presumably, heads – through one of several metal rings that were mounted on walls, like sideways basketball hoops.

After the warlike Toltecs successfully invaded Chichén Itzá around 800 AD, bringing with them human sacrifice, the games got rough. Members of the losing team were sometimes killed, or the captain of the losing team was sacrificed to the gods. Of course, interpretations vary from site to site across the wide-ranging former Mayan empire. Every game wasn't do or die. Sacrifices did not occur in the western Mexico area. They mostly occurred in the Yucatán and the more southerly locations in present-day Guatemala and Belize.

I am not a transcendentalist. I do not believe in life after death, and my capacity for ESP is nil. I have never astral travelled. But, standing alone in the middle of that ball court at Lubaantum, questions darted like the exotic birds around us: Why do men build places like this? What compels men to defeat one another, to seek glory, like rutting goats high on adrenalin? What is the nature of human sacrifice?

Less grandly, why have I returned to playing competitive soccer in my fifties? How can soccer be so barbaric and aesthetically pleasing all at once? Why don't more women think we are ridiculous?

Pablo obligingly took some photos of me, posing like a fool at midfield, where I usually play. My camera had been stolen two days earlier, north of Placencia, so he promised to send them to me later – which he did.

At Lubaantum I felt an uplifting camaraderie with those ghosts who had chased and kicked a spherical object with all the single-minded verve of a dog chasing a stick. If I closed my eyes, I could hear them shouting encouragement to their teammates beneath the jungle canopy, and cursing their adversaries for good measure, the way I did every Sunday morning with my team, the Legends.

On the jet fuel of testosterone, it was an easy journey through time from Lubaantum to Granada. You don't need to partake of the local weed to feel yourself transported from 800 AD to the glorious moment when you lace up your boots to do battle with some guy who used to play for Real Madrid.

As I listened to the rustling of the wind, I knew if I had lived at Lubaantum, I would have risked life and limb too. Competing for glory in the middle of the ninth or tenth century would have been an inescapable fate, just as it had been for me growing up in a suburb in a sedate country in the middle of the twentieth century.

All over the planet we are obsessed by the allure of eternal combat. At some gawdawful, archaic, and even monstrous level, we can't help ourselves. We want to play soccer – or

Pablo Bouchub

I visited several ball courts in Lubaantum in southern Belize, and this one was the smallest.

something like it – to the death. The attraction is so potent for some of us that we are willing to spend about six thousand dollars apiece in order to travel to southern Spain to play one game before we give up the ghost.

At Lubaantum, as I stood at midfield and it finally began to rain, I knew my animal desire to kick a ball and chase it was deeply embedded, and no amount of rationalizing was going to change that. When I'm ninety years old, I'll still have an eye for a pretty girl, and if an errant soccer ball rolls my way, I'll still have the urge to kick it.

Playing soccer passionately is either hugely pathetic or frighteningly noble. It can be one or the other, but never somewhere in-between. If you want to play in-between, don't bother showing up.

PART ONE

SOCCER IN CANADA

Frances Metcalf

Fidel Bacelic, our best player.

GROWING UP SOCCER-POOR

Football is a language everyone can speak. – Roberto Baggio

Pelé and Maradona and Garrincha and Ronaldinho grew up in dirt-poor neighbourhoods, but they were soccer-rich. The South American soccer federation, CONMEBOL, was founded in 1916, before any other continental association. Ever since Uruguay won two Olympic goal medals in 1924 and 1928, the South Americans have been equal with the Europeans in terms of soccer knowledge and skill. By comparison, most North Americans have grown up soccer-poor.

When I was living for my Saturday mornings, high on the drug of anticipation, hoping to score goals and get my name in the local paper, I knew next to nothing about the sport I played. In the 1950s, those of us who were raised on the West Coast of Canada, separated from the rest of the world by the Rocky Mountains, inherited a tendency to believe everything we did was original, unblemished by history.

I played most of my games at Ambleside Park near a shopping centre called Park Royal, not knowing Ambleside and

Park Royal were places that already existed in England. In my youth all teams used the 2–3–5 formation, not knowing England had adopted the 2–3–5 formation for its national team in 1884, followed by the Scots in 1887.

We never dreamed of playing in the World Cup, for the simple reason that we had never heard of it. The only Cup we knew was the Stanley Cup, for hockey. Our netminder was called a goalie, like in hockey, never a keeper. We didn't have a striker; we had a centre forward. A stopper was something you put in a sink. A derby was a horse race in Kentucky or a hat. A clean sheet meant laundry.

Then one day my father took me to see an astonishing documentary film in the gymnasium at the West Vancouver recreation centre. As soon as they turned out the lights, I had an eerie premonition that this footage would prove nearly as unforgettable as those black and white newsreels of concentration camps. That night we saw images from a 1954 soccer tournament in Switzerland and a 1958 tournament in Sweden. The 1954 film featured the formidable Hungarians led by Ferenc Puskas, the "Galloping Major." The 1958 film showed a grinning, seventeen-year-old Brazilian who, for some unknown reason, had only one name.

And they called it football.

Around that time a German-born coach told my parents I should go to play in Europe. He said it was the only way to guarantee that I would continue to get better, to realize my potential. He volunteered to arrange it. He thought I could make it professionally.

This was the early 1960s. I would have been about eleven or twelve. In those days, we played until age sixteen and that was it. Therefore, the essence of all sports, except hockey and

In days of yore, I was a threat to score – no more. This game was played at Ambleside Park in West Vancouver.

baseball and the brand of American football that was played by the B.C. Lions and Toronto Argonauts, was amateurism, as preached by the Olympics. One of my sports heroes was Abebe Bikila, the Ethiopian who won the marathon at the Rome Olympics in 1960, running barefoot. I also liked Bobby Orr, who wore number 4, and Hank Aaron, number 44.

It wasn't possible to have soccer dreams. My parents were middle class, but barely. People who tried to play sports for a living were hopeless cases, like actors. They only did so because they weren't capable of being doctors or lawyers. The meaning of life was upward mobility. The idea of going to Europe for a professional soccer career was so far-fetched that it was not even lightly considered. England, maybe. But Germany? Few people imagined that there would ever be an Owen Hargreaves.

The last thing our family needed was another separation anxiety. My parents, Betty and Art, who had dutifully attended my games, rain or shine, were caught inside the prolonged process of their divorce. How could I possibly go east of the Rockies? I might as well have dreamt of being an astronaut at Cape Canaveral.

My parents kept clippings. One year we won a provincial championship. Another year I played on an all-star team from North Vancouver, outside of my district. Trophies were stored in cardboard boxes (never on display, because that would be boasting). My upbringing was profoundly Canadian. To want anything more from life would be tempting fate.

At seventeen I graduated from high school and looked around. My parents had split up, and I was painfully in love with a beautiful girl who was one year older than me. Rather than follow my brother to university, I went hitchhiking in Europe, where I tried to grow my first beard and read Herman Hesse novels. I tried to convince myself I was doing something courageous, but looking back at this period, sleeping in the Kennedy Airport terminal (because I was afraid to go into New York City) and taking the cheapest flight possible via Icelandic Airlines, landing in Luxembourg, then freezing my ass off in the Pyrenees, maybe I was just delaying the responsibilities of growing up.

Like millions of others, as a candidate for the counterculture, I had read *Be Here Now* by Baba Ram Dass. Soccer didn't exist anymore. The whole time I was over there, I never saw a game. It was one of the coldest European winters on record. From the Pyrenees I hitchhiked to southern Italy, temporarily lost my passport in Brindisi, and, in search of warmth, took ferries to Crete, where I lived in a cave at

Matala for six weeks. This was where Joni Mitchell later wrote a song entitled "Carey." I got beach tar on my feet, just like she did.

I essentially traded in the soccer ball for the guitar, assuming the latter might help me get girls. Although if I got one, I wasn't sure what I would do. I was still pining for the girl back home. That winter I read all of Dostoevsky's novels and lived like a pauper.

It was an endurance test, and one I was failing. I didn't visit any tourist attractions except the Parthenon. About six months later, I finally returned to Vancouver from my forty days and forty nights in the wilderness. After two or three shoebox novels, I married Tara. She was still one year older than me. She was twenty-two and I was twenty-one. We had a string of old cars and dogs, plus two children. I lived by my wits, wrote some books, published a quarterly newspaper. Around the midway point of my life, on some reptilian brain level, I realized I must make a choice: chase women or chase the ball.

I joined an over-thirties soccer team. I told everyone I was playing again because I couldn't abide jogging and I hated golf. The truth was I craved those Saturday mornings when I was six, when there was always something to look forward to, always something to dream about, when I could be the cock of the walk, and I missed the joy and the camaraderie of being on a team, the relief of being part of a struggle beyond myself.

A brain tumour operation intervened in 2001. About two years later, against the well-meaning advice of everyone, I showed up for an informal kick-around at Carnarvon school on a Sunday morning, dreadfully out of shape, and I managed to score twice. A congenial character with a clipboard asked me if I was interested in playing on his over-fifties team. I was very surprised to learn from Ken Falk that there was a well-established league for players fifty years or older.

I haven't scored twice since.

In 2005 we went to France and played well, beating various village teams in the Toulouse area, but I was sidelined by a serious thigh muscle tear, mostly relegated to serving as our coach. It was a dreadful experience, being unable to play. I craved an athletic opportunity for redemption.

In April 2006, the organizational mainstay behind our Point Grey club, Alan Cook, sent out this message:

Hey Guys,

Our trip to Spain next year is shaping up. Myles Ellis has set up a game for us in Granada, a small city just north of the coast near Malaga on the Spanish Riviera. Myles has relatives that live nearby and he is familiar with the town. Granada is away from the madding crowd and a little cooler.

Although it sounds a bit like lambs to the slaughter, we are playing against an old-timers team made up of ex–La Liga (Spanish First Division) players, a couple of whom are reported to have played for Real Madrid.

We will play them in a stadium in the evening under the lights. They have promised to announce it in the local paper (next to the ad for the bullfights). There will be other games arranged, but that sounds like the big test.

Having become the manager of one of our two teams in the over-fifties, along with Alan Cook, only I knew that Alan had judiciously edited out one sentence from Myles's communiqué:

I think they see our defeat on the pitch as certain as the bull's death in the ring.

That's how we got the ball rolling. I began to insist that we must have at least one game with a "level playing field." I advised Alan that I would gather the ages of our players and send the median age of our version of the Mackenzie–Papineau Battalion – Canadian volunteers who fought in the Spanish Civil War – to Myles, our bilingual organizer. In this way, I hoped and presumed, Myles would be able to ensure we would have at least one fair contest, a chance to test ourselves against European peers.

THE HISTORY OF SOCCER
IN ONE CHAPTER

Serious sport has nothing to do with fair play. It is bound up with hatred, jealousy, boastfulness, disregard of all rules and sadistic pleasure in witnessing violence. In other words, it is war minus the shooting.
– George Orwell

On St. Mary's, in the Scilly Isles – located forty-five kilometres southwest of the United Kingdom's most southwesterly mainland point – the Garrison Gunners and the Woolpack Wanderers have been playing all their games against each other for forty consecutive years. They play thirteen games per season. Every year the same referee volunteers to orchestrate the same match-up on the same windswept field.

The weather is too unpredictable to allow the island's footballers to compete in the Cornish Sunday League on the English mainland, so every year two captains divide the island's forty available players. Every one of the island's sixteen hundred inhabitants can tell you the Gunners have won the league title slightly more often than the Wanderers, and one championship was shared. It's like the Montagues and the Capulets, or the Hatfields and the McCoys, with pints at the pub afterwards – and some basic human need fulfilled.

What on earth compelled British and German soldiers during the First World War to disobey their superiors and declare a truce on Christmas Day in order to exchange gifts and play an impromptu "friendly" in no man's land, then retreat to their godforsaken trenches in the French countryside on December 26, in order to set about blowing each other to bits? Was there a referee? Did those guys bother keeping score?

If soccer is the world's most-played sport, can connections be made between our natural instinct to kick something and our natural instinct to fight? The Romanian philosopher Emil Cioran, quoted in Tim Parks's *A Season with Verona*, once wrote, "The civilizing passage from blows to insults was no doubt necessary, but the price was high. Words will never be enough. We will always be nostalgic for violence and blood."

Maybe the Mayans got it right. Maybe it would be better if the loser were killed. Maybe that's what we're really after.

After my visit to Lubaantum, I became increasingly curious about the global origins of the world's most popular sport. The more I learned, the more I came to realize that an obsession to play or watch soccer is a socially acceptable form of madness in most countries. The validity of soccer as an integral human activity in most countries seems to be right up there with eating and sleeping.

Sport can be as fundamental as Earth, Water, Fire, and Air. Sex is sacred, Taxes are here to stay, scientists aren't making much progress getting rid of Death, but in order to elevate humans out of our primordial soup, I boldly predict Religion will be jettisoned before we are willing to renounce Sport. Certainly, in free societies, it seems more people are willing to debate the validity of Religion than the validity of Sport.

Every day, in every society, all over the planet, we collectively seek the adrenalin rush of *beating the other guy* – and yet we shake our heads in dismay at the proliferation of war and violent crimes. George Orwell wrote in 1945,

I am always amazed when I hear people saying that sport creates goodwill between the nations, and that if only the common peoples of the world could meet one another at football or cricket, they would have no inclination to meet on the battlefield.

Even if one didn't know from concrete examples (the 1936 Olympic Games, for instance) that international sporting contests lead to orgies of hatred, one could deduce it from general principles. . . . If you wanted to add to the vast fund of ill-will existing in the world at this moment, you could hardly do it better than by a series of football matches between

Jews and Arabs, Germans and Czechs, Indians and British, Russians and Poles, and Italians and Jugoslavs, each match to be watched by a mixed audience of 100,000 spectators.

⊛

Published in London in 1906, *The Book of Football* suggests that the origins of Association football (a.k.a. soccer) are Biblical, asserting that Adam and Eve could have played footie with an apple in the Garden of Eden. For those who are atheists, it's much easier to imagine Genghis Khan and his mates playing a spirited game of polo with a severed head, minus their horses.

In *Manwatching*, Desmond Morris suggests anthropological links to soccer, equating the thrills of the sport to the pleasures of pack hunting. "Viewed in this way," he writes, "a game of football becomes a reciprocal hunt. Each team of players, or 'hunting pack,' tries to score a goal by aiming a ball, or 'weapon' at a defended goal-mouth, or 'prey.'"

Picking up where Freud left off, Morris also cites the sexual element. "The essence of the ancient hunting pattern was that it involved a great deal of physical exercise combined with risk and excitement. It involved a long sequence with a build-up, with strategy and planning, with skill and daring and ultimately with a grand climax and a moment of triumph."

Desmond, old boy, that's a lovely quote, but presumably you have never watched a nil–nil NASL draw on your telly.

For the record, the earliest known football fatality was recorded by Cicero (106–43 BC) after a ball was errantly kicked into a Roman barbershop, resulting in the death of a luckless man receiving a shave. Many would argue strenuously that it has been a cutthroat game ever since.

Before the Roman and Mayan empires, as far back as 500 BC, the Chinese played a game called *tsu chu*. Players took turns kicking a ball through a narrow opening between two poles, more than ten metres high, adorned with coloured silks. It is not known whether the town crier shouted the Chinese equivalent of "Goooooaaaaaaaaaaal!!!!!!!" Five centuries later, Li Yu (50–130 AD) hung a Taoist poem on a bamboo goalpost. "A round ball and a square goal suggest the shape of the Yin and the Yang. The ball is like the full moon and the two teams stand opposed."

Li Yu's poetic full moon evocation has yet to be adopted by the movers and shakers at FIFA, the Fédération Internationale de Football Association, founded in 1904, or the International Olympic Committee (IOC), sponsors of a goal medal competition for soccer since 1900. FIFA and the IOC are both highly conservative and profitable organizations, created by Frenchmen, that maintain cloistered corporate headquarters in Switzerland, a Taoist poetry–free zone where the League of Nations had its headquarters and the Nazis stashed their loot.

Around the time they were supposedly inventing democracy, the Greeks played footie with a ball made of hair and linen, sewn together with string, before they went high-tech with an inflated pig bladder wrapped in leather. The ox- or pig-bladder ball, encased in leather, remained *de rigueur* for about two thousand years, until rubber bladders were manufactured.

The prolific playwright Antiphanes of Macedonia, around 35 BC, described a throwing and kicking game called *episkyros* that was separately played by both nude men and women in Ancient Greece. At the National Museum of Athens you can see a marble relief of an older *episkyros* player showing a boy how to balance a ball on his upraised thigh. This image appears on the trophy presented annually to the top club in Europe.

Just as Romans adopted and renamed Greek gods, Romans adapted *episkyros* to create a new game called *harpastum*, using a smaller and harder ball. Clement of Alexander described two teams, consisting of five to twelve players per side, simultaneously competing to maintain possession of the ball in their half of a rectangular field. Popular during the reign of Julius Caesar, *harpastum* was a game of endurance, skill, and passing strategies, often played before spectators in a stadium, to maintain the fitness of soldiers. The main rule for this rugby-like encounter was that only the player in possession of the ball could be attacked.

When the Roman legions reached the British Isles, at least one recorded game of *harpastum* was played between the invaders and the natives, giving rise to violent forms of ball games that evolved into football. According to British folklore, English workmen dug up the skull of a detested Dane in a former battlefield and kicked it around, *circa* 1075 AD. How they knew that skull belonged to an invading Dane is not to be questioned; the story endures as one of the earliest bits of propaganda to suggest that soccer is deeply English.

In his history of London, published in 1174, William Fitzstephen, biographer of Thomas à Becket, described how London youths ventured into the fields "for the very popular game of ball. The students of each school have their own ball; the workers from each city craft are also carrying their balls."

Games of football were initially chaotic, outdoor brawls involving hundreds of players. Elders were aroused with "a stirring of natural heat by viewing so much activity and by participation in the joys of unrestrained youth." So from its outset, football was a spectator sport, more akin to cockfighting than ballet. Kick or be kicked.

In 1287 the Synod of Exeter banned "unseemly sports" from churchyards. "Forasmuch as there is a great noise in the city caused by Hustling over large balls," warned the Mayor of London and King Edward ɪɪ's ministers in 1314, "from which many evils may arise, which God forbid, we command and forbid, on behalf of the King, on pain of imprisonment, such game to be used in the city in future."

Similar edicts were issued by King Richard ɪɪ in 1389 and by King Henry ɪv in 1401. In France rough ball games were similarly banned by Philippe v in 1319 and Charles v in 1369. Initially the ball was carried into an opponent's zone, as in rugby or American football, but by the late fifteenth century it was also being kicked.

In 1519, having worked as headmaster at Eton College and Winchester, William Horman provided one of the earliest English references to football in his Latin textbook, the *Vulgaria*: "We wyll playe with a ball full of wynde."

In 1583 Philip Stubbs wrote in *Anatomy of Abuses*, "Football . . . causeth fighting, brawling, contention, quarrel-picking, murder, homicide and great effusion of bloode, as daily experience teacheth." Writing in Latin in the mid-1600s, poet and scholar Robert Matthew concocted a line translatable as "We may play quoits, or handball, or bat-and-ball, or football; these games are innocent and lawful."

An "innocent and lawful" tradition of village street ball and field ball endures in the British Isles to this day. Every year annual outdoor contests are held, sometimes between married males and unmarried males, or with teams divided by local geography. Given that more than five of these outdoor affairs are held on Shrove Tuesdays, some sociologists have suggested links to pre-Christian fertility rites. According to Mircea Eliade in *Patterns in Comparative Religion*, "The contest and fights which take place in so many places in the spring or at harvest time undoubtedly spring from the primitive notion that blows, contests, rough games between the sexes and so on, all stir up and increase the energies of the whole universe."

Riotous, beer-induced football rites are still being staged at Kirkwall, Orkney; Duns, Borders; Workington, Cumbria; Alnwick, Northumberland; Sedgefield, County Durham; Atherstone, Warwickshire; Corfe Castle, Dorset; and St. Columb, Cornwall. At games held in Derbyshire, the goals are five kilometres apart, separated by streams. In Sedgefield – where a Pamplona-like madness attracts as many as a thousand participants – the game cannot commence until the ball is first passed through a small ring, known as the Bullring, on the village green, a tradition that reminds us of the rings on Mayan ball courts.

An Aboriginal form of football called *pahsaheman* was recorded in North America in 1610. Not to be outdone, the French concocted a football-like equivalent called *soule*, the Germans played *Knappen*, Inuit in the Arctic played *kalagut* (weather permitting), Russians played *lapta*, and the Japanese had a sport called *kemari*, a ball game similar to the non-competitive sport of "keepie uppie" in which players in a circle try to keep one ball from dropping to the ground.

In Australia a ball game identified as *marn grook*, played by Aborigines, allegedly served as the forerunner of

Australian Rules Football, which also draws heavily from Irish influences. The rules of Gaelic football were codified in Ireland by Maurice Davin in 1887.

The earliest football-like rules were codified for a costumed version of a sixteenth-century game invented in Florence. In 1580 Count Giovanni de' Bardi di Vernio wrote guidelines entitled "Discorso sopra 'l giuco del Calcio Fiorentino." Leonardo da Vinci was an avid spectator of *o calcio storico* (kickball in costume), the Florentine game played by young aristocrats in Piazza della Novere or Piazza di Santa Croce during the period between Epiphany and Lent. Machiavelli, Pope Clement vii, Pope Leo ix, and Pope Urban viii were reputedly all *calcio* players. Their tactics must have been interesting.

Calcio entered the history books when Florentines ignored a siege by the troops of Charles v, Holy Roman Emperor, in order to play and rip their own expensive garments to shreds. Although the non-political violence of unrestricted football was mainly destructive of property, authorities in most countries have recognized how soccer and militarism can be linked as twin passions. If mobilized by radical or government forces, gangs of marauding youths can be formidable forces for revolution, or for repression.

Anyone who has thumbed through Franklin Foer's engaging but misleadingly titled *How Soccer Explains the World* will learn how soccer hooliganism has been manipulated by powermongers around the globe. As football historian James Walvin observed, "Quite apart from the injuries to players, medieval observers were more alarmed by the wider social unrest caused by football. . . . It was, in brief, a game which at times came perilously close to testing to the limits the social control of local and national governments."

King Edward ii condemned "hustling over large balls, from which many evils may arise," in 1314. Edward iii dismissed football as one of several games that was "stupid and utterly useless" in 1349. Henry iv signed an edict against the game in 1410. James i of Scotland banned "fute-ball" in 1424. Henry vi officially denounced it in 1447. It was banned from Oxford in 1555. Queen Elizabeth banned the game from the City of London in 1572.

But soccer players endured, as impossible to eradicate as rats. By 1615 there were reports of "greate disorders and tumults" caused by football in London. In Manchester, long before Alec Ferguson was knighted, "a companye of lewde and disordered persons" were reportedly engaged in the unlawful practice of "playinge with the footbale in ye streets of the a said towne breakinge many men's windows and glasse."

As early as 1592, Shakespeare had added the word *football* to the lexicon of English theatre, when a character in *The Comedy of Errors* complained:

> Am I so round with you, as you with me,
> that like a football you do spurn me thus?
> You spurn me hence, and he will spurn me hither;
> If I last in this service, you must case me in leather.

Later, in *King Lear*, the Earl of Kent remarked, "Nor tripped neither, you base football player!"

After Charles ii approved the game in 1681, football gradually became a respectable pastime for the upper classes. T. Frankland's *Nugae Etonenses*, published in 1766, contains a reference to the "Football Fields" of Eton. After one player was killed during a Shrove Tuesday match in 1796, at Derby, authorities alleged the game was "disgraceful to humanity and civilization, subversive of good order and Government and destructive of the Morals, Properties and very lives of our Inhabitants," but the sport could not be suppressed because rich men's sons had entered the fray.

In time the English custom of playing unregulated football in the streets fell victim to urban sprawl and industrialization. As fewer common areas were available for wide-ranging games of football, boundaries had to be added to the game. The death blow for unregulated football was the Highways Act of 1835, prohibiting football on public highways. Perpetrators could be subject to a fine of forty shillings.

The games gradually became regulated and locally controlled, giving rise to the birth of the world's first and oldest football club, Sheffield Football Club, founded in 1857. Most historians like to suggest the English game had its codified origins soon thereafter. Representatives of twelve English teams signed a gentleman's agreement in a London tavern in 1863, consenting to adopt a set of rules that had been drafted at the University of Cambridge in 1846. So by the middle of the nineteenth century, carrying the ball and kicking your opponent were officially disallowed. "Kicks must be aimed only at the ball." This gave rise to the nuances of the modern game with eleven players per side.

In 1871 it was decided one player, the goalkeeper, could use his hands. The London-based Football Association also sponsored the first FA Cup final in 1871. Off-the-pitch referees were added to the game in 1872, the year Scotland hosted the first international soccer match versus England.

On an experimental basis, a wooden crossbar was added atop two goal posts, replacing the traditional belt or rope, in

1875. The throw-in was added by the English in 1882, the year in which four Home Nations (England, Scotland, Ireland, and Wales) formed the first international football association. The International Association Football Board (IAFB) insisted on the fixed crossbar and staged the first international football tourney, the Home Championships, won by the Scots in 1884.

Professionalism was resisted by many until it was legalized in 1885, the year Preston recorded the most lopsided FA Cup win, 26–nil versus Hyde. The first professional to appear for England had to wear a blue shirt while his teammates appeared in white. Real gentlemen didn't need to play for money, but winning gradually took precedence. The Scots, often credited with introducing positional play, would not allow professionalism in their games, so English managers travelled north and poached some of the better Scottish players. The Preston "Invincibles," under the management of Major William Sudell, soon had ten Scottish pros.

By 1891 Scotland was forced to accept professionalism, creating their Scottish League in 1893. Clubs evolved a transfer system whereby they had to pay an opposing team to acquire one of its players. The players themselves were not necessarily directly compensated. Maximum salary levels were imposed for each division, typically around three times the average salary in England.

Initially women were granted free entrance to soccer games in Scotland and England, but their increasing presence required admission fees by the mid-1880s. Women first played an organized soccer match in Inverness, Scotland, in 1888. The wonderfully named Nettie Honeyball – of whom you will hear more – organized the first women's match in England in 1895.

According to British academic James Walvin, who wrote *The Only Game: Football in Our Times,* there were 158 professional football clubs in Britain by 1914. The preceding year more than 120,000 spectators had watched Aston Villa beat Sunderland to win the FA Cup at Crystal Palace.

The parameters of the pitch were clearly outlined with lime by 1890, when nets were added behind each goal. The following year referees stepped onto the field to run alongside the players. Referees introduced the penalty kick, twelve paces from the goal line, to obviate the butcher tactics employed by defenders whenever the opposition got into scoring range. Too many players were being killed.

Scottish schoolteacher Alexander Watson Hutton is generally credited with introducing the game to Argentina in 1882. Buenos Aires had its own championship competition by 1893. Legend has it that Brazilian-born aristocrat and cricketer Charles Miller did much the same for Brazil when he brought two leather footballs from England to São Paulo in 1894. Ten years later São Paolo had its own league. Another Scottish teacher, William Leslie Poole, formalized the first Uruguayan football club within the Albion Cricket Club in 1893. Englishmen organized the first international football contest between Argentina and Uruguay, in Montevideo, in 1889.

The English began to lose their twentieth-century grip on both the rules and athletic superiority as early as 1904, when seven countries formed the Fédération Internationale de Football Association in Paris. When the organizers of FIFA offered the presidency of the fledgling body to England, as an enticement to join, the English snubbed them, giving rise to the presidency of a Frenchman, Robert Guérin.

When England finally did join FIFA in 1906, Guérin was replaced by Englishman Daniel Burley Woolfall, but political turmoil and economics scuttled any major growth. In the aftermath of the First World War, Dutchman Carl Hirschmann managed the floundering organization until Frenchman Jules Rimet took over as president in 1921. The English Football Association left FIFA in 1926.

Ever since then, England has failed to call the tune, regaining its global supremacy only once with its dramatic 4–2 extra-time victory over West Germany, at home, in 1966, captained by Bobby Moore.

⚽

David Goldblatt's impressively overwritten 978-page book, *The Ball Is Round*, is rife with examples of how football and violence have been linked. After the first major soccer catastrophe occurred at Ibrox Park in Glasgow in 1902, when a rebuilt terrace gave way, killing twenty-five people and wounding five hundred others, Glasgow gained the dubious distinction of playing host to the first soccer riot in 1909, at gigantic Hampden Park, a stadium that had attracted a record crowd of 121,452 spectators two years earlier.

In 1985, when Liverpool fans attacked Juventus fans during a European Champions Cup final at Heysel, Belgium, the alarmed Italian fans panicked and a wall collapsed, killing thirty-nine people. Four years later, in a karmic twist of fate, ninety-six Liverpool fans were crushed to death at

Hillsborough Stadium during their team's semifinal match with Nottingham Forest.

After the Hillsborough tragedy, authorities were suitably shocked and appalled. Academics studied hooliganism and published reports. Journalists infiltrated the violent gangs. Movies were made. Stadiums were reconfigured. Policing methods were improved. But the age-old reputation of soccer as a cauldron for violence remains dodgy.

Tim Parks quotes a nineteenth-century Italian, Giovanni Maria de' Bardi, who wrote: "Football is a public game of two groups of young men, on foot and unarmed, who pleasingly compete to move a medium-sized inflated ball from one end of the piazza to the other, for the sake of honour." But the honour of football is all too frequently sullied by vicious tackles, spitting, swearing, jersey pulling, fake injuries, fake penalties, and exaggerated displays of self-glorification. Hooliganism, game fixing, and stadium disasters have also become notorious.

The disastrous head-butting incident involving Zinedine Zidane and a foul-mouthed Italian defender at the World Cup final in 2006 was followed by the Italian game-fixing scandals of 2007. These embarrassments arose during a period when the game has become stultified by defensive tactics. Or as Edson Arantes do Nascimento (Pelé) once put it, "In my day we played to win; now, they play not to lose."

The average number of goals scored in recent World Cups has certainly been decreasing. The standard goal size for soccer – eight feet high, eight yards wide – evolved in accordance with the number of goals that were deemed generally desirable for a contest between two sides. Therefore, with the improved training, the increased size, and the acrobatic prowess of goaltenders at the highest levels of the game, it's rational to suggest the size of the soccer goal needs to be slightly increased.

⚽

The first World Cup was staged under Jules Rimet in Uruguay in July 1930 to mark the centenary of Uruguay's constitution. Rimet commissioned French sculptor Abel Lafleur to make a golden trophy known as the Goddess of Victory, but it became later known as the Coupe Jules Rimet. Although Uruguay's magnificent Centenario Stadium wasn't ready for the opening-round games, and only four European nations accepted Uruguay's all-expenses-paid invitation to participate, the host nation could declare its tournament a resounding political and economic success after beating its closest rival, Argentina, 4–2, in the first World Cup final.

It is often noted that Brazil's reputation for soccer supremacy, and Pelé's elevation to the world's first global superstar, was greatly enhanced by the fact that their 3–1 World Cup victory over Uruguay was the first World Cup final to be broadcast around the world in colour.

The economics of football altered drastically with the onset of television, corporate sponsorships, and club-related merchandising. The combination of these three revenue streams has eclipsed the traditional revenue source of match-day receipts in major markets.

As upper-echelon clubs gained greater revenues, transfer fees for players skyrocketed. Whereas the record transfer of one thousand pounds paid by Sunderland for Alf Common in 1905 equalled approximately thirteen years of average

English earnings, the record transfer fee paid by Manchester United for Juan Veron in 2001 matched approximately one thousand years of average English earnings. As revenues increased, players, the first of them Pelé, acquired agents to negotiate better salaries.

The advent of Pelé as a soccer icon increased the public appetite for great players. The importance of playing on a World Cup championship squad has increased with globalization, so the likes of Di Stéfano and George Best often don't get their due. Now that David Beckham is following in the steps of Pelé and ending his career in North America, where the most lucrative promotional deals can be made, perhaps he too, like Pelé, will start comparing himself to Beethoven and Michelangelo, and referring to himself in the third person.

The game is truly global. Even Canada, of all places, has hosted the world's second most important FIFA championship, the men's Under-21 tournament, and most of the world's soccer balls are now being made by Pakistan. But Britain still claims to be the primary source of the modern game.

The world's oldest soccer ball was discovered in the 1970s within the walls of a castle that once housed Mary, Queen of Scots. According to a 1999 Reuters report, "the ball – about a third the size of those used in today's very different game – was found hidden behind paneling in the Stirling Castle bedchamber of Mary, the Catholic pretender to Queen Elizabeth's throne in England." This 450-year-old pig's bladder, covered by deer hide, was shipped from the Smith Museum in Scotland to Germany in April 2006 for display at the World Cup tournament, the largest and most successful sporting event in the history of mankind.

That unprecedented extravaganza was held in June 2006 – exactly one year before my team played its own equivalent of the World Cup in Spain.

INTERVIEW WITH A MISTRESS #1

My relationship with the ball has grown into an intimate and enduring love affair. I can't keep it private any longer. After five decades, in honour of Nettie Honeyball, who founded the British Ladies Football Club in 1894, I have given my mistress an identity. Her pet name for me, in return, is Sir Stanley, a reference to Stanley Matthews.

I can only imagine that Nettie Honeyball was a passionate woman, on and off the field. In 1895 she said, "I founded the association late last year, with the fixed resolve of proving to the world that women are not the 'ornamental and useless' creatures men have pictured. I must confess, my convictions on all matters where the sexes are so widely divided are all on the side of emancipation, and I look forward to the time when ladies may sit in Parliament and have a voice in the direction of affairs, especially those which concern them most."

ALAN: Morning, Nettie.

NETTIE: Sir Stanley, I presume.

ALAN: I would have called, but I've been busy.

NETTIE: You mean you couldn't sneak away from the wife.

ALAN: I've never pretended things were going to be otherwise.

NETTIE: You spend so much more time with her. And she gets you on the holidays.

ALAN: How many times do you have to make me say it? I'm
         more passionate with you, for ninety minutes at a
         time.

NETTIE: I just wish you wouldn't leave me out in the cold like
         this. When you ignore me I get so . . .

ALAN: Depressed?

NETTIE: Deflated.

ALAN: I'm sorry, love. She doesn't like me to bring you into
         the house. It's much better if you stay out here in the
         shed, with the garden tools. She thinks you're dirty.

NETTIE: So what brings you out here in the moonlight? Are you
         feeling romantic? Or do you just want to take a leak in
         the fish pond?

ALAN: I came because I want to talk about us. About our rela-
         tionship.

NETTIE: What happened? Has your subscription to *Four Four
         Two* expired? Have you been reading *Cosmopolitan*?

ALAN: Remember last year when we went to France together?
         And we played in that tournament?

NETTIE: It was lovely.

ALAN: Well, this time we're going to Spain. To celebrate our
         anniversary.

NETTIE: You remembered!

ALAN: Yes. Soon it will be fifty years since I took you out on
         my own, in the backyard. The cherry tree had all those
         beautiful pink blossoms. We used that new stone wall
         my dad built.

NETTIE: And you were so gentle with me. And so devoted.

ALAN: I was very clumsy.

NETTIE: But your heart was in the right place. It was pure. It
         was innocent.

ALAN: And we can have that again, Nettie. I want it to be better than ever. This time our team will play against guys who played in the Spanish First Division. For Barcelona and Real Madrid.

NETTIE: *The* Real Madrid? The team David Beckham plays for?

ALAN: Yup. The New York Yankees of European football.

NETTIE: I'm impressed. They have won more Spanish league championships than any other team. They've got to be one of the most famous football teams on the planet.

ALAN: Right up there with Manchester United, Juventus, AC Milan, Bayern Munich, Boca Juniors, and Chelsea.

NETTIE: Will David Beckham show up to watch?

ALAN: Ah, I highly doubt it. He'll probably be back home in England with Posh Spice. Besides, we won't be playing in Madrid. We'll be farther south, in Granada, the place with the Alhambra.

NETTIE: By the Moorish walls?

ALAN: Yes, that's right. Yes, yes, yes. By the Moorish walls.

NETTIE: "He kissed me under the Moorish wall and I thought well as him as another –"

ALAN: We'll go to the beach. We'll drink sangria. We'll read Lorca.

NETTIE: "– and all the queer little streets and pink and blue and yellow houses and the rose gardens and the jessamine and geraniums and cactuses and Gibraltar as a girl where I was a Flower of the mountain yes when I put the rose in my hair like the Andalusian girls –"

ALAN: That's not Lorca. That's James Joyce.

NETTIE: "– and first I put my arms around him yes and drew him down to me so he could feel my breasts all

perfume yes and his heart was going like mad and yes I
said yes I will Yes."

ALAN: Nettie, I've given this matter a great deal of considera-
tion. There's something you need to hear. Something
really important.

NETTIE: Don't worry. I'm not naive. I won't be expecting you to
win.

ALAN: Of course not. We can't realistically expect to beat these
guys. That's part of the appeal. Playing against the odds.
We just want to prove that we can still compete. You
can't expect a bunch of guys from Vancouver, Canada, to
outdo a bunch of Spaniards who used to play professionally. But hopeless causes are the best kind. That's
why Norman Bethune went there to fight in the Spanish
Civil War. We should call our team the Bethunes.

NETTIE: But you guys won that tournament in the south of
France.

ALAN: That was different. We were playing teams from small
towns. We used Hans's son, who was in his late twenties, and also the French boyfriend of Serge's daughter.
And we borrowed a goalie.

NETTIE: You had Bill Allen, and he was in his seventies! And
you allowed Bruce's daughter and her friends to play.

ALAN: The Granada Veterans won't be like that at all. It will
be more like an international match. Canada versus
Spain. It will be advertised in the Spanish papers. I'm
going to try to get them to agree to a median age limit,
either fifty-five or fifty-six. Trouble is, they might not
have enough guys in that age category who are fit
enough to play.

NETTIE: So no Zidane?

ALAN: Zinedine Zidane was born in Marseilles in 1972. The year after that, I got married. Even though Zizou is balding, I'm old enough to be his father. Do the math!

NETTIE: So what did you come out here to tell me?

ALAN: This won't be a fantasy getaway. It won't be a carefree romantic holiday. It will be much more complicated than that.

NETTIE: Why?

ALAN: Tara is coming. It's time we faced reality, Nettie. We're all in this together. I've thought it through. It's what I want.

NETTIE: How will we possibly get along? Won't she be jealous?

ALAN: I'm tired of being split in two. I just can't take it anymore. I want the truth to be out in the open. I love you both. For once, I want everything to be above board.

NETTIE: You're just being selfish. You want to have your cake and eat it too.

ALAN: Spain could be a new beginning for all three of us.

NETTIE: This is how you plan to celebrate our silver anniversary? As a bigamist?

ALAN: She's never even seen me play!

NETTIE: I've known you longer than she has.

ALAN: Not really. There was that twenty-five-year period when you and I didn't even see each other. I sank into an abyss. I tried golf.

NETTIE: But you always wanted me. You were just in denial.

ALAN: True. But try not to be negative. This is going to be the trip of a lifetime. Remember when we made a soccer trip to France, and we visited the shrine at Lourdes? This time we'll visit the Alhambra. We might even stop in Barcelona and see the stadium where Ronaldinho plays. It will be the football equivalent of a pilgrimage to Mecca.

NETTIE: You're crazy.

ALAN: No, I'm just turning fifty-five.

The superbly named Nettie Honeyball was one of the founders of women's football in England.

WEE WILLIE

Often the goalkeeper is a more complex individual than the outfield players. – Declan Lynch, "The Loneliness of the Long-Term Goalie," *Irish Independent*

All over the planet there are soccer teams like ours, comprising men who are past their sell-by date, but we're unusual by virtue of being typically Canadian: that is, more than two-thirds of our players were born outside of the country, mostly in Europe.

As middle-aged men we tend to think about sex and soccer and money, but increasingly not in that order. We all dream of heroics, as if we were young again, and we all like to believe we're slightly better athletes than we really are. You can't play sports otherwise. For instance, if the median age of our team going to Granada is fifty-six, I'm a youngster.

We're all over fifty. Most of us played soccer in our youth and have returned to the game after a lengthy intermission called marriage. One of us, Ed, had a brief career as a professional hockey goalie for the California Seals. None of us played soccer professionally.

Our league doesn't keep standings. Slide tackles are disallowed, and the referee can send players off the field at any time, for any reason, to cool them off. The league evolved over a thirty-year period from a Scottish-based side that was co-founded by one of our most beloved teammates, Bill Egan, an Irishman who is as charming off the field as a nursery rhyme character, and as intrepid on the field as Paul Scholes.

Bill Egan makes you want to believe in Guinness, leprechauns, and joyful football. With his munchkin-like size and speedy legs, he could be one of those generous goblins in a video game who provides valuable keys to unlock vaults, or, in a less modern context, that Mother Goose character Wee Willie Winkie, transmogrified to soccer. Instead of running through the town "upstairs and downstairs in his nightgown" to make sure all the Scottish children are asleep, our Irish adult version of Wee Willie creates havoc for the public good by waking everyone up with his good-natured audacity and Puckish grin. Bill Egan is a sprite-sized Merlin out of a sports fairy tale, a good gnome who can be frolicsome and wise at the same time.

It's satisfying to remember that Wee Willie, as much as anyone else, can take credit for our weekly misadventures. If Harpo Marx ever appeared in a football movie, he would have played goalkeeper like Bill Egan. Once each game, always for no apparent strategic reason, Bill Egan startles everyone by leaving his goal and making a semi-calculated run up the wing. Instead of handling the ball and taking a conventional punt, Bill drops the ball at his feet and dribbles as far as he can beyond his own penalty box. Like a runaway pet seeking a taste of unleashed freedom, he sometimes gallivants as far as midfield, and, like alarmed characters in a storybook, we can never refrain from shouting, "Stop, Billy, stop! Kick it out!"

This event occurs repeatedly, like a predictable bedtime story. Each time it happens, we are appalled, and we secretly love it. Bill Egan, the rascal spirit, courts danger for the fun of it, scrambling the established order of things, then scampering back to his goal line in the nick of time.

It's a circus act without a tent. His apoplectic teammates are usually too overcome with relief to register any complaints. No harm has been done. On the contrary, our blood is flowing faster, our adrenalin is up.

We are alive!

Bill Egan's nearest professional equivalent would be the Paraguayan goalkeeper José Luis Chilavert, who takes all the spot kicks for his team and holds the world record for goals by a netminder. Unable to touch the crossbar if his life depended on it, Bill often completes his weekly stint as the league's shortest goaltender and switches to play forward in the second half. He never plays midfielder or defender, only striker or goalie. I'm pretty sure he once announced we could play him anywhere, as long as it was forward or goalie.

When Bill goes up front, another transformation occurs. He somehow gets bigger. Instead of jeopardizing his own team, Bill becomes dangerous to the opposition, making darting and intelligent runs that are equivalent to those of an attacking warrior half his age. Instead of becoming a potential laughingstock, Bill is a potential hero, both sly and athletic.

Any defender who underestimates Bill due to his age and size – not to mention his enduring appetite for cigarettes and booze – risks being embarrassed by a goal. He doesn't score nearly as often as he used to, but he always provides glimpses of what a terrific player he must have been in his prime, and why he can never stop loving the game.

We have another player in his seventies who is like that. The other Bill, Bill Allen, anticipates and executes with such consummate grace that it must be painful for him to consciously avoid physical contact, to merely hint at the player he must have been. Bill Allen played at a semi-pro level in England, and his superiority is evident each time he touches the ball. But whereas Bill Allen keeps mostly to himself, perhaps awash in soccer memories, Bill Egan continues to scamper through his field of dreams in the present tense. He remains immune to melancholy, and is good for at least fifteen or twenty minutes of sprinting football, then off to the pub for a convivial pint. Unlike some of our Scottish-trained players, who are prone to strategic tackles that can be viewed as cynical challenges, Bill has evolved a more lyrical approach to football, rarely complaining to the referee, rarely berating his own teammates, laughing as much as possible, and playing like a gentleman. If Bill Egan has negative assessments of others, he mostly keeps them to himself.

In the land of the blind, they say the one-eyed man is king. And Bill Egan is a king. Even though he lost the sight from one of his eyes forty years ago, he knows more about the game he loves than most of the players in Canada do. Formerly an avid coach, Bill now sets an example for the rest of us – how to age gracefully. Whenever he comes to one of our games to watch, leaning on the fence rather than sitting in the stands, I know Bill is seeing more than others, and yet there is always a twinkle in his one good eye.

Raised on the eastern coast of Ireland in a family of ten children, he received some training as a meat cutter, but his prospects were grim. "I didn't want to keep shuttling back and forth between Ireland and England," he says. "I wanted to make a new start on my own."

When it came time to emigrate, instead of joining his two older brothers in Fremantle, Australia, he chose that big pink country on the map, Canada, where he didn't know a soul. "I knew just enough about Canada to know people spoke French in the eastern part," he says, "so that's why I came to Vancouver. I couldn't speak any French, and I had always lived close to the ocean. I could see that Vancouver was on the ocean. It was that simple."

In the 1960s there were plenty of jobs in British Columbia for young men in construction. Bill worked as a cook on massive dam projects and in logging camps. "At one place they wanted to get rid of me for singing," he says. "I enjoyed myself too much. These guys would come into the mess to eat at the end of another long day, and I would be too happy."

When the so-called counterculture took hold in the early 1970s, Bill Egan lived in Kitsilano, now a yuppie enclave, but formerly Vancouver's equivalent to San Francisco's Haight-Ashbury district. During that hippie era, there were plenty of drugs to be had, and he was not averse to a toke or two. "But I never, ever sold it," he says.

When the cops busted his shared apartment one day, finding a few bags of marijuana and hashish, Bill Egan took the fall for his buddy. "The other guy, he had a job. I wasn't working at the time. So I said the stuff was all mine. It was better if I went to jail than him." Bill spent six months in Oakalla Prison, where he worked in the kitchen and organized soccer games. It was quite common in those days for otherwise law-abiding young men to get nabbed like that.

Driving home after a night of drinking at the Fraser Arms pub, Bill's party-hearty lifestyle eventually caught up with him at age twenty-two. When they dragged him out of his vehicle, his face was disfigured and he had permanently lost the sight from one eye. That car accident was the turning point. He understood it was inevitable; he had brought misfortune upon himself, and there was nobody else to blame. He still remembers hiding beneath the sheets, afraid to let anyone see him after he had gone "home" to Ireland to recuperate among his family.

But instead of wallowing in self-pity, Bill returned to Vancouver and fell in love with a woman – a woman who was already engaged. A year passed before he learned that Myrna never went through with her marriage plans. Bill married her and she helped him turn over a new leaf. He got some first aid training.

"It was a real turnaround," he says. "Instead of butchering animals as a meat cutter, suddenly I was healing people."

Children followed. He kept his nose clean, he worked hard, and he started to organize soccer again. In the 1970s there were very few places for men over thirty to play soccer, and no league. So Bill Egan started one.

There were only about five or six teams in the whole city at first, and Sunday-morning kick-arounds were held at the park directly across the street from his house. Those kick arounds are still held at the park across from Bill Egan's house, thirty-five years later, and Bill's garage has become the unofficial headquarters for trophies, soccer nets, orange pylons, and soccer balls.

Still married to Myrna, still working graveyard shifts as a paramedic, Bill regards himself as a lucky man. He remains active as a player, the unacknowledged heart and soul of the B.C. Oldtimers Soccer League that has expanded to include ninety-six teams with eighteen hundred players. He won't be making the trip to Spain with us, but he'll be with us in spirit. Long may he run.

⚽

Other team sports, notably American football, rely heavily on pre-arranged strategies with innumerable stoppages (a made-up hockey word). Plays are conceived on blackboards or computer screens. They are numbered. Players are pawns; coaches are generals. Improvisation is secondary to militaristic manoeuvres. But we have come to understand the beauty of sports, and soccer in particular, is that much of it is improvised, made up on the fly.

Although there has been an effort to introduce "scientific" coaching to soccer, it's a ruse. The rule book for American football is about three inches thick, whereas soccer has relatively few rules, with relatively few whistles. The emphasis is on skill, teamwork, and improvisation, sometimes individual, sometimes combined. Coaches cannot call timeouts and there are minimal substitutions. The joyful expression of improvisation in soccer is artistry on a grass canvas. At its best, soccer is Picasso wearing cleats. It is a game of spontaneous courage.

We will be travelling a great distance, at considerable expense, and we will likely lose our big match against the Granada Veterans, but we are committed to losing courageously, in accordance with Thucydides, who wrote, "The secret to happiness is freedom; the secret to freedom, courage."

This is why we play. When we get on the airplane for Spain, Bill Egan will not be with us. Instead there will be a guy seated ahead of us, wearing a scythe and a black hood. Most people don't see him, but if you to care to join this entourage, you will get some glimpses of this fundamental character. He is usually on the sidelines during our games, like a mascot.

Most of us are not yet over the hill. We see the hill in the distance, but we're not there yet. We may look old, but some of us don't play old once the whistle blows. Some of us, like Hans Hart, are tenacious tacklers; some of us, like Fidel Bacelic, can still put the ball in the net from all angles with the deftness of a Thierry Henry. Some of us, like Dave Naphtali, are still remarkably fast and fit. A few are still crazy enough to get into fisticuffs.

If you're fit in your fifties, it is possible to play at a high calibre, as long as your opponents can't run one hundred metres in ten seconds. That's because soccer is a team game that requires wits as much as muscle. We are not particularly gifted, but we are dedicated to our sport. Most importantly, we are playing within a culture that promotes fitness in a temperate climate. As part of the Me Generation, we are baby boomers who refuse to get old. Nearly all of us are sufficiently advanced in our parenting to squeeze adequate leisure time out of our daily lives to avoid a beer gut.

We are lucky enough to play year-round in a place with the highest average life expectancy for males on the planet. British Columbia, Canada, according to a 2006 report, has surpassed Japan in this rating. It's a good bet, statistically, that I will live at least 79.2 years. Hence we avoid the terms Old-timer or Weekend Warrior. Every week I try to play better. Every week our team wants to play better. We look forward to our weekly soccer game as much as we did when we were kids. At least we now know what we'll be missing if we can no longer play.

When you're young, you never stop and ponder what your life would be like if you couldn't play football. You take the game for granted, like oxygen or summer holidays. But this is different. This is better. The presence of Death on the sidelines heightens the drama and satisfaction of our encounters with the opposition, and our sense of camaraderie as a team.

When we show up at the pitch, we are glad to see one another and often we shake hands. We joke. We are not only concerned with how well we might perform as individuals; we are also sensitive to the requirements of communalism. Everyone feels the difference. It is a privilege to be able to play.

Your next injury could end your career. For every athlete, it is ever thus, but as a youth you don't think that way; you barely think at all. You are too busy performing. You are lost in the moment. You don't see the game as a highlight in a prolonged continuum.

We are old enough to know there are two game clocks going at once. There are the ninety minutes allotted to the match, as calculated by the referee's wristwatch, and there is another invisible timekeeper, far less predictable than the referee, who likes to blow his whistle on a whim. The drama of waiting for full-time enhances every fresh encounter.

CHURCH OF SOCCER

Years have gone by and I've finally learned to accept myself
for who I am: a beggar for good soccer. – Eduardo Galeano

After games I often wake at three or four in the morning. They say there are physiological reasons for this, something to do with muscles or circulation, and various pharmaceutical remedies are available, but I'd rather moan and groan.

Suffering to grow is a form of stupidity I inherited from my father. He, I presume, inherited it from his father, and so on. My father played several sports well, despite a leg that wouldn't bend at the knee. In his youth he probably thought he was brave by avoiding medical interventions, stiff-legging it around the bases, never stopping to imagine that he was impaired, but his athletic heroism only brought him to a dreadful end. Stubbornly in denial, he fell victim to a lethal combination of untreated prostate cancer and Alzheimer's disease.

The two physicians on our team, Richard and Bruce, both take ibuprofen or Advil before games. I tell myself doctors are notorious pill-poppers who are given free samples by drug companies. I prefer to punch channel 113 instead.

When I wake at four in the morning, stiff and sore, and sneak downstairs wearing my wife's cotton bathrobe – in the darkness it's often difficult to distinguish between the two white robes hanging on the antique coat stand – I shuffle-walk to get a glass of milk from the refrigerator, tiptoe into the TV room, and find the correct black remote. For compli-cated reasons that I refuse to have explained to me, we now possess three channel switchers for one television set.

Having invested more than $250 for a newfangled box that will enable me to see all the World Cup games, I cover myself in a blanket, put my feet on the coffee table, and search for my soccer fix. The news programming from American stations makes me cynical, I haven't watched a sitcom from beginning to end since I was twelve, and I lack the patience for old movies. I am even past the age where I want to watch dumb-looking girls in their late teens or early twenties pretending to be sexy, wearing skimpy bathing suits, writhing on demand for chat-line commercials.

Gimme soccer.

I don't care if it's the Argentinian league, the Mexican league, or Bundesliga. I have gained access to 140 channels in order to watch the only one that regularly shows soccer highlights.

I don't care whether it's Sunderland versus Portsmouth. I don't care whether it's the top ten saves of the week, the top ten goals of the week, or the latest news about the injury of some player I have never heard of. Do Not Disturb.

I am deluding myself into thinking that by watching the game being played properly I can transform myself into a better player. I am compensating for all those decades when I never had any access to television soccer. I am broadening my knowledge of the game in much the same way that gullible, lonely souls watch fire and brimstone preachers giving long-winded interpretations of the Bible. I am trying to be born again.

I was unwashed. I was unclean. I dwelt in ignorance. But now I am learning the names of the stadiums and managers. Arsène Wenger (the one who reminds me of a turkey) begat Arsenal. José Mourinho (the one who struts like a peacock) begat Chelsea. Alex Ferguson (the one who doesn't need to strut) begat Manchester United. And so on. The range of characters is Biblical.

I have fallen under the spell of the Reverend Eric Cantona, the maverick French striker who played for Manchester United, then resurrected himself as a bearded Billy Graham of soccer, proselytizing about *Joga Bonito*, The Beautiful Game, for a series of Nike commercials featuring Ronaldinho, Rooney, and Cristiano Ronaldo. I believe everything he tells me.

"You cannot be a great player without being intelligent," Cantona says. "You need to be very quick to read the runs of teammates. In one second you have to imagine a lot of possibilities and decide immediately. It's like geometry in your head. Sometimes there are sixty thousand people in the stands and you give a good ball to somebody to score and nobody could see the ball. Why? Because you have something special and can read things nobody else could."

At first I didn't even know who Eric Cantona was and I didn't realize that *Joga Bonito*, roughly translated, means Play Beautifully. But when I compared the bearded pitchman's commentary about soccer with the drivel that passes for expert commentary on most Canadian hockey broadcasts, I became convinced that Cantona's viewpoint was superior.

"Maradona was like Kasparov. He could see ten moves ahead. Platini was like a chess player. So was Cruyff. So is Zinedine Zidane. It is about creativity. I don't like people who say: 'I paint so I am an artist.' You are an artist if you create something."

I talk back to the TV. "Yes, I agree with you, Eric. What you say is absolutely true. I lack the Kasparov gene to make the game beautiful. Even though I steal the ball more than other players, these days I can only excel at playing the game defensively. The players you glorify are all goal creators. That's not me anymore. I have lost my scoring touch."

When the mute button silences the commercials, one is capable of clear-minded revelations at four in the morning. Even if I could possess superior "pace" (a relatively new word in my vocabulary), I would fear being caught upfield. More than I trust my abilities, I fear irresponsibility.

"This is one of the many weaknesses of my style, Eric. I will intimidate with a tackle, but never by dribbling. I will often pass the ball because I fear the embarrassment of losing possession."

I know that the beautiful game necessarily involves risk, experimentation. If you are afraid of looking foolish in the offensive zone, you will never succeed in making an opponent look foolish.

"Brazil have the heart and soul," Eric Cantona says. "Brazil have everything. They are very passionate, and skilful. When they give a ball to someone, it's like a gift."

Praise the Lord. Instead of dreaming in my bed upstairs, I am downstairs with Eric Cantona. Together we are watching Ronaldinho in Barcelona, and it's weirdly akin to the pleasure one experiences watching a beautiful woman walk down the street. It's not a crime to admire the insouciant sway of a woman's hips along the sidewalk. You don't have to be making love with a woman to take great pleasure from the way she moves. It's part of nature. And the way the Portuguese Ronaldo flits down the sidelines, prancing in a slightly effeminate way, well, sometimes it makes you wonder, What's it all about, Alfie? It *is* beautiful, and mesmerizing. And it can be correspondingly tragic.

A few weeks ago we had a game in Richmond, against the Pioneers, one of the better teams. Too many of our weaker players showed up. Although we had most of the scoring chances, they scored twice. One of their goals was probably offside, but it hardly matters now. I only remember the moment in the second half when I failed to make a pass. Fidel was open. Just after I had stolen the ball and slipped past one of their players, the rush of adrenalin, mixed with fatigue, got the best of me. Fidel was only five metres away, to my right. We were about fifteen metres from their penalty area. He was calling for the ball. Instead of making the simple play, I wasted my remaining energies on a long shot that was easily handled by the keeper.

Fidel is our Kasparov, and I failed to deliver the gift. Instead of relinquishing control to a more dangerous offensive player, I lifted my harmless shot towards the goal. Fidel cried out, and I could hear the disappointment in his voice.

Soccer can be a painstaking game of snakes and ladders. Even though I had played smartly for eighty minutes, climbing as many ladders as I could, seldom faltering, helping my teammates climb their ladders, injecting boldness, I suddenly landed on the wrong square, and I could feel myself sliding downwards on a snake of selfishness.

Nobody else on the field would have noticed except Fidel. Minutes later, when there was a free kick from long range, he took it, and the ball sailed far right, nowhere near the goal. In retrospect, I probably should have taken the free kick from that distance, but Fidel took it, possibly because I hadn't passed him the ball. That's how teams can fall apart. And that's why it seems right to watch soccer at four in the morning, not just to learn how to play, but also to learn how not to play.

When I was young, playing in the offensive end, scoring goals, the game was easy for me, and life was uncomplicated. To the victor went the spoils. I could replay moments of glory in my head. Now that I am older, in the second half of my life, playing more in the defensive zone, I am wary of mistakes. This more cautious approach is not without its rewards. In my optimistic moments, I hope I am adapting some of the lessons I learn from soccer to life.

Forgive us our trespasses. Albert Camus once wrote, "All I know of morality and duty, I owe to football." That's actually a fairly dumb, overblown statement, but there are times – around four in the morning, when the raccoons are prowling the streets – when it almost sounds profound. In the church of soccer, we conduct our religious studies at all hours of the day and night. It only takes one fall from grace to ruin the game.

Against the Pioneers I played fiercely. I blocked several shots from close range, I headed the ball more than anyone, I intercepted more passes, and my corners reached the heads of my teammates. But those moments of proficiency were doomed to quickly fade from memory, eclipsed by one blemish, a failure to make a simple pass.

I pray I am not haunted by similar trespasses after we play in Spain.

KENNY GOES DOWN

A lot of guys play soccer like they go through life.
– Ken Falk, defender, age fifty-seven

When Cathy Falk says she doesn't understand why guys need to chase after a ball, like dogs with their tongues hanging out, she means it. Her husband has been playing the game he loves ever since high school, longer than he has known her. It all began when his track and field coach asked him to join the soccer team at Richmond High because he could run fast.

Ken had mostly played baseball, American football, and ball hockey. "Big subdivisions were going up like crazy. A bunch of us would take off in the morning and go for miles, organizing ourselves for games somewhere. We made up our own rules, depending on how many people we had. Our parents never knew where we were, and it didn't matter. We pretty much policed ourselves."

In university he heard about a half-assed soccer league for young engineers, doctors, and architects. As an aspiring architect for William Graham Consultants, Ken first played on a team called the Graham Wafers, with turquoise shirts and orange logos. A crushing bodycheck into the boards while playing hockey in a rink at one in the morning convinced him it would be better to stick to soccer.

Ken remembers the day a lean and fit guy showed up at Prince of Wales school, wondering if either side needed an extra body. That day Dave Naphtali played for the opposing team, but at the end of the game Dave walked over to Ken and said, "I'd like to play for you guys." Ken was twenty-seven; Dave was twenty-eight. In those days Ken could still run like a gazelle, but he never had a nose for the goal. Dave was much the same. They have been playing soccer together ever since.

By the time they graduated to playing in the Metro League, in which teams rise or fall in various divisions, there were about one hundred Metro teams, mostly guys in their twenties. Ken and Dave decided they could only remain competitive by improving their fitness, so they would get up at six in the morning, three times per week, to go jogging through the University Endowment Lands.

"When we were in the Metro League, we used to have a real coach!" Ken says. "We used to have practices, serious practices. Roy Bendall, he was an old-time Brit. We'd do all these drills. We'd do all this fitness and stretching. I kept telling people there were other games I was good at!"

Gradually Ken and Dave both relegated themselves to the back line, where they have gelled into a nucleus, relying on their grit and their smarts and their familiarity. Whereas Dave has been known to mix it up a bit, how Ken keeps his cool is a welcome mystery. If somebody behaves badly, throwing a tantrum or indulging in violence, he never seems perturbed, or even judgmental. They have seen malcontents and misfits fall by the wayside while superior sportsmen endure. Flashier players have their mini-epochs of glory. Carlos was a hotshot from Brazil. Lynn was a star from Wales. Ace, a prolific goal scorer, moved to South America. Most guys quit playing to raise kids.

One Sunday morning Dave arrived with champagne for everyone, instead of cigars, because his second son, Corey, had been born just hours before the game. Ken hasn't been sidelined by domesticity either. If you saw Ken play just one game, you might not notice him much. If you watched him week after week, you'd begin to realize that Ken is a pillar of consistency.

Gradually you would see how his sophisticated geniality makes him stand out as much as his baldness. He has an IQ that is much higher than most, but he chooses not to assert it, except when we are driving to a game, when he cannot resist providing detailed information regarding the superior route. It must be the architect in him.

Although Ken is not motivated by the will to power, he is deeply enamoured of the will to efficiency. As Bobby Moore says in his memoirs, always make the easy pass. That's Ken. He cuts off attackers like a draftsman with a protractor, measuring the angles perfectly. Never fancy, always economical. And yet he is someone habitually prone to merriment. Ken is that rare sort of person who, when telling amusing stories, likes to include exclamation marks at the end of his sentences – and you don't mind.

One of the goalies of yesteryear was a bouncer who came directly to the games on Sunday mornings from his work on Saturday nights. "This guy was six foot six," Ken says, "and the meanest and ugliest son of a gun. One day he announced he was quitting. He said he was afraid of getting marks on his face. It could ruin his movie career!"

Ken has probably told this anecdote twenty times, but his glee is undiminished. There is a twinkle in his eye when he recalls another teammate who had a sex change. Human beings amuse him. Ken rarely expresses disdain, and neither does Dave. This probably helps to explain why they have been able to build teams around themselves.

Surprised to discover there were organized teams for over-forties, they melded with a group of Scotsmen who were playing informally on summer mornings at Trafalgar Park. "When we went to the pub and they dropped into their brogue," Ken says, "I literally couldn't understand half of what they were saying." The club was called Vancouver Thistle. Bill Egan, who lived across from Trafalgar Park, usually showed up to play on Robbie Burns Day wearing a tartan tam.

Ken gradually took over management of the Sunday-morning kick-arounds in the summer, more or less by default. For more than a decade, as guys from all over the city gathered at Trafalgar Park at ten in the morning, it was always Ken who greeted everybody, holding his clipboard, writing down everyone's first names, improvising lineups for as many as fifty or sixty players.

Ken performed the same role in the gymnasium on Thursday nights during the winters. He calmly and astutely divided everyone into teams that were invariably equal in strength. Obviously he had devised some sort of system for splitting us up, handing out the coloured pinnies to be worn over shirts, but nobody every questioned how he did it. That would be like asking a magician to explain how he pulled a rabbit from a hat.

Throughout those hundreds of Sunday mornings and Thursday nights, Ken rarely raised his voice except to laugh. Often his laughter came at his own expense. When he and his family visited China as a guest of a leading Chinese industrialist, he was feted with a gigantic banquet where they drank a lot of Scotch. "I was introduced as Canada's leading architect!" He appreciated the compliment, but the absurdity of it was even more delightful.

Some of Ken's vivacity came from his mother, who played competitive softball into her forties on a team called the Thompson Tillies. "They had a pitcher called Torchy," he says, delighted, "because she had red hair. The other day my mother went out to have lunch with Torchy, who is eighty-five!"

Despite tracing his ancestry to two Norwegian-born parents ("I'm a purebred!"), Ken doesn't seem to mind his nickname, Ken the Kaiser, a flattering but ludicrous reference to Franz Beckenbauer, the German field general. Calling him the Kaiser is like calling a six foot six guy Shorty. As a central defender, Ken has a herky-jerky style, completely at odds with the smoothness of Beckenbauer. If a newcomer assumes Ken must be a German Canadian, he doesn't bother to correct them. The confusion adds to his merriment.

All of which serves to explain why everyone was so shocked to hear that Ken, our indomitable father figure, had leukemia.

☉

One day Ken went for a routine checkup and was told something was wrong with his cell separation count. The next day he had a new identity: cancer victim. Ken was certain somebody had made a mistake. "This is all bullshit," he said to his doctor. "I don't have any symptoms." Ken had never been in a hospital in his life.

Feeling as healthy as ever, he attended an architects' convention in Las Vegas. Upon his return he and Cathy went to the hospital, where they learned the results of a biopsy. The diagnosis was the same. He had acute leukemia.

Stunned, he and Cathy were walking down a hospital corridor, wondering where the rest of his life would take them, when they bumped into Bruce Fleming, a sturdy midfielder who doubles as a doctor in the Vancouver General Hospital (VGH) emergency ward. Bruce's non-medicinal response to Ken's news was concise and memorable.

"Oh, fuck," he said.

Ken, Bruce, and Cathy went to the hospital cafeteria to talk things over. That same night they all went out to dinner. This is a role that Bruce and the other physician on our squad, Richard, have adopted by default: team medical officers.

"I was still bitching," Ken recalls. "This can't be true!"

Dr. Power, a lovely woman from Ireland, agreed to review all the information. Ken was also sent to Dr. Neville, a hematologist, to find out more. Entering the Heather Pavilion of VGH, Ken noticed a large sign saying Heather B-4 Leukemia.

After all those hundreds of hours jogging through the Endowment Lands, after all those soccer games, it didn't add up. "What am I doing here?" Ken asked himself. "I've never had anything to do with the sick world!"

The day before he was scheduled to start his chemotherapy, a Sunday, Ken played soccer for us. He played a full game at fullback, as usual. After the game we all went to a nearby restaurant called Enigma. I can't even remember who we played against, and I've long since forgotten the score of that game, but I recall leaving the restaurant with Ken and a few others.

As we said our self-conscious goodbyes, embracing Ken on the sidewalk, I told him what a friend of mine had told me once. "If I had to pick someone who I thought could get through this," I said, "it would have to be you." I was hoping, illogically, that this might somehow serve as a verbal good luck charm. I had come through my brain surgery unscathed. And the statement had the added benefit of being true.

I didn't see it myself, but apparently Ken cried on the sidewalk as he was talking to Dave. That would make sense. Most of us had only known Ken for a few years; he and Dave were the founders of the team. They were like brothers.

Usually when someone is afflicted with cancer, you want to stay away; you want to let them have their privacy. It's not cowardice so much as respect. You know that almost whatever your mouth might say, it will sound inadequate or facile to your brain. With Ken, however, most of us *wanted* to see him. Everyone wanted to participate in his drama, as if making his turmoil into a team effort might somehow help him. Sometimes sympathy can be an invasion of family intimacy, but in Ken's case I found our pack mentality was curiously uplifting. Ken was loved. It was as if we were a herd of elephants and one of us was wounded.

The family took precedence over the team, but Ken's gregariousness was a healthy part of his personality, and it needed to be allowed to continue. After we got the heads-up from Cathy, Fidel and I visited Ken near the beginning of his hospital stay, before he was unduly weakened by the chemo treatments.

The pretence of normality functioned like a bandage that could be taken on and off. Ken took his laptop so he could stay in touch with his architectural firm. Cathy was keeping me posted, on a daily basis, so that I could alert everyone when it became a bad idea to visit.

That first day Fidel took Ken some freshly cooked lunch in his frying pan. It was the same pasta dish with sausage that he had whipped up for Ken and Cathy in France, when we had played in a soccer tournament near Toulouse. The memories were still fresh – everyone eating and laughing together on a veranda overlooking a farmer's field near Gaillac.

Fidel and I had stopped en route to the hospital to get a French baguette. We knew it was the way Ken would prefer to play it. With the intravenous tube in his chest, Ken chuckled and dished out some of the pasta with a wooden spoon. We brought him presents like it was a birthday party. Fidel also brought one of his abstract paintings to hang on the hospital wall, to personalize the space. I gave Ken a hardcover book on the history of architecture. When you go into combat, it's good to be fearless. There was a robust energy in Ken's eyes that prevented everyone around him, except Cathy, who had the most to lose, from falling prey to fear.

That day Fidel and I had to assiduously wash our hands in a special washroom for medical personnel and visitors. In order to keep your hands free of any germs, you leaned your thighs against a bar to make the water spray down into a stainless steel trough. I had a sense of déjà vu.

In France, Fidel and I had taken a side trip to Lourdes. It was a miserable, cold, wet day. We visited the grotto where Bernadette Soubirous supposedly saw the Virgin Mary. Although I frequently verge on being anti-religious, I am curious about the power of belief. For Fidel it was different. Raised in Catholic Croatia, he lined up to touch his hands against the rock face of the grotto, while I stood back, not wanting to spoil the experience of others. After Fidel had joined the lineup and brushed his hands against the grotto, we walked through the drizzle to the tents where pilgrims lit candles. It was his idea to light eleven candles, aligning them in the shape of our football team, using the 1–4–4–2 formation.

At the hospital the running water in the stainless steel sink reminded me of the water dripping from the rock face of Bernadette's grotto. Here we were again, making another pilgrimage, only this time it was for real, this time it was much closer to home. Instead of putting our faith in God, we were placing our bets on science, but our feelings of hopefulness mixed with helplessness were fundamentally the same.

As Fidel and I stood silently, side by side, washing our hands with the disinfectant, I realized that neither of us had wanted to go and see Ken by ourselves. Instinctively we knew we were more powerful together. Possibly we were the new Ken and Dave, but we hoped not.

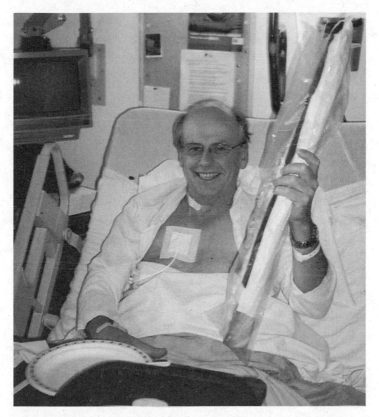

Stalwart defender Ken Falk attributed his resiliency as a leukemia patient to family support, his Nordic heritage, and four consecutive decades of soccer.

⚽

Ken sailed through his chemotherapy. Even the staff was amazed.

On the day he was released from hospital, Ken wore a Norse helmet, with two protruding horns. It was a Viking victory. St. Olaf resurrected. The treatments continued with daily visits to the hospital, but Ken continued as a model patient. He sent me various messages of optimism.

> Things are going very well. We go to VGH every day for a fluid top-up. I hit bottom today on one of the blood counts. We are trying to do this. I get a transfusion of platelets tomorrow. That means I am starting the road up! One to two weeks to restore counts. Let's get going on Spain '07!

> At the moment I am cancer-free. If a biopsy confirms that, then over the next few weeks I will have two rounds of consolidation chemo as an outpatient. I feel pretty good currently, albeit with no energy. We also got some good lab news yesterday that I have normal cytogenetics.

> Catherine says she misses writing you every day. We are now in a new routine dealing with Blood Count Land. I have very much appreciated the support given by all you guys. Wish I could play Sunday. I might stop by and yell at you guys from a distance!

After only several months, Ken was given a clean bill of health. For the next two years, he would be vulnerable to the leukemia reasserting itself, but basically he had managed to make himself into an ex–cancer patient in near record time.

His football resurrection was less auspicious. One of our two teams was playing against South Hill, an experienced but cynical team, at the newly reopened field on the Musqueam reserve, near the university. Ken showed up for the match in civvies, presumably to cheer on his mates, but when he unzipped his jacket I could see his team jersey underneath.

South Hill didn't run much, but they had played together for years and they had one midfielder who formerly played semi-pro. They also had by far the best keeper in the league, an old-school goalie from England who didn't wear gloves. His positioning was always perfect, and he took control of his box with unerring confidence.

The scoring opened abruptly. With only five minutes gone, they lofted a seemingly harmless ball into our box. Either it took a crazy bounce on the rough pitch, or else one of our defenders wasn't alert – probably a combination of the two – but our keeper's hesitation, not coming off his line soon enough, created a chasm of opportunity for one of their forwards, who tapped it home.

Thistle equalized only five minutes later. It was nice three-way passing play, unusually efficient, like a diagram on a chalkboard. The right back, Fred, brought it up the line and tapped it ten metres inwards to a midfielder, Eddie, who had the presence of mind to quickly deflect the ball back down the line again. Our forward, Trevor, took the angled pass behind their outside defender, about ten metres from the touch line. By the time he had gained control of the ball, he was almost out of bounds, but he swirled quickly, without looking, and drilled the ball from a severe angle. To everyone's astonishment, Trevor's shot caromed off the near goalpost, then lodged in their net just inside the far post.

For the rest of the first half, Thistle dominated the flow of play, but didn't get any scoring opportunities. South Hill didn't panic. They held their positions. At halftime a few substitutions were made, but Ken stayed on the sidelines. He mentioned to a few of us that he intended to play for a few minutes, but at the same time he seemed apprehensive.

South Hill scored about ten minutes into the second half, due to another defensive miscue. One of our slower players had failed to clear the ball cleanly. Our goalie was upset with the goal, seemingly unaware that he had made an even more obvious error in the first half.

When one player overreacts, the team's cohesiveness often suffers. Thistle stopped displaying any strong belief in their ability to win the game. They began to hope for a lucky goal, rather than concentrating on creating one with skill. The defence did not move forward with any authority.

With about twenty minutes left to play, Ken announced that he would give it a try. Instead of inserting himself in the middle of the back line, where he usually played alongside Dave, Ken substituted on the right, at the back. When the referee was alerted to an incoming player, nobody appeared, because Ken was struggling to remove his black sweatpants while seated in a lawn chair.

As soon as Ken stepped onto the field, our team started applauding. The applause lasted for about half a minute, as Ken jogged into position, and was unadulterated by any comment or explanation. South Hill must have wondered what the fuss was about.

Ken looked somewhat dazed, even fragile. Instead of running towards opponents with intimidating zeal, he was tentative. When he made his first kick, the ball skittered off his boot. Even though he had shed about twenty pounds, Ken was stumbling as much as he was running. Clearly he had the jitters and was physically weak. When he bent to pick up the ball for a throw-in, he had difficulty grasping it. Instead of sending it assertively down the line, he threw it only about four metres to the closest man. He stayed on the field for another eight minutes, as if he was relearning how to play, then took himself off.

"I just wanted to be able to say I did it," he said.

Nobody is going to remember that 2–1 loss to South Hill. But I'll always remember Ken struggling to get out of his sweatpants in the lawn chair.

About two months later, Ken was still in recovery mode. Fidel and I joined Thistle for their match against Croatia at the Adanac field. (Adanac is Canada spelled backwards.) It was one of those desultory performances during which the players look old. In over-fifties soccer the team that moves the ball most efficiently can soon tire their opponents. We were being outplayed tactically. The Croatians, who usually dissembled by bickering at one another, were firmly in control of the ball. We lacked forwards who were able to put sufficient pressure on their back line. It was going to be another game to forget.

Then, towards the end of the first half, after some minimal contact, Ken went down. He stayed down like a boxer who is dizzy, unable to get up from the mat. The ball was kicked out of bounds while everyone huddled around him, worried. This was so unlike Ken that everyone immediately felt nervous for him. It took him about two minutes to get up and hobble to the sidelines.

During those two minutes, dark thoughts drifted overhead, like ominous clouds. Flying to Spain without Ken would be like Columbus sailing west without an anchor. It was unimaginable.

In the second half, Ken took another tumble, and he didn't bounce back. It could have been any one of us, at any time, but it was Ken, twice in the same game. Stumbling, weak, *old*.

Later Ken made a joke about needing a massage, but when he fell a second time you could see he was scared. Bruce and Richard, our two doctors, were away that game. As Ken left the field, I ran towards him and said, "Ken, I think you'd better take it easy." He nodded and understood completely. I was no doctor, but I had a licence to dispense advice. I play with a medical alert bracelet. Four years earlier, Dr. Christopher Honey had removed a benign meningioma from my head.

In sports there is nothing sweeter than a come-from-behind victory, nothing more satisfying than a comeback. The dark clouds passed. A few weeks later, Ken was fine. As good as ever. Better.

Ready for Spain.

I PREFER TO WIN

Football is a thinly disguised re-enactment of hunting;
we played it before we were human. – Carl Sagan

How competitive should an amateur sports team be?

It's a question that nags every amateur athlete and every amateur team. Are those life-and-death juices circulating in our veins? Or are we simply playing for fun and fitness?

Early in 2006, after all three of our teams in the Point Grey Soccer Club were inexplicably clobbered on the same Thursday night, the issue of competitiveness versus recreation rose to the fore. Ken Falk sent a terse email to everyone, in large lettering, listing a combined score line.

POINT GREYS 2

LATIN UNITED / COLUMBUS / TEAM CHILE 16

Regular Sunday clinic will be held at 9:30 at Trafalgar School.
Among the topics to be covered:

- how to recognize a teammate on the field
- locating goals without GPS
- appropriate times and locations for daydreams

It wasn't exactly Tolstoy asking his famous question, What
is to be done?, but it did the trick. To what extent were we
content to be casual footballers? And to what extent did we
want to play to win?

A few of us were glad for this collective whipping. We
started talking among ourselves about what we wanted from
soccer, and we wondered aloud about our ability to imple-
ment changes. Our poor collective showing provided a
window of opportunity for those of us who were bold enough
to consider revolutionizing our team.

The status quo, if you're paying attention, never exists. It's
a bit like marriage. You can either keep making things better
or else you start getting worse. There are losing streaks in
matrimony and sport.

Having worked in public relations and advertising, Alan
Cook showed more than a knack for communications when
he announced that he had secured a year-round practice
pitch for Tuesday nights:

We are in dire need of a serious coordinated practice time for
any of us to progress as teams. I suggest that we use it exclu-
sively for Point Grey practice. No outside visitors. I have some
ideas I'd be happy to share with like-minded enthusiasts

who care about the Point Grey soccer teams becoming a force to contend with, rather than the easiest teams to beat in the league.

I'm talking about RESPECT, gentlemen. How about brainstorming on how we can bring this to fruition? Let's each team nominate an individual to decide on the strategy of how we approach these Tuesday evenings. I doubt any of us want to show up to do drills, as we used to do in our youth, but the practice games could at least be a little more constructive by working on one play a week, etc. What say you various pundits and jokesters? Let's build this club into a place where legends are made!

I liked Alan's use of that word *legends*. It had a ring to it, dignified but ambitious, comical and catchy. One team in our league was already called Classics. Another was Euro-Stars. If we wanted to reflect higher ambitions for ourselves, Legends could serve nicely. A name change couldn't hurt.

Our situation reminded me of my early teens, when I had played in a succession of neophyte rock 'n' roll bands. After a few gigs, sometimes only one, we would feel obliged to give ourselves a new name. That way our reputation might not precede us to the next house party or community dance. We went through so many names between grades seven and nine that I can't recall if any one of them ever stuck. I was usually the one who came up with the new names for the band.

Having failed to gel as a team called United, I figured it was time we raised the stakes and called ourselves Legends. To push the revolution forward, some other basic steps could be taken with minimal fuss. I made a list.

1. Make sure we all confirm in advance whether or not we're showing up.
2. Get to the games on time.
3. Warm up properly.
4. Bring enough soccer balls.
5. Get lineups figured out in advance.
6. Take an organized approach to making subs.

It wasn't exactly rocket science. As well: (7) we had no strategies for corner kicks, (8) we were too slow to take free kicks, (9) we were slow to take throw-ins, and (10) we chronically mixed up our positioning during a game, rather than restrict players to one position per game.

The best team in our league, Columbus, had played together for years, and it showed in their passing and organization. They made few substitutions. They had a coach. They did not worry about equalizing their playing times, as if they were peewees just learning the game. They played their best players until they built up a lead. And they arrived early enough to warm up.

Some of our aging brethren got carried away and suggested we take the radical step of actually hiring a coach to run us through drills. They might as well have suggested inviting a dentist to our practices to use dentistry drills. For most guys in their fifties and sixties, many of whom were university professors or managers of large enterprises, the notion of taking instruction from anyone, about anything – unless it was from a much higher female power, our wives – was anathema.

Somebody knew a national B-licenced coach who was a former member of Canada's national men's team, someone who had played professionally in Holland and for the Toronto Blizzard. Most of us were not impressed by these credentials. Sure, he might still be a better player, but was he going to be smarter than us? If he was so smart, why would this guy be willing to make a few extra bucks coaching a bunch of old guys?

Ian Hutchinson, a geography professor, provided this cautionary response:

> Walter Winterbottom coached the England football team from 1946–1962. In 1955 he showed up in Newcastle to conduct a clinic with promising young players. I have no memory of what drills we went through that day; the only thing I do remember was that we sat around in a circle after the scrimmage and he said, "How many of you lads take ballet lessons?" Nobody said anything, but afterwards the general opinion was "No wonder England lost 6–3 and 7–1 to Hungary in the last two years." Be careful what you wish for!

Indeed. It was a tad silly to be anxious about how well we performed in a league that didn't keep track of standings. But you don't need to conduct a scientific survey to prove that losing isn't as much fun as winning.

Losing is seldom ennobling. One exception, one of the few laudable losses in football history, occurred in 1974. After drawing the first game of their home-and-away series against Chile, played in the Soviet Union, the Soviets refused to play the return match of their World Cup qualifying series in Chile's National Stadium, which had been used by the military dictatorship of Augusto Pinochet for the execution of political prisoners. Although the Soviets knew they would be disqualified from World Cup competition, they made this gesture in support of the democratically elected government of Salvador Allende, ousted with CIA complicity one year earlier. The match went ahead as scheduled, without any visiting team. The Chileans appeared on the field, dribbled down the pitch after the opening whistle, and kicked the ball into an empty net. Triumph! They claimed the victory, but thereafter Chile failed to win a single match during the 1974 World Cup in Germany.

Losing may be something to avoid, but tinkering with a team can be a conundrum. I have always enjoyed the axiom "If it ain't broke, don't fix it," so if we dared to reformat one of our teams, how could we be certain we would not cause irreparable damage in the process?

Brian Phillips suggested to Alan Cook that we get all our players together "and see if we find some common ground, then develop an action plan." That seemed harmless enough. But I have always been leery of democracy in such matters. Some people's ideas are downright goofy and require rejection, not integration, and it's hard to do the rejecting as a group.

To avoid the perils of group-think, I talked to key players on my United team and deduced there was a consensus about our projected degree of seriousness. In a nutshell, WE WANTED TO WIN!!!!

Our casual, enlightened approach to football was generating frustration. Our most serious player, Fidel, welcomed these discussions about reformation. "Hey, smart boys. I'm totally happy that this has finally happened . . . Two and a half years of waiting . . . We are a very intelligent group. We don't need to practise on the field . . . First we sit in the clubhouse and talk, then we go onto the field . . . This is a big day for Point Grey . . . Rule number one. Start playing without the ball in our feet."

And of course Fidel was absolutely right. In our fifties physical ability and skills could not be improved much, but we could *think* better football.

I've improved every year as a writer, because I increasingly make fewer mistakes and I never make things worse when I tinker. It can be the same with football. One gradually learns to become a more efficient player. Not faster, not stronger, but more efficient. For instance, one can learn to be more responsible and committed off the ball. It's not a matter of stamina or brawn, it's a matter of concentration and self-discipline, as well as leadership and organization.

Fidel knew more about how the game should be played than any of us, and yet he wasn't running the team. Worse, everybody knew Fidel knew the game best, and yet he was not being consulted about its management. If we were really so smart, why weren't we asking Fidel what to do? Was it because he was new to the team? Was it because he still spoke with a Croatian accent? Was it because some of us were too insecure and jealous of his abilities?

Our win–loss record for the summer was okay on paper – nine wins, four losses, two ties – but we were not playing satisfying football. Everybody knew that. When we were bickering about our playing times or lack of strategy, we didn't feel like a team at all. The more I thought about my team, the more I didn't want to remain on it if most of the guys weren't willing to consider improving. Why should some of us feel badly if we wanted to play better soccer?

This, more or less, is how the Legends were born.

Another way of telling the story is simply to confess that Fidel and I decided we wanted to play our final years of soccer together, and the transformation of United into Legends followed from that. But that's a narrow view of the situation that fails to register the complicity and dedication of others. Everyone had their own particular notions of how to play football correctly, gleaned from boyhoods in different countries. But we lacked cohesion. We lacked team spirit. We lacked leaders and followers. So somebody had to imple ment changes.

It was a simple revolution. We lacked a dedicated goal-keeper and a striker, so Fidel and I recruited Tony Arimare, an excellent fifty-year-old keeper, and Menny Marangoudakis, an excellent fifty-year-old striker. First we took Tony for a coffee, then we met Menny for a Guinness. We didn't have any signing bonus to offer, there wasn't any dickering with their agents, it wasn't exactly a tense bargaining process, but there *was* a courtship process.

Top players need to feel valued. So we offered them respect. It was the only collateral we had to put on the table. In return for their agreement to join us, we promised our comradeship. The unofficial constitution of the Point Grey Legends took the form of a paper napkin with a simple diagram. In a straight line, from our goalmouth to the opposition's goalmouth, we would have strength up the middle: Tony, me, Fidel, Menny. That was the Magna Carta.

Issues of team chemistry and philosophy could be addressed in due course. Ostensibly generated by a reorganization committee and born of consultation, the reorganization memorandum was drafted by the person who happened to be the only professional writer on the team.

After citing Alan Cook's and Ken Falk's preceding memos, I invited each United team member to vote Yes or No to five envisioned changes. They were asked to vote Yes only if they agreed with all five of the proposals.

1. Name change. The name of our team would be changed from United to Legends.

2. Organization. A maximum of fourteen to fifteen players would be asked to dress for each game, and lineups would be published two days before each game.

3. Substitution policy. Substitutions would be minimized. Players would play for longer periods, rather than running in and out of games, generating confusion. Players would be asked to assume more responsibility for taking themselves on and off the pitch if tired or injured, resubstituting themselves into their designated positions to encourage continuity.

4. Roster. Our roster of twenty players would include five half-fee members to be rotated into the lineup, enabling the team to field its strongest possible lineup against tougher opposition.

5. Future growth. Changes would be in effect for one year, subject to revision. Pirate-ship democracy would prevail: I could be replaced as manager at any time.

⊛

It was a gamble, a risk. There was absolutely no way of knowing that our team would not implode, or even that our play would necessarily improve. And I knew some feelings would be hurt. But if you want to make an omelette, you gotta break some eggs, etc.

Although it appeared as if Ken Falk's email had triggered the reformation process, the reconfiguration process primarily stemmed from discussions between Fidel and me about one year in advance of the referendum. We were now enacting a cultural revolution, and I was the self-elected engineer of human souls. The survey of opinion had the appearance of sweet reasonableness, but one could also view it as a blueprint for a bloodless coup. In essence, I was taking over our team.

Is the lover who successfully woos his bride into matrimony not a plotter too? And is the bride who successfully persuades her husband-to-be that his pursuit of her has been successful, when in reality she has controlled the courtship game all along, also not guilty of plotting? If I was manipulative, I was at least mindful of everyone's feelings. I did not want to kick anybody out of the lifeboat; I just wanted us to play better soccer against the better teams.

The first eleven responses received to the Reorganization Committee Memo, with its vaguely Stalinist title, were all Yes. These results were quickly circulated so that none of the remaining nineteen players would suffer the embarrassment of being out of sync if one or two of them voted No. Obviously if they wished to register a dissenting opinion, they were still free to do so, but they had to realize that an overwhelming majority were in favour of taking a more competitive approach.

We wanted to beat the top team, Columbus. We wanted to avenge our 5–1 loss. Admitting that this was what most of us wanted, deep down, felt much better than pretending not to want it.

Most sports teams resolve their roster issues via executive fiat. We took a different approach. Everyone voted against the status quo, fully cognizant of the ramifications. If, in the process, we were choosing to sell our souls to the Devil in order to play better soccer, well, okay. We were adults.

It might appear ludicrous for an over-fifties soccer team to undertake strategic management manoeuvres as if we were Manchester United, but this process enabled us to admit to ourselves that we were passionate about the game. I have no doubt that a women's volleyball team in northern China is wrestling with the same issues, along with an amateur swim club in Canberra, say, or a cricket team in Jamaica. Amateurs can be as passionate as professionals.

Yes, we are grey-haired amateurs. Yes, we have slowed down a bit over the years. Yes, we are guilty of thinking we are better players than we are. But we want to be better than those other grey-haired amateurs we are playing against. And that is not sinful. It is sport.

And so we crossed the Rubicon.

INTERVIEW WITH A MISTRESS #2

NETTIE: A peseta for your thoughts.
ALAN: They use Euros now.
NETTIE: Whatever. So what's the matter? Why the hangdog look?

ALAN: I can't *not* think about the big game. And it feels a bit childish, thinking about soccer at my age. I feel guilty about the way it takes up so much space in my imagination.

NETTIE: A fantasy life is healthy. It's perfectly normal. The imagination can be like a performance-enhancing drug.

ALAN: I should be thinking about important stuff. Like the ozone layer.

NETTIE: If it feels good kicking me around, let yourself feel good. Just do it. Why do you have to complicate your pleasure?

ALAN: Yesterday I had this terrible thought while I was shaving: What if my grandmother, who is 101 years old, suddenly gets seriously ill? What happens if she dies? What happens if there's a funeral? Do I cancel my trip or do I go to Spain?

NETTIE: Geez, the suspense is killing me.

ALAN: I knew what my answer would be by the time I finished shaving.

NETTIE: Go with it.

ALAN: You know, I go back and forth between resenting you and craving you.

NETTIE: Pray tell.

ALAN: For most of us, going to Spain is going to serve as a defining contest. It will be our equivalent of the World Cup. It's our chance to be transformed, to aim for glory. All our games prior to this one could be reduced to footnotes in our football memory banks. We could be torn to shreds. The score at the end of the game isn't going to matter. I just want to be able to walk off that field knowing I was the best that I can be, not just as a player, but as a person. I want some nobility out of this.

NETTIE: Seems out of character. You'd rather win the game.

ALAN: Not if it's my final game. Nettie, I haven't told anyone yet. Just you. I'm considering hanging up my cleats.

NETTIE: So it's *Last Tango in Granada*. The tryst to end all trysts. You want to paint yourself as Mr. High 'n' Mighty, retiring from the chase, but that's a load of hooey. I *know* you. There's a movie in your mind. Granada is where the Moors built the Alhambra. You guys are all from *British* Columbia. You want to be Richard the Lion-Heart. In your heart of hearts, this trip is some sort of warped religious crusade. From the way you're talking about this match in a bullring, you guys ought to be called the Canadian Crusaders. You're seeking the ultimate soccer climax.

ALAN: All right. Fine. I admit it. It's all barbaric.

NETTIE: That's better. Embrace it. Desmond Morris is right. Football and sex and hunting are all connected.

ALAN: Do you think Ronaldinho has these conversations with himself?

NETTIE: He doesn't have to. Ronaldinho is not an intellectual. And Ronaldinho is not a writer. He's a real soccer player.

ALAN: Gawd, how marvellous that would be.

NETTIE: All those soccer commercials on television telling millions of kids "Be like Ronaldinho" are really only making millions of kids and overgrown kids like you unhappy. They will crave whatever products are being sold to compensate. Maybe that's why you often feel your love of soccer is childish.

ALAN: You mean, it's like Castro telling his fellow Cubans "Be like Che," even though he knows Che Guevara was a self-inflated creep? Fidel Castro hung Che out to dry in Bolivia, but he knows if he uses the idea of Che, he can make all his citizens feel inadequate. And that way they will buy into his idea of socialism.

NETTIE: You've lost me.

ALAN: If I were a psychiatric patient on a sofa and you were Sigmund Freud on a chair, you could tell me all sorts of insightful analysis, but you couldn't stop me from dreaming about Ronaldinho. Did you see that clip on the Internet? The one where he bounces the ball off the crossbar four times in a row without letting the ball hit the ground, shooting from outside the penalty box?

NETTIE: That was trick photography, you ninny.

ALAN: It's not considered standard psychiatric behaviour for the shrink to laugh at her patient.

NETTIE: Ultimately it can all be reduced to male potency. It's all about scoring.

ALAN: Laugh all you like. But I love the way Ronaldinho smiles after he scores a goal. It's beautiful. It's angelic. You can tell a lot about a player by the way he responds when he scores a goal. I've been thinking about this lately . . . it used to be that the goal scorer would automatically celebrate with his teammates, but the game has been changing for the worse. The players nowadays are developing celebratory routines. It's as if the new breed of professional soccer player hopes to score in order to have a licence to make an impression on the crowd or the television audience *after* he scores. Scoring a goal has turned into an act of self-conscious theatre. In the process the goal scorer is demeaning the purpose of the goal, and diminishing the value of the game. It amounts to athletic corruption.

NETTIE: Like I told you, deep down you're a puritan.

ALAN: For the old-fashioned player, the goal itself is the ultimate experience, not the celebration of the goal afterwards. A goal is what his team needs. The unselfish celebrant maintains his dignity and promptly returns to his side of the field, respectfully accepting the congratulations of his teammates en route. He does not attempt to embellish his happiness by drawing further attention to himself. He does not sprint towards the section of the stadium that contains his most exuberant fans in order to bask in their adoration. He does not seek to further humiliate the opposition with his showboat antics. The old-fashioned player will never sprawl on the grass as if he has been mortally wounded by his own joy.

NETTIE: You've really got a bee in your bonnet.

ALAN: Most importantly, the old-fashioned player would never be seized by an uncontrollable urge to remove his jersey. Fortunately there are still some referees who are willing to allocate yellow cards for this nonsense. The trouble is, as soon as the referee lifts his arm for a yellow card, penalizing the player for his exhibitionism, he is prolonging the amount of screen time allocated to the scorer. The yellow card forces the television commentators to talk about the goal scorer even more.

NETTIE: But the fans like it.

ALAN: It's okay for the Brazilians to act crazy – maybe they can't help themselves – but the other day I saw a game on TV and an *Englishman* was doing it! He was prancing

around like a madman, bare-chested, waving his jersey
above his head. I loathe this form of self-marketing.
Scoring should be a pure act for the tribe, not a vindica-
tion of self.

NETTIE: What's wrong with prolonging ecstasy?

ALAN: Must your mind always be in the gutter, Nell.

NETTIE: So I can look up at the stars.

ALAN: You stole that line from somewhere. It's not even
original.

NETTIE: There's nothing new under the sun.

ALAN: You're incorrigible.

NETTIE: Thanks for sharing.

RONALDINHO'S SMILE*

*The great fallacy is that this game is first and last about winning.
It is nothing of the kind. The game is about glory: it is about
doing things with style.* – Danny Blanchflower

It is a warm spring afternoon, and I am thinking about
Ronaldinho's smile.

---

* Ronaldo de Assis Moreira, a.k.a. Ronaldinho, was born on March 21,
1980, in Porto Alegre, Brazil, where he is commonly known as
Ronaldinho Gaúcho, a reference to his origins in the cowboy state of
Rio Grande do Sul. Twice named FIFA's footballer of the year and twice
named European footballer of the year, he led Brazil to the World Cup
championship in 2002.

I am thinking about Ronaldinho's smile as I pump air into my wife's bicycle, the blue one with the brown basket at the front and the black basket at the back, the one she sometimes uses to get groceries. I am thinking about Ronaldinho's smile as I put the soccer ball in the rear basket and start pedalling slowly through our neighbourhood, swerving lazily from side to side along the suburban streets littered with the delicate pink blossoms of the Japanese cherry trees, not wearing a helmet. I am thinking about Ronaldinho's smile as I gradually accelerate, trying not to think about the hairline fracture in my left femur, wrapped in an adhesive bandage, and my torn calf muscle, and how the bruising has drained into the ankle area, turning it blue and yellow.

Those injuries are temporary inconveniences. It's my knee problem that puzzles me. I've never had a knee go kaput like that. Bobby Orr was forced to quit hockey with a bum knee. Much the same thing happened to Ronaldinho's older brother. It frightens me a bit. It's not getting any better. When I wake up in the mornings, I can't walk. And our summer league starts in two weeks.

I know nothing about knees. I only know I must get into better shape for our big game against the Granada Veterans. If I let myself turn to mush, I'm doomed.

What happened was this: I collided with a much bigger, younger player out at the university, about three weeks ago, during a noon-hour pickup game. One of my cleats somehow freakishly caught in his shoelace. What are the chances of that happening? A zillion to one. As he fell one way, I was twisted sideways in the other direction, like a heifer jerked at the end of a rodeo rope. I've been gimped ever since. The inside of my right knee burns, and yet there's no swelling. There's got to be something seriously gibbled up inside the joint. That's my diagnosis. I could go to a physiotherapist, but they might bring bad news. Worse, they might give me exercises to do. I'd much rather think about Ronaldinho and his guileless smile.

It's not just his skill that enabled Ronaldinho to eclipse David Beckham as the world's highest-earning player; it's his smile, the most famous grin in sports, unchanged after twenty years. If you have ever seen footage of Ronaldinho as a child, performing tricks with a ball in a gymnasium, you'll know what I'm talking about. All over the world, no matter what language you speak, you get the same message: Ronaldinho epitomizes the joy of soccer.

Two years ago, I hadn't heard of him. Up until recently, I was a soccer illiterate. I had no idea Ronaldinho once scored twenty-three goals in one game (at age thirteen), or that he scored a thirty-five-metre free kick against England during the 2002 World Cup. Millions of people on the planet have known for years that he was dubbed Ronaldinho, or "little Ronaldo," to differentiate him from Brazilian striker Ronaldo, whose own 1994 World Cup jersey had read "Ronaldinho" to distinguish him, in turn, from an older teammate with the same name. But not me.

It was his smile that got me hooked. It's not the smile of an arrogant multi-millionaire; it's the smile of an impish, unspoiled boy inside a man, a Peter Pan with bulging thighs. Like the nursery rhyme character who sucked on his thumb and pulled out a plum saying "Oh, what a good boy am I," Ronaldinho inhabits a different world from the rest of us, a magical world of delight.

Ronaldinho has the creativity, skills, and character to transport us consistently into the realm of fantasy football.

That's why the "Brazilian Ping-Pong" video of Ronaldinho is so alluring. There he is, seated on the grass, slowly putting on a new pair of golden soccer shoes. He juggles the ball thirty-five times, keeping it aloft, as he proceeds to the top of the penalty area and strikes the ball off the crossbar four times in succession, without letting the ball touch the ground. Even if two of the four rebounds off the crossbar were faked with CGI, as many have claimed, we want to believe Ronaldinho *could* do that trick four times in a row.

It's as if Ronaldinho, more than any other player, still plays the game to discover what he can do next. Or, as his manager at Barcelona, Frank Rijkaard, said, "Instructions? I don't give him instructions, just complete freedom to do what he wants." The soccer field is a wide playpen for Ronaldinho's imagination. It makes sense that Brazilian comic book author Mauricio de Sousa has created a series of cartoon characters based on Ronaldinho, his brother, and his mother. He elevates the game with moments of brilliance that are almost cartoonish in their otherworldliness. Imagine scoring twenty-three times in one game.

More than anyone else, including Zidane, Ronaldinho reminds everyone that soccer, at its best, is an art form.

When I reach Carnarvon school, I lean the bike against a chain-link fence and fumble with the unfamiliar lock. I have always made it a point of principle to own a bike that isn't worth stealing; therefore I have never bothered with bicycle locks before. I would rather have someone steal my bike than be paranoid all the time. Therefore I must borrow my wife's bike, because I don't own one.

The four-digit combination is 3516, the same numbers for our street address. Our shared bank account has a password with four numbers too, based on our four first names. This is how marriages work, I think. This is why people stay together. They amass savings of memory, shared history, and it becomes the currency of shared intimacy. Gradually, after thirty-five years together, you begin to feel rich. All those photo albums are better than money in the bank. Somebody knows you; you know them. You are not alone. Marriage is a river raft that won't sink or flip over. You think it's about romance when you start out, but love turns into a form of memory banking to get security.

There is a brick wall on the side of Carnarvon that adjoins the playing fields, about twelve metres high and twenty-five metres long, without windows. Between the ages of six and twelve, I attended a school that also had a windowless wall, not as wide, but higher, made entirely of cement. Whenever I couldn't find anyone else to play with, I spent many happy hours with that wall.

Almost fifty years ago, like Ronaldinho, I too was once safely inside my own world of fantasy football, immune to the anxieties of adulthood, ignorant of death. It only occurs to me that the walls of Carnarvon school and Pauline Johnson school are connected by a half-century of soccer *after* I start to tentatively warm up, one kick at a time, reawakening physiological memories.

Without giving it much thought, I have made my way back to a neighbourhood playground to play with myself in the most innocent sense of the word. Evidently soccer can be a form of reversion therapy. My soccer past is a magnet, pulling me back towards boyhood. This doesn't feel at all like a retreat from reality; it feels instead like a better version of reality.

I cannot possibly explain this to anyone, or even attempt to talk about it, but it seems to be happening to me, at age fifty-four, and I am not going to fight it. If I keep thinking about Ronaldinho's smile, the world seems to turn into a better place. "In life, there is light and there is obscurity," he says. "Why stay in the dark and be sad? I have always chosen the light side. I am in good health, I have a fantastic family, I play football. My personality is to have fun in everything I do. How could I not be happy? I have always approached life in that way. I am not scared of facing the pressure of the club, the fans, and the press. I know that my role is to make people happy. I like that, and I will play football all my life for this reason."

Initially I don't pound the ball against the wall. My right calf muscle can't take it. So I just try to keep the ball in constant motion. For weeks I have been troubled by my free kicks. My corners have been fine, but my last twenty or thirty free kicks have been frustrating. I am losing my self-confidence, and I worry that my teammates must be losing confidence in me.

I need to practise. I need to concentrate. I need to kick this ball against the wall. It is not a form of penance; it is more like a form of prayer. I am praying to the soccer gods to give me back my strength and my accuracy. And I am entirely certain that if Ronaldinho could read my thoughts, he would understand my situation perfectly.

Here I am an invisible almost-old guy. Three Chinese-Canadian kids are playing basketball on the asphalt court nearby, taking absolutely no notice of me. A father walks by with his four-year-old and I stop kicking the ball until they pass out of range, the way a polite driver might stop for a pedestrian at an intersection. I don't even merit a cautious glance. Perhaps ten years from now I'll look old enough to be noticeable on the playground as an anomaly, but so far I have only morphed into nothing special.

Two seasons ago, I was asked to show my driver's licence three times after our games. The opposition didn't believe I was over fifty. When my wife didn't know I was listening, I could sometimes hear her happily mentioning this to people on the telephone, to friends and relatives. But last season it didn't happen even once. So I must be aging.

I'm still contending. I'm still a contender. I'm not pathetic yet, I tell myself, as I keep kicking the ball against the wall with the furtiveness of an alcoholic. Maybe soccer is just a foolhardy habit. Maybe I shouldn't be looking forward to this trip to Spain quite so much. Maybe it's mere escapism. Maybe Ronaldinho's smile is devilish. Maybe I'm being lured into a humiliating trap. Maybe pride comes before a fall. Maybe I need to be more careful. Maybe my right knee is never going to heal. Maybe I'm never going to be a better player.

The day I start to take pride in *still* being able to play, I hope I will be able to quit. Right now, it's not like that. The ball caroms off an outcropping in the bricks, flying sideways towards the street. A young woman jogging along the sidewalk sees it rolling towards her, and she stops running and retrieves it for me, the way people do, out of courtesy, and timidly kicks it back to me. There is a pleasant exchange of smiles, even though I am old enough to be her father. As they say in one of those old Monty Python routines, "I'm not dead yet!"

So I start to experiment. I visualize what it must be like to curve the ball around a wall. I imagine an eight-foot-wide goal painted onto the brick wall. I imagine a wall of five players standing before me, about ten metres away, with their hands covering their privates. I place the ball for a free kick. My strategy is more fanciful than athletic. I decide I will simply turn myself into Ronaldinho and use wishful thinking to curve the ball around the wall.

This is not exactly the best way to learn new techniques, but when you don't have a coach, and you're probably too old to be coachable, you have to start somewhere. When I was a boy, curving the ball was inconceivable. The game has evolved, and I have not evolved with it. So I must learn a new trick in order to prove that I am not an old dog.

In all my years of playing soccer, taking hundreds and hundreds of free kicks, I have never once attempted to "bend it like Beckham," but today is the first day of the rest of my life, et cetera. Nobody on the entire planet gives a damn whether I make a fool of myself or not. I am amazed to realize I have not lacked the ability to curve the ball around a wall so much as I have lacked the imagination to do it. Whether or not Ronaldinho really did hit that crossbar four times in a row, keeping the ball aloft the whole time, is secondary to the *idea* of doing it. Before you take a trip to an exotic land, first you must be inspired to plan the journey.

My experiment goes poorly at first. Most of my shots into the invisible wall are hapless, and feeble. I'm like an infant taking baby steps. I tell myself I am not genuinely trying to curve the ball, I'm just trying to help my body mimic the technique, to introduce an idea. I soon discover if I run at the ball straight on, the way I do when I want to send the ball flying forward like a missile, a low screamer, it's never going to work. It's mandatory to approach the ball from an angle. It only takes about three tries before I begin to get a feel for the geometry involved.

I am seeking a glimmer of hope, a sliver of success. It's a matter of body control, balance. To generate some spin, it becomes necessary to sacrifice some velocity in order to twist my foot at the point of impact. Swinging my foot in a wider arc, using the inside of my boot, feels unnatural at first. It's like trying to teach yourself to swing a golf club. This is not something the body has learned to do over millions of years. It requires tedious measurements. It's science meeting art.

I have to retrieve the ball after each errant shot. My legs are getting sore. I am reminded of that teenage girl in *Bend It Like Beckham* who practises in her backyard in London, trying to curve the ball around her mother's laundry hanging out to dry. That was the best soccer sequence in the whole film. Her mother scolds her, but only half-heartedly. If you want to play the violin, you have to sound terrible at first, but who can fail to appreciate when someone makes the effort?

Enduring humiliation is the first step in learning. Possibly this is why we learn about Buddhist monks whipping novices. Once or twice I succeed in spinning the ball with a forceful kick. But if I reach the invisible goal almost twenty metres away, it's a fluke. The sideways approach complicates my sense of accuracy. The invisible wall of defenders has little to fear.

After about thirty attempts, my knee is starting to cry foul. But I finally make a breakthrough. One of my shots curves about thirty centimetres. Then another. I try to allow my body to take the shot, as much as my brain. I soon discover there must be a balance between the two. If I relax my mind during the split second prior to impact, it enables my body to do the job for me, the same way I take corner kicks.

It's like golf. If you think too much about the mechanics, you're going to hit the ball into the woods. If you try to isolate your concentration on just one part of what you're doing, that will guarantee a dreadful shot too. Instead I'm Ronaldinho, and I'm *enjoying* taking the kick. It is a wonderful privilege to be sweating and panting like an old dog, hitting wildly inaccurate shots against a brick wall. Without knowing how or why, I suddenly take one shot with my left arm outstretched as I sweep towards the ball. This is the element that was missing!

For mathematical reasons only a physicist could explain, the outstretched arm serves as a balancing rod, a crucial component of the kick. Immediately I try this again, and I know it's right. If that left arm is extended, it somehow guides the right leg swinging sideways. I forget about the imaginary wall. I concentrate on the left arm, measuring its effect, not bothering about where the ball goes. This leads to some integral fine-tuning. I discover it is absolutely essential to drop the outstretched arm just before the foot makes contact with the ball. There is something about the downward motion of the arm that helps provide some control on the curve. If the left arm remains outstretched during the kick, it just feels like bad golf. If that arm suddenly drops to point at the ground, the torso can twist in unison with the right foot.

Even so, I'm now certain that if Ronaldinho or Roberto Carlos or Beckham manages to curve the ball around the wall and score into the corner of the net, there has to be an element of luck involved, because the more you practise this shot, the more you realize you cannot be looking at the goalkeeper or the net at the moment of impact, or during the follow-through. The head has to be down. Again, there's an analogy to golf. Keep your eye on the ball, and your head down.

All I will have to do now is practise this shot for an hour a day, every day, for the coming year, and then . . . My legs hurt and my back is stiff. It's time to go home.

I have just had my first violin lesson. I will never play like a maestro, but one day I might be able to scratch out a tune. If we are playing in Spain and there is a free kick just outside the box, you never know what might happen. It's something to think about while I'm riding home. It is permissible to dream.

PART TWO

THE ROAD TO GRANADA

Back Row: *Ross, Hans, Ed, Christian, Alan C., Myles, Ken, Dave N., Serge.* Front Row: *Tony N., Nick, Ian, Tony A., Alan, Fidel, Trevor, Bruce.* Missing: *Randey, Dave T., Richard.*

WORLD CUP 2006

Humankind has grown larger and richer in my heart with the addition of other peoples. – Mongolian novelist Galsan Tschinag

Some people climb church steps on their knees. Others run the Boston Marathon. I was called upon by God to watch every game of the World Cup. In June 2006 amateur football-ogists all over the planet, from Vladivostok to Woodstock, from St. Petersburg to Pittsburgh, from Rio to Tokyo, vowed to watch all sixty-four matches, not merely pulling for favourite teams, but cheering for brilliant soccer.

Even before it was over, I didn't want it to end. As a tele-vision gathering of the tribes, the 2006 World Cup brought us together better than the first moon landing. It didn't matter whether you were a Sufi in Mali or a Malibu surfer, watching the World Cup felt like a vaguely humanitarian gesture. WE ARE THE WORLD. WE ARE THE PEOPLE. We all com-plained in hundreds of different languages about the same referees; we all guessed who was faking injuries. We all kept track of the number of times they showed Maradona in the stands looking tanked, or Posh Spice, David Beckham's wife, in a tank top.

Some of us even persuaded ourselves that watching the World Cup from Germany *meant* something, as if our seden- tary global wave of open-mindedness was an antidote to the fear-mongering of the White House. Watching World Cup 2006 was better than a peace march with placards, because we didn't have to go far from the refrigerator. Best of all, my month-long spiritual retreat to the sofa marked the onset of mental preparations for my own team's international match exactly one year hence, in Spain.

I especially enjoyed seeing all thirty-two teams lining up before their games, beneath the stadiums, holding hands with innocent mascots, shifting their feet like nervous gladi- ators, waiting for the face-painted crowds to rise at their appearance. No matter how many times I watched that prelude being repeated, I never ceased to wonder what those players could be thinking, and how those children beside them must have felt.

Most players avoided eye contact with anyone, retreating into themselves, but the Brazilian captain, thirty-six-year-old Cafu, was an exception. He made conversation with his fair- haired escort, making her smile and laugh, respecting her in a fatherly way. No wonder everybody loved the only non- European team ever to win the World Cup in Europe. Even better, the Samba Boys played their drums on the team bus on the way to games and were told by their coach that it was okay to have sex during the tournament.

One-third of the entries in my team's soccer pool picked Brazil to win. The votes were Brazil (13), England (6), Italy (4), Netherlands (4), Argentina (3), France (1), Czech Republic (1),

Croatia (1), United States (1), Ukraine (1), and Germany (1). I cast that lone vote for Germany because

- the home team always has an advantage;
- only Brazil had scored more goals in World Cup play;
- I was impressed by German coach Jürgen Klinsmann's congenial, short-sleeved approach on the sidelines. As a newly retired player, "Klinsy" wasn't acting like a dictatorial father figure, or an imported guru hired to be impartial;
- I remembered the immortal words of English striker Gary Lineker, who said, "Football is a very simple game. For ninety minutes, twenty-two men go running after the ball, and at the end the Germans win."

After the final whistle, the number of times the ball strikes the crossbar is no longer relevant, red cards and corner kicks are gradually forgotten, tantrums from coaches turn into obscure footnotes, and incidents of gentlemanly behaviour fade even faster, so I decided I would monitor the action closely in the hopes that I could appreciate the game beyond the memory of who wins and who loses.

If you don't write things down, you don't get to remember Iran's brazenly handsome goalkeeper – looking oddly like a muscular Errol Flynn – presenting the ponytailed Mexican captain with a bouquet of flowers prior to the kickoff at Nuremberg on June 11, 2006.

If you don't write things down, you don't get to remember the dangerous collision on that same Nuremberg pitch between a very blond Swedish attacker and a very black fullback from Trinidad and Tobago and the way they both picked themselves up, grinned, and embraced, enjoying their decisions not to enact the manly pretence of hostility.

Such judgments at Nuremberg are never recorded in history books, but these are the moments that keep us watching, as much as the goals. When civility triumphs over barbarism, everybody wins.

Having downloaded my BBC Sport World Cup 2006 Wall Chart in order to keep track of all the scores, I proceeded to join the largest television audience in history, priming myself for our encounter with the Spaniards, which loomed large on my sporting horizon. At fifty-four, I was losing my World Cup virginity, and it was none too soon. The 2006 World Cup was the starting line for the Granada encounter, a crash course in international soccer relations.

✪

Already the prospect of playing in Spain was making me anxious. My relations with the less skilled players were becoming strained. Worse, I didn't know how to shut myself up. I began to hear myself yelling at my fellow players during our games, chiding them for inferior passes, and grimacing aloud when they flubbed a shot. A steady diet of three World Cup games per day would be just what the doctor ordered. I would be brought down to earth by the feast of talent.

Instead of fretting over my own team's aging ineptitude, I became happily distracted by pre-tournament shenanigans. Would the president of Brazil apologize for saying Brazil's striker, Ronaldo, was too fat? Would the Spanish coach, Luis Aragonés, apologize in person to French striker Thierry Henry for calling him a "black shit" back in 2004?

Sports as valium. I seriously questioned if perhaps our

embittered world might turn into a better place if all males could watch two or three international matches per day, 365 days per year. If only George Bush Jr. could develop a passion for *real* football. If only the Taliban could have access to my channel 113. The nuances of the stock market or the latest nightmare in Iraq were rendered insignificant. Watching football each day felt entirely natural, like eating three meals a day, or praying five times to Mecca.

It was much more important for men around the world to sit in coffee shops and discuss the relative merits of the 4–4–2 versus the 4–5–1. We learned that thuggish-looking English striker Wayne Rooney was recovering from a broken bone in his foot, but Liverpool striker Djibril Cisse couldn't compete for France, after breaking his leg. Michael Ballack, the Chelsea-bound midfielder, was rumoured to be having a tiff with coach Klinsmann; Togo's entire team was threatening to boycott their games because they weren't getting paid.

For one month, *this* constituted the news.

When Togo's German-born coach resigned less than a week before his squad's opening match, the Togo football federation let it be known that Otto Pfister drank too much. Pfister threatened to sue. Then he reappeared on the sidelines for Togo's opening match against South Korea.

Four Central African teams were making their World Cup debuts. All four would lose their opening matches, and several would have grounds for questioning referees' decisions. Two of the Central African teams, Côte d'Ivoire and Angola, were ranked fifth and ninth respectively on the United Nations index of most corrupt nations, but it was Italy that was burdened with a major football game–fixing scandal going into the tournament.

The fifth African team was Tunisia. The only African nations to previously advance beyond the opening round were Nigeria in 1994 and Senegal in 2002. Voting with my head, I had picked Germany, but voting with my heart I would be pulling for Togo, Côte d'Ivoire, Angola, or Ghana. Or, failing a miracle, France.

Eight years earlier, my family had watched Zinedine Zidane & Co. beat Brazil while we were vacationing in southern France. That night my wife fell in love with Zidane, and I entirely approved. I felt much the same way about him. I wanted France to win, because I wanted Zidane to win. Like me, he looked like an old guy still trying to prove himself.

Like Hansel dropping bread crumbs, to prevent myself from getting lost in a Black Forest of football mania, I kept my World Cup diary religiously up to date, one game at a time, maintaining special interest in the French, the Germans, the English, and the rapidly improving Africans.

⚽

For England's first match, I rose at five-thirty in the morning and drove to an ex-Englishman's house to watch several former Englishmen, now Canadians, watch their former nation tentatively rise to the occasion. Jam was spread on croissants, coffees consumed. There was no raucous cheering, no leaping off the sofa in front of the high-definition feed. Ever since Becks had slipped onto his arse while taking a penalty, and had also managed to get himself ejected from a World Cup game, his photogenic, matador-like presence on the pitch mostly inspired trepidation. With a metrosexual like Beckham for a captain, England could not realistically hope to repeat their triumph of forty years earlier, back in those glory days of 1966, when the English lads in their tight-fitting white trunks had been gallantly led by a "hard man" like Bobby Moore.

The sense of reluctance to invest faith in England was palpable. Prior to Beckham taking his umpteenth free kick, when he adopted that classic pre-kick pose of his, as if he's modelling for Madame Tussaud's or competing for attention with *The Discus Thrower*, one of the ex-Brits quipped, "There you are, boys. That's what a generous lover looks like."

After growing up in traditional English households, it was difficult for these guys to swallow the preening and poised style of modern players, who needlessly stepped over the ball as they raced down the field. They had never learned such skills themselves. Most of the ex-Brits had more faith in the likes of Steven Gerrard, an all-rounder, or their tough-as-nails defender, John Terry. To them, Beckham and the likes of Cristiano Ronaldo were pussyfooters, while Frank Lampard and Gerrard were two-way players who performed like do-or-die soldiers. Either of them would have made a better captain.

For my friends around the TV, football demanded sacrifice of body and soul. It was necessary to exhibit this sacrifice by never displaying weakness. And yet the game was evolving into something more inventive, something more *delicate*, and something more theatrical. To make matters worse, much of this evolution was being fostered in the Premiership, where grown men were seen rolling around on the field, clutching their ankles, and screaming like banshees. According to racist stereotypes, that sort of behaviour belonged in Argentina or Italy, not England. Oh, how the mighty were falling.

After England barely beat Paraguay, we all thanked our host for a lovely breakfast and drove away beneath the speed limit. I pulled out of the driveway behind Alan Cook. Back in England, Alan Cook's father, a long-distance cyclist, used to watch the Brazilians on the telly with disgust. He distrusted their style of play, all those nifty, short passes. He called it pit-pat football. Real men didn't eat quiche. And real men don't indulge in pit-pat football.

Even though Alan might have lost a step or two as he approached age sixty, he still played with a stout heart. He had inherited a style of play that was brave and unembell-ished. He had one move to outwit the opposition, the simple but effective about-face by stepping on the ball. It worked every time. He always gave his best effort and could be counted on to make the prudent pass. He was someone you wanted on your team because he never said or did anything to detract from it.

Some games I watched with my teammates, and others I watched alone. The most-watched game in the world was Brazil's opener with Croatia. Fidel's ten-year-old son, Tonko, watched that match in the town square of Fidel's hometown in Dalmatia, Croatia, having received permission to leave his Vancouver school early and visit relatives in the old country. After seeing the match outdoors, with the other towns-people, Tonko telephoned his dad with a game report.

It reminded me of the World Cup eight years earlier, when I had scheduled a family vacation to the south of France, not realizing we'd be there during the World Cup games. The four of us watched the final game in a tiny village bar along with several other tourist families who cheered as Zizou scored those two headers to beat the Brazilians 3–nil.

Determined to find some celebratory action, my eldest son, Jeremy, and I drove in our rented car to Uzès, but we could only find a few dozen young people listening to loud rock music, honking their horns. The city fathers and mothers of Languedoc had evidently all gone to bed, and we were left to assume either that this, like much of southern France, was rugby country, or possibly the dark skins of the victorious French team, led by a balding guy with Algerian parents, didn't set the locals' hearts on fire. We drove home that night along an otherwise deserted country road lined with elm trees, their trunks all painted white at eye level. Both of us were drunk, and we felt as if we were in a movie, giddy with laughter, happy for France even if most of the French couldn't be bothered.

I turned off the headlights and we drove by the light of the moon.

Eight years later, in 2006, everyone was talking about Nike's Dream Team commercials in which two Spanish youngsters pick sides, inviting twenty-two of the world's best players for a game on their sandlot. The split-second editing of those commercials made repeated viewings tolerable, but they also promulgated the growing notion that superior football was some form of hyperactive ballet, fast-paced entertainment for people with an attention deficit syndrome.

Around the world we were being persuaded by Nike to accept that free-spirited South American football was superior – *Joga Bonito*, and all that stuff. But did trickery and flamboyance and individual creativity really prevail over stamina and disciplined teamwork? The more I watched, the more I came to suspect the goalkeeper was generally the most important player on the pitch, not the player who could balance the ball on the back of his neck. The striker who didn't panic and calmly placed the ball into the net with the side of his foot, à la Thierry Henry, was more valuable over the course of a long season than the acrobat who scored once every year with a spectacular bicycle kick. But the ads told a different tale. I began to wonder if fast-paced advertising was altering the game more than the Brazilians were.

Does fierce resolve over ninety minutes beat nine seconds of finesse? Should you want to play on a team with stout-hearted men? Or should you want to play on a team composed of men with flair?

The World Cup was an ideal place to look for answers.

EUROPE RISES

There is no greater drama in sport than a team trying to validate its national character in the World Cup. – Jeff Rusnak

One-quarter of the thirty-two teams in the 2006 World Cup were debutants, but only one of these (Ukraine) went as far as the quarter-finals. Only six non-European teams made it to the Round of 16, resulting in the first all-European semi-finals since 1982. After my African longshots were eliminated, I concentrated my hopes on Germany, my soccer-pool pick, and I retained a soft spot for France. I tried not to pull for England. Cursed by a false sense of superiority gleaned from colonialism, the English national team was always a tragedy waiting to happen.

Only 15 per cent of Germans believed their team would

win the World Cup, but Germany was ranked third most likely to win by the bookies. I sided with the bookies. Germany looked unbeatable in the early stages, noticeably more cohesive. With apparent ease, their Polish-born striker Miroslav Klose emerged as the tournament's top marksman.

Blitzkrieg. That word must have been used in headlines around the world after Germany pulverized Sweden with a barrage of shots, winning 2–nil. Their superior team mentality was apparent at four minutes when their other Polish-born striker, Lukas Podolski, raced to the sideline to celebrate his goal with his teammates. Coach Jürgen Klinsmann leapt into the melee, as if forgetting he was no longer one of the players.

The quarter-final encounter between Germany and Argentina built slowly to a climax. Evenly matched with contrasting styles, the two countries had tied their previous two meetings, they had won five World Cups between them, and they had met in the finals twice. During a scoreless first half, there were precious few serious attempts on either goal, but Argentina had superior ball possession.

The Argentinians scored first on a corner kick by Riquelme, headed home by their defender, Roberto Ayala, at forty-nine minutes. After a goalmouth collision, the South American keeper was replaced by his backup. Hoping to preserve his slim lead, Argentina's coach, José Pekerman, removed two of his best offensive-minded players, Riquelme and Crespo, in favour of more defence. Adding the speedy David Odonkor, Germany grew stronger and equalized on a cross from their injured leader, Ballack, that was headed onward by Tim Borowski, and headed once more by Klose for his fifth goal of the tournament, at eighty minutes.

The only thing settled by the thirty minutes of extra time were the German nerves. Having gained the ascendancy in the second half, Germany entered the penalty shootout with a psychological advantage. Their side had not lost in a penalty shootout since 1976. In eighteen attempts, the only German to miss a spot kick in World Cup shootouts was Uli Stielike, in 1982 against France.

Riquelme and Crespo could only watch as four German players in succession took flawless penalty kicks and Arsenal netminder Lehmann stopped shots from Ayala and Esteban Cambiasso. "We were convinced that if we got to penalties we'd advance," said Klinsmann. The mental toughness of Germany won the day.

My selection of Germany to win fitted my concept of how the game must be played. The Germans don't stop. They don't lie on the ground and wail. They go at you for ninety minutes. Their stamina is frequently (and unfairly) described as machine-like. This is how I believe football must be played – with the intensity of hockey. There must be a tremendous amount of will involved over 90 minutes (or 120 minutes). As a young team with a vibrant and upbeat coach, the Germans were not dedicated to winning by trickery or fancy footwork or suffocating defence. As I saw it, they were out-teaming their opponents.

Watching the first semifinal match between Germany and Italy in a local cinema proved to be appropriate. The match turned out to be one of those unbelievable Hollywood thrillers. The Germans were playing their semifinal in noisy Dortmund, where they had not been beaten for fourteen games, stretching back to 1935. Literally the last kick of the match was a goal.

Italy, much to their credit, matched the Germans in the first half, gaining greater ball possession and creating better chances. German playmaker Michael Ballack was smooth and noteworthy, but he failed to penetrate the Italian box. Arguably Ballack was hampered by the disappearance of his aggressive tackling midfield partner, Torsten Frings, suspended by FIFA after an Italian television network supplied some incriminating footage of a Germany–Argentina postgame squabble.

In the second half, Italy began to fade noticeably. Like a boxer on the ropes, Italy protected itself as Germany thrust forward again and again, sparked by darting runs by their sparkplug fullback, Philip Lahm. Of course, Italy's captain, Fabio Cannavaro, was outstanding, but I felt it was only a matter of time before Germany would prevail. The Italians were once more feigning injuries that were laughable when viewed on the replay.

When Klinsmann substituted his speedster, David Odonkor, he put his arm around him, chatted him up, and even rubbed his belly. The Germans were making optimistic runs, and Klinsmann was hoping Odonkor's pace might deliver the knockout blow. It appeared the Germans had superior fitness. But Italy's Marcello Lippi countered by adding his own speedster, Vincenzo Iaquinta.

After ninety minutes nothing was settled, but Italy had only thirty more minutes to avoid the shootout. As if scripted by Hollywood, the semifinal suddenly revived into a noble struggle between two dedicated and evenly matched sides. Neither team approached the waning minutes with cynicism. Italians Alberto Gilardino and Gianluca Zambrotta both hit the German uprights in the opening two minutes of added time. It was as if a Catholic angel had whispered into the ears of the Italians, "Boys, remember, these guys haven't been able to score on you either."

The midfields for both teams tended to evaporate during back-and-forth rushes, and millions of viewers nervously hoped for one side or the other to score – any side – just so long as this memorable battle would not be decided by a penalty shootout.

After 118 minutes, the popcorn eaters got their surprise ending. Midfielder Andrea Pirlo, the man of the match for a second time, gained possession at the top of the German box, and he didn't panic. Instead of attempting to shoot, he retained possession, moving sideways, avoiding several German defenders, until he was able to slip a five-metre pass to Fabio Grosso. With two German defenders between him and the German keeper, the young Juventus defender deftly curled the ball with his left foot into the far corner of the net. It was a glorious goal that sent Grosso charging across the pitch, rolling his head from side to side, as if he was equally shocked by ecstasy and disbelief.

Of the twenty-three players on Italy's roster, thirteen would be affected by the game-fixing scandal back home in Serie A. Seven of the eleven starting players for Italy played for the four teams that appeared destined for demotion: Milan, Juventus, Fiorentina, and Lazio. And yet Italy had somehow managed to rise above their domestic scandal to ruin the party of the home team.

To legitimize this triumph and further vanquish ignominy, the all-time Juventus goal-scoring leader, Alessandro Del Piero, who had replaced Luca Toni in added time, put Germany out of its misery with a breathtaking second goal that started with an interception by Cannavaro back in Italy's own box. As the beneficiary of a splicing run by Gilardino, the aging Del Piero curled a masterful shot into the right corner of Germany's net, once again giving Lehmann no chance. The Mexican referee blew his whistle. Germany was dead.

At the outset of the broadcast, when the BBC commentator had wondered aloud if Italy would be Machiavelli or Michelangelo, his comment had sounded like one of those contrived slogans, like One Small Step for Man, One Giant Leap for Mankind, invented by an ad agency or a public relations firm. But afterwards, when Italians all over the world, including Vancouver, were waving their flags and honking their car horns as if they had scored the winning goal themselves, it explained the arc of the story.

Whether or not the Italians deserved to be Michelangelo didn't matter so much to them, but appearances did. Italy had won ugly over the United States and Australia, but if you had to behave like Machiavelli to attain the privilege of looking in the mirror and seeing Michelangelo, well, that was just part of the Devil's bargain. That was sport. And my godless but dogged Germans were relegated to the consolation game versus Portugal.

⚽

With their balding superstar, Zidane, the French were a bunch of nearly over-the-hill guys, not unlike my own team, so they qualified as sentimental favourites. Their most capped player, Lilian Thuram, at thirty-four, had been persuaded to come out of his international retirement by

Zidane, also age thirty-four. "In football," Thuram said, "the egos are very big but you just learn to put others first."

France struggled at the outset of the tournament, barely surviving in their group. In the seven hundredth World Cup game ever played, Spain's rising star, David Villa, scored at twenty-eight minutes on a penalty resulting from a push in the box by Thuram. After five offsides were called against their striker, Thierry Henry, the French looked close to feeble, but then Franck Ribéry equalized at forty-one minutes, slashing through the Spanish back line to collect a well-timed Patrick Vieira pass and swerving to avoid the outstretched dive of Spanish keeper Iker Casillas.

It was over in Hanover for the Spanish at eighty-two minutes when Henry successfully faked an interference foul against defender Carles Puyol, who later commented, "If anything, it was a foul on Henry." Vieira's header off the resulting free kick by Zidane luckily caromed off Sergio Ramos into the Spanish net. After viewing the replay, only the crassest observer would allocate the goat's horns to valiant Puyol.

Much to their credit, the French had consistently outfought and outpassed the Spanish in the second half prior to Italian referee Roberto Roselli's lone questionable call. Surging with confidence, ahead 2–1, France had a more thrilling ascendancy at ninety minutes, when Zidane held onto the ball instead of shooting, outwitting a defender and coolly beating "St. Ikes" with a well-placed shot into the corner of the net.

Smiles of rejuvenation and relief on the faces of the French players signalled a new optimism. Zizou was back! The star of World Cup 1998 heartily embraced Henry and walked arm in arm off the pitch with Fabien Barthez, both grinning like schoolboys.

Spain's loss to France was the fourth successive World Cup match in which the team with the least ball possession won the match. In the preceding three encounters, Ghana had more ball possession than Brazil, Switzerland had more ball possession than Ukraine, and Australia had more possession than Italy. In those four games, the men of the match were defenders Patrick Vieira and Zé Roberto, and goalkeepers Gianluigi Buffon and Olexandr Shovkovsky. So what, if anything, did this tell us about the state of the game?

Spain had shared the goal-scoring leading during the round robin with Argentina and Germany, and the skilled Spaniards had been unbeaten in twenty-five games since Luis Aragonés had taken the helm in 2004. But the defensively strong French had stifled the offence of Spain and gained their victory mainly because Thierry Henry was able to concoct a phantom foul called against Puyol.

I drove to my Tuesday-night game wondering about defence versus offence. Sure enough, our side had at least 65 per cent of the ball possession that night but ultimately lost 4–3. We outran them, we outtackled them, we outshot them, but we lost due to miscues at the back, as well as an inability to capitalize on scoring chances.

From watching the World Cup and attempting to play the game hours later, I realized that confident ball possession was essential. I was able to set up two of my team's goals, the second of which was – ahem – described by one of my teammates as "Zidane-like" because I had retained possession, waiting for the right moment, rather than nervously distributing the ball at the first opportunity, as I often do.

Confident ball possession was more important than duration of ball possession, and the gallant Ghanaians were an obvious case in point. They had exerted tremendous pressure on Brazil, but their feverish attacks ultimately fizzled due to panic-stricken finishing attempts. In contrast, the Brazilians often appeared to go about their business in a leisurely, almost lazy fashion. Many people observed that Brazil only played well enough to win, and that was their style. That was part of a sophisticated intimidation approach: if the Brazilians appeared to be enjoying themselves while their opponents were struggling furiously to keep pace, it was one of the many ways one team could diminish the confidence of the other.

Confidence was almost everything. It explained why six of the eight quarter-finalists were countries that had previously won the World Cup. France, Portugal, Italy, and Germany made it to the semifinals, and they were all European teams. Despite the vibrancy of soccer on other continents, the old guard held sway. With Zidane rejuvenated, France had a player who could outdazzle the Brazilians, and that's precisely what he did. Zizou rose to the occasion in Frankfurt, effectively erasing the mystique of Brazil's much advertised superiority.

The quarter-final game between France and Brazil justified all the games that came before it – and all the 2006 World Cup games after it. Even if you weren't supporting France, your heart could not fail to quiver as the unshaven Zizou exhibited his masterful skills in the midfield, holding onto the ball for just the right amount of time, each time.

Again, confidence was the key. The Brazilians hadn't lost a World Cup game since the French had beaten them eight years earlier, bested by two goals from Zidane's head, and the Brazilians must have been unsettled by this fact. For once, Brazil stepped onto the pitch knowing they were beatable. For the French, it would be a case of déjà vu. Zidane didn't score, but it was his accurate free kick that Thierry Henry smashed into the top of the Brazilian net with a volley at fifty-seven minutes that made all the difference.

Although the 1–nil victory for France was monumental, another statistic was even more remarkable: Brazil only managed one shot on goal, a relatively feeble effort by Ronaldo in the ninetieth minute.

A spell was broken. It was the first time Brazil had been shut out in consecutive matches by the same team. Brazil's World Cup winning streak was halted at eleven games. The highly touted youngster Ricardo Kaka was mediocre when compared to the energetic runs of Franck Ribéry and Florent Malouda. The chunky striker Ronaldo did not become the first player in history to win his second consecutive Golden Boot. And for the fifth consecutive game, Ronaldinho was inconsequential. Angry fans destroyed a seven-metre statue of Ronaldinho in the Brazilian city of Chapecó, and he was severely criticized for partying with Adriano in Barcelona two days after the match.

French midfielder Patrick Vieira, one of six veterans on the team from France's World Cup win in 1998, was every bit as valuable as any Brazilian on the pitch, and Henry needed only two seconds to prove he was the most dependable striker in football. Experts had suggested Brazil was only playing as hard as they needed to play, but when finally faced with cohesive and talented opposition, Brazil showed they did not know how to swing into a higher gear. Midfielder

Zé Roberto cried and said, "The unity that we had outside the pitch was lacking inside it."

When Brazil fell behind 1–nil, they could not inject a collective sense of urgency. As talented individuals, they were either stylistically incapable of exerting themselves at full speed for ninety minutes or else they had been lulled into a false sense of security, seemingly drugged by adoration. Taking their superiority for granted, Brazil had only played one warmup game prior to the World Cup, a relatively meaningless 4–nil thrashing of lowly New Zealand. "Brazil arrived at the World Cup like globetrotters and were expected to go out and win it, but they never turned up," said former Brazil star Leonardo. "They relied on their individuality and never created a spirit to win the World Cup."

For all their storied reputations as mostly poor kids who learned their football on the streets and on the beaches, they had forgotten how to fight for their lives. It was the first time Brazil had failed to reach the semifinals since 1990, but if the Brazilians were emotionally shaken by their loss, the cameras never showed it. Upon announcing his retirement, along with Cafu, Juninho Pernambucano said all players over thirty ought to retire from the team.

France had grown stronger during the match, despite the age of their players, and fully deserved their victory, becoming the first country to beat Brazil three times in World Cup play. Praise was heaped on Zidane. "He made the difference, even more than in 1998," said Brazilian coach Parreira. "This was probably his best performance in the last eight years. He showed a lot of personality and creativity." Never shy to take an opportunity to ensure he remained elevated at the top of the pantheon of Brazilian players, the great Pelé added,

"Zidane is the master. Over the past ten years, there's been no one like him. He has been the best player in the world."

In the semifinal against Portugal, Zidane notched the only goal on a penalty after Portuguese defender Ricardo Carvalho tripped Thierry Henry at thirty-three minutes. With the exception of an uncharacteristic bobble by goalkeeper Fabien Barthez at seventy-eight minutes, the French enjoyed clear sailing in a forgettable second half, as if they were well aware they hadn't lost to Portugal since 1975. Ultimately the Portuguese deserved to lose as much as the French deserved to win. Marooned by his lacklustre midfield, the highly touted Portuguese striker Pauleta was substituted at sixty-eight minutes, having scored only one goal in the World Cup. Dubbed a pantomime villain, Cristiano Ronaldo was booed for his diving tactics, but he was clearly the lone viable Portuguese threat to score. Zidane donned Luis Figo's sweat-soaked jersey at the end of the game, knowing full well he would have the opportunity to finish his career on a high note, whereas his Real Madrid teammate would be burdened with regrets.

The stage was now set for Zizou to make a grand exit in Berlin.

THE WHITE BEAR

Sport is a preserver of health. – Hippocrates.
But then he never had a TV. – Annalisa Barbieri

With that wisecrack about television debunking Hippocrates, Annalisa Barbieri concluded her column about sports in the

June 16 issue of the *Guardian Weekly*. Hers was a timely piece about the need to pursue more important matters. I enjoyed it thoroughly. It was, after all, mostly about football.

Like someone who was renouncing smoking or alcohol – or men – the Italian-raised Barbieri was advocating *not caring* about the World Cup. The notion of writing an article about rejecting the world's most popular sport reminded me of a game invented by Leo Tolstoy and his older brother when they were young: they would go into a corner and try *not* to think of a white bear.

When I wasn't playing or watching the World Cup, I was writing about it and talking about it every day with Fidel. The night before, we had played one and a half games of football. We were riding on a merry-go-round of football, and we didn't want to get off. Football even pervaded my dreams. So this was the ideal time to come across Barbieri's viewpoint.

Knowing that four of the top Italian teams were in the process of being demoted from Serie A due to a fixing scandal involving the manipulation of Italian referees, possibly Barbieri was trying to distance herself from the game on some subconscious level. The last time there was a major scandal within Italian football, back in 1980, Italy went on to win the 1982 World Cup. But she didn't mention that. She only confessed that she had watched every game Italy played when her homeland had reached the semifinals of the World Cup in 1978 and won the damn thing in 1982.

Regardless of her motives, I was thoroughly taken with Barbieri's rational response to football. She noted that watching all sixty-four games of the World Cup required football fanatics to tape at least eight of them (because sixteen matches were played at the same time, in tandems, to prevent teams from strategizing to lose in order to avoid playing certain teams in the succeeding round). I suspected anybody who cared enough to know such things about the tournament must have sneaked a peek at at least a game or two, but Barbieri claimed to have gone cold turkey.

I am not one to deny a fellow journalist the chance to harmlessly tweak the truth for the sake of a paycheque – her subject, after all, was *only* sports – but the chances that Annalisa Barbieri had avoided seeing any footage of that awful Italy–U.S.A. encounter, in which an Italian had bloodied the nose of an American with a deliberate elbow, were next to none. A modicum of research revealed that Barbieri had written a Dear Annie column for the *Independent*, so she likely lived in football-mad England, where the games on the telly would have been unavoidable.

Barbieri's most compelling argument was that a great many people (she didn't say "men") devoted more time to sports than marriage. This was funny and true. I had drawn that same conclusion many times, particularly after miserable rounds of bad golf during my frustrating forties, before I returned to football. I had publicly rejected golf cold turkey on the Barbierian grounds that it was time-consuming and ridiculously expensive, while privately knowing I had quit the game mainly because I wasn't nearly as good at it as I thought I should be. Nonetheless, I accepted Barbieri's aversion to sport as wasteful, particularly regarding the amount of geography and water golf courses appropriated.

Although Barbieri didn't go so far as to suggest everyone should henceforth divorce themselves from the World Cup on the grounds of social irresponsibility, she was clearly suggesting that watching sports and talking about sports and thinking about sports, when bundled together, mostly added up to a colossal waste of precious time. And I thought, well, gee, good for her.

All I knew was that when one of our two over-fifties squads was faced with the prospect of playing with ten men, I immediately felt obliged to drive across town to Richmond for half an hour, as if I was a one-man version of the cavalry, and bolster their midfield. This was, of course, a clear-cut case of ascribing a noble motivation to a self-serving action. Fidel and I privately admitted it was really something quite different: I joked that we were soccer whores. We would play anywhere, with anyone, given half a chance.

Leaving that first game at halftime, driving halfway across Vancouver with Alan Cook to join my own club, I felt alive. Much the same sensation can be gained by chasing women one isn't supposed to chase. This is an aspect of sport that Annalisa Barbieri didn't investigate in her article – how and why sport is actually good for marriage.

As we drove across town, Alan Cook remarked that it was good that our wives approved of our playing. Even though they laughed at us sometimes, making jokes about us, and even though they gave us those I-told-you-so looks when we returned home injured, mostly they *liked* the fact that their husbands were still foolish enough to play football in their fifties.

Alan Cook suggested they were generous-minded for doing so, but I saw it differently. "When it comes to appearances, women care ten times more than we do," I said. "If they can have husbands who look relatively young and fit, it makes them look good too." The more I thought about it, the more I suspected this could be true.

I could have devoted those five hours of playing football to my marriage; we could have taken a long walk and fed the ducks or seen some silly Hollywood movie, but we have been married for more years than I can usually remember. Lessee now . . . we met in high school in 1968, and we were married in 1973. What year is it now? The last time I checked, my wife's eyes were blue, I think.

Reading Annalisa Barbieri's article, I wondered about her marital status. As much as I agree that sports can be viewed as an opiate of the people (my words, not hers) and that politicians often secretly care more about cricket than un-employment (her words, not mine), I felt she was cheating by not admitting, to herself or us, that she was making her point from a privileged position. That is, her team had won.

"In 1978 I grew so superstitious," she wrote, "that an entire month was taken up making Italy flags for various ornaments and toys to hold. After our 1982 triumph I looked away for good."

So that explained it. Annalisa Barbieri could go to her grave knowing her country had reached the zenith of world football. All her superstitious zeal had paid off! Once she had experienced the elation of watching an unforeseen hero, Paolo Rossi, win the Golden Boot by scoring six goals, what more could she possibly hope to gain from football?

Such a degree of communal joyfulness (when she was young?) could never be eclipsed. If my country ever won the World Cup, I might feel liberated from the game too. If

I could travel to the moon like Neil Armstrong, I might renounce any interest in visiting there a second time. Meanwhile, for as long as we can run, Fidel and I will continue to pick up a game wherever we can, and talk about football when it can't be played.

After Croatia was knocked out, Fidel had complex emotions, none of which were new. Croatians, he said, knew they always had something missing inside. Their talented team had imploded from lack of discipline, lack of belief. Croatians always feel guilty about something, he said, and so they blame others.

The Croatian coach blamed his players for their tie with Australia. At the same time, he was playing his own son on the team. In Croatia, soccer politics were inescapable. "I would hire a foreign coach," Fidel said, "and I wouldn't let any of the politicians anywhere near the team. In fact, I would hire a foreigner to run the country."

The complexity of soccer in Croatia was encapsulated in one incident that was not shown on the BBC's World Cup television broadcast. Nearing the end of Croatia's intense battle with Brazil, which Croatia nearly won, a young man wearing a Croatian jersey managed to get himself onto the pitch at Berlin. At the eighty-sixth minute, as reported in the Croatian media, a twenty-year-old named Ante Zuanic evaded security personnel long enough to kneel and kiss the boots of Croatian Dado Prso. To prevent harm coming to the well-meaning intruder, Prso, a striker for Glasgow Rangers, escorted the intrepid fan off the field. The young man was later fined 140 Euros for the disturbance. Contacted at his home in Split, Dalmatia, the boy's fifty-four-year-old father,

Mateito Zuanic, told reporters his son had been a promising player in Croatia during his teens, but the Zuanics had refused to pay a bribe to the local team, Hajduk, in Split, so Ante could never advance professionally. "He's quick like the wind," said Ante's father. "I'm going to pull his ears when I see him. Then I'll shake his hand. I'm so proud of the way he fooled all the German police."

Fidel was glad his son was in Croatia watching the game, so Tonko could see what was good and what was bad about Croatia, and he could begin to see more clearly what was good and bad about Canada. People in Fidel's hometown were deeply upset by Croatia's failure to advance, but Tonko informed them that they shouldn't feel that way because it was clear the team didn't *deserve* to go forward. Fidel was proud that Tonko had not been swept into a ritual of teeth-gnashing and accusations, consumed by a national feast of resentment and self-pity.

This, too, is why we play and watch football. When Hippocrates said sport was a preserver of health, I suspect he was not limiting his definition of health to physical well-being. For a ten-year-old to travel to a foreign land and tell his relatives they were responding foolishly to their team's failings is remarkable, something that is learned from watching and playing the game at a high level, learning to impose high standards on oneself.

We don't just play the game to win. We also play the game to teach ourselves the best ways to survive, and how to live.

MY WORLD CUP RUNNETH OVER

*Complaining about boring football is a little like complaining
about the sad ending of* King Lear: *It misses the point somehow.*
— Nick Hornby, *Fever Pitch*

Of course the North American media accentuated the diving,
faking, and poor refereeing decisions that tarnished a few of
the games in the Round of 16 – as if to explain why Canada
and the United States were unwilling to take the game as
seriously as other countries. And naturally Australian fans
were miffed about the dive in their penalty box during the
final minutes of their game with Italy that produced a fatal
penalty – but the growth of the Internet was leaving that sort
of narrow criticism in its wake.

Everyone was getting connected. Everyone was making
their own independent assessments and gathering their
own bits of arcane information. Was it significant that so
many teams had fullbacks as their captains – such as Rafael
Márquez (Mexico), Cafu (Brazil), Fabio Cannavaro (Italy),
Carles Puyol (Spain), Jean-Paul Abalo Dosseh (Togo), and
Olof Mellberg (Sweden)? Or that only three players had
beards (a Saudi, an American, and an Italian)?

Was it significant that this World Cup had more countries
with double-barrelled names than ever before – South Korea,
Serbia and Montenegro, Côte d'Ivoire, United States, Costa
Rica, Czech Republic, Saudi Arabia, and Trinidad and Tobago?

Did it matter that after England's victories in the round
robin, players' wives and girlfriends were able to visit their
partners in their hotel rooms, while players for Ukraine and
Costa Rica, on the other hand, were told to remain abstinent?

Did it matter that while more than half the teams had foreign-born coaches, all four teams to reach the semifinals didn't? Or that while the German staff of Jürgen Klinsmann analyzed their opponents' strengths and weaknesses by watching countless hours of videos, French coach Raymond Domenech took his players to visit museums and art galleries?

Even though Brazil was out of the tournament, they were not removed from the mental proceedings. World Cup watchers around the globe knew Brazil remained in the tournament as the measuring stick against which other teams would be judged. If Portugal could have prevailed, it would have been their first World Cup; if France, it would be their second. Near neighbours Italy and Germany had competed in their semifinal to determine which team would have the right to advance to the final and try to become only the second team to win the World Cup at least four times – second place on the all-time World Cup list.

FIFA made laudable efforts to mount an anti-racism campaign in conjunction with the World Cup, but ironically the unfolding spectacle made it difficult not to draw assumptions about national characters. The World Cup was a festival of prejudice made palatable by the fact that many citizens made much harsher assessments of their own country's failings than outsiders did. Clichés were reinforced. Italians were drama queens. Portuguese were deceitful. Germans were clinical. The French were unpredictable. The Spanish and Mexicans always choked. And the English were unimaginative.

Described as sterile by the announcer, England's 1–nil win over Ecuador will only be remembered because David Beckham scored the lone goal on a curving second-half free kick from thirty metres at sixty minutes, temporarily silencing his detractors by becoming the first Englishman to score in three World Cups. Wayne Rooney's tantrums outnumbered his goals. Ashley Cole was the English hero, making a remarkable recovery to deflect an early shot from striker Carlos Tenorio off the crossbar after a major miscue by John Terry, who was nonetheless selected as man of the match. As Rob Smyth observed in the *Guardian* after the game, "England's progress in this World Cup continues to startle only because it is so humdrum."

Having been blessed by a relatively easy draw in the "Group of Health" in the opening stages, the English side continued to play as if burdened by the tired illusion that somehow they deserved to win. Fidel said they could have placed a cardboard cutout of coach Sven-Goran Eriksson on the sidelines for all the emotion he displayed. Prior to their quarter-final showdown with Portugal, the cold fish Svengali did put his arm around Frank Lampard, presumably telling his midfielder not to worry if he had taken more shots than any other player in the tournament and still not scored, but evidently Eriksson failed to give directions to his mercurial striker, Wayne Rooney.

In their quarter-final match against Portugal, Rooney was red-carded at thirty minutes for stepping on the crotch of the prone Portugal player Ricardo Carvalho, then pushing his Manchester United teammate Cristiano Ronaldo. Reduced to ten men by the Argentinian referee, Eriksson added storklike striker Peter Crouch as a target for long-ball clearances, but at the expense of removing his most adventuresome player, Joe Cole. It did help a great deal more when he replaced his half-invisible captain, Beckham, with young speedster Aaron Lennon. England attempted twenty shots to Portugal's nine, but ultimately England endured for their ninth nil–nil draw in World Cup competition.

In the shootout, Portugal's Ricardo became the first goalkeeper in World Cup history to stop three penalty kicks (by Lampard, Gerrard, and Jamie Carragher). Only Owen Hargreaves, FIFA's man of the match, beat Ricardo. British fans were quick to note that Hargreaves was "sort of a German anyway" because he played in the Bundesliga. It was England's third consecutive World Cup loss in penalties. The *Guardian* had correctly predicted England would lose in a shootout in the quarter-finals. When I watched the England–Portugal game with Fidel, he correctly predicted Frank Lampard would not score in the shootout. He *knew* Lampard was doomed just by looking at his body language. Fidel suggested all the English players had been scared. "They need a coach from a warm climate," he said.

Only twelve hours after his team's third straight loss to a team coached by Scolari, David Beckham resigned as captain before the pressure to do so was overwhelming. "I wish to stress that I want to continue to play for England and help in any way I can," he said.

This earnest farewell didn't impress Richard Williams, who noted in the *Guardian* that Eriksson's successor "may feel that a 31-year-old winger whose effectiveness has been reduced to taking free kicks is surplus to requirements." Williams's acidic post-mortem suggested that England's footballers were chronically unable to learn that confidence must be earned; it cannot be inherited by birthright.

When Lampard said after the match that England had "deserved" to win, he was inadvertently exposing the problem at the heart of the team's consistent inability to scale the highest peaks. Earlier in the campaign Beckham had said England would get to the final because they "deserved" to be there. Since no deeper analysis was forthcoming, his listeners were left to infer that the evidence in support of his contention might have included any or all of the following:

- England's historic role as the game's mother country
- The popularity of the Premiership at home and abroad
- The inflated pay and celebrity status of its players
- The attention lavished on the public appearances of their wives and girlfriends

This attitude represents a culture of complacency at work, and it could be seen in the shootout against Portugal, when three of England's penalty-takers failed with attempts in which the slackness of their body language and their shooting spoke of men who were ready to put their trust in the belief, as England players have believed for several generations, that their reputations would be enough to ensure their success.

Or, in other words, the English invariably looked backwards at their lone victory in 1966, like Lot's wife, who looked back at Sodom and turned into a pillar of salt.

Clearly the World Cup is more of a theatre for failure than it is a theatre for success. Only one team every four years gets to feel otherwise. The consolation match to claim third place, this time between Portugal and Germany, lacked dramatic appeal. All goals came in the second half. Germany won 3–1.

Schweinsteiger, as a surname, means pig killer, but the young German midfielder Bastian Schweinsteiger added the definition Portugal killer by scoring twice on long blasts and taking a free kick that resulted in an own goal, enabling both Germany's veteran goalkeeper, Oliver Kahn, winner of the Golden Ball Award in 2002, and the host country to exit the tournament in high spirits.

To avoid the press, both the Italian and French teams went into seclusion. The Italians had played their semifinal game like they were French, and the French had played their semi-final game like they were Italians. Who could possibly know which squad would prevail? The Italians had a more vibrant and varied team, but the French had some grandeur about them, some inner calm. The French were relying on their defence, peppered with some inspiration from Zidane, and were playing only Thierry Henry up front, whereas the Italians, notorious for their defence, were playing more adventuresome football than usual, particularly when they substituted Iaquinta near the end of each contest. They would designate the tough-tackling Gattuso to stifle Zidane.

The oddsmakers gave Italy the nod, but the heart mostly went for France.

THE BERLIN FALL

What kind of game is this – demonic and divine? – Marguerite Duras

If you were hired as a football detective and your job was to pinpoint the seemingly insignificant moment that unlocked the secret to the most significant drama of the month-long World Cup – to find the hidden clue to Zinedine Zidane's downfall from grace, the footballing parallel to the angel Lucifer dropping from heaven in *Paradise Lost* – you might do well to rewind the footage of the infamous France–Italy finale more than one hundred minutes prior to his repugnant head-butt on the Italian defender Marco Materazzi, and freeze-frame the tape during the coin toss.

The coin toss is every bit as significant as the national anthems. It is the moment at which two teams begin to submit their fates to the football gods. As soon as the coin is sent flipping skyward, mere luck is involved.

And so the theatre of football begins, even before the ball is first kicked. The captains meet at the centre of the pitch like leaders of opposing tribes. In Berlin on July 9, 2006, as both team captains met with the businesslike Argentinian referee, Horacio Elizondo, it was the duty and responsibility of Fabio Cannavaro and Zinedine Zidane to represent their teams at the highest level, as football ambassadors, as sportsmen beyond nationalism, as exemplary men.

Cannavaro put a smile on his face, to at least enact the pretence of fraternalism, but Zidane was not in the mood for either artifice or courtesy. Having played 151 games for Juventus from 1996 to 2001, Zidane thought he knew Italians. Now, with the eyes of the world upon him, he behaved as if he knew they could not be trusted, and so he would not deign to treat Cannavaro as an equal. In doing so, Zidane was undermining the motto of the country he was representing, "*Liberté, Égalité, Fraternité.*"

As someone who had grown up on the rough streets of northern Marseilles, Zidane joined the ceremonial coin toss with the grim, unshaven face of a warrior. He had evidently decided in advance that to behave otherwise might be to admit weakness. When it came time to shake hands, Zidane, who had been glaring at Cannavaro like a boxer before a fight, chose to avert his eyes from the man who is acknowledged as possibly the best defender in the game of football and instead let his opponent become aware that his handshake was as cursory as possible, almost as dismissive as a slap in the face.

Approximately 110 minutes later, this relentless hostility would lead to the incident that stunned and appalled billions of viewers: when Europe's best player head-butted Marco Materazzi in the chest, leaving his team leaderless. With only ten men, the tournament's projected storybook ending became impossible, and Zinedine Zidane, the man with perhaps the most gifted feet in the world, was revealed to have feet of clay.

In the parlance of pop psychology, perhaps Zidane was too tightly wound. His failure to respectfully recognize Cannavaro as a worthy opponent, and even as a person with a face, revealed a fault line within the masterful dribbler, a weakness of character that would ruin his exit from the game: a faith in hostility.

⚽

You don't have to be a football expert to see there is a magnificence about the way Zinedine Zidane moves. He was selected as the first male model for Christian Dior for reasons beyond football. When Zidane squints through his hawklike eyes and walks across the field without moving his head, with perspiration dripping down his cheeks, his stare is eerie and menacing, like an animal captured through a telephoto lens on the plains of the Serengeti. Or as the French rock singer Jean-Louis Murat put it, "Nobody knows if Zidane is an angel or demon. He smiles like Saint Teresa and grimaces like a serial killer."

Zidane's teammates over the years have enthused about his powerful presence as much as his creativity. According to French team manager Jacques Santini, "He never shies from responsibility either on the field or off it. That's why he is such a good influence on the game and such a captain. He is never afraid." Zidane has a reputation for fearlessness, and this is a powerful form of leadership – but it should not be mistaken as the only form of leadership, or even the best.

Certainly in sports it is admirable never to show fear. Zidane has always had a lethal air about him, but advertising to others that You Cannot Beat Me is a relatively crude form of intimidation. Ruthlessness comes with a price – and Zidane ultimately paid it – but how sad and pathetic and disturbing his display of ruthlessness turned out to be! You knew, as soon as you saw Zidane head-butt Marco Materazzi, that you would remember the moment for as long as you lived. For Zidane lovers all over the world, this was as devastating as a car accident. After Zidane left the field, disgraced, the end result of the match became secondary. You knew you would be having as many conversations about Zidane's flawed character as you would have about the outcome of a sixty-four-game tournament.

There were dozens of high-definition cameras to record his football crime. As soon as the referee ran over to the linesman and asked him what had happened behind the play, and the linesman spoke for no more than two seconds, you had a sickening foreknowledge that a red card would be forthcoming. For those who had grown to idolize Zidane's football as flawless, watching the replay of his head-butt was about as easy as repeatedly watching those two airplanes crash into the Twin Towers. It was pure ugliness, only worse in one highly significant way: you knew Zidane got what he deserved. Judging by the way he walked directly off the pitch, he knew it too.

At the game's seven-minute mark, Zidane was very lucky. After Florent Malouda had gained a penalty in the box at the expense of Materazzi – who was a prominent figure throughout this game, involved in all four of its major incidents – Zidane stepped confidently to the penalty spot. With a calmness that bordered on insouciance, Zidane cheekily chipped his shot towards the net, allowing time for Gianluigi Buffon to dive too soon to his right. But instead of exhibiting Zidane's mastery of the situation, this shot caromed off the crossbar and plummeted down, bouncing once just behind the goal line before it spun out towards Zidane. He celebrated immediately, but very few others were sure if it was a goal or not. There was a strange interval of disconnection. The referee had to confirm for everyone that Zidane had indeed scored. And so the joy of that goal was missing from the event. The great Zidane had triumphed – but with luck. His French teammates could have been emboldened by the knowledge that they had just scored the first goal in the tournament against Buffon, other than that own goal Italy had allowed against the United States, but instead Zidane's goal was impure, as if Zidane had scored on a technicality.

The unconvincing nature of the strike mostly galvanized the resolve of the Italians. Within ten minutes, Italy responded with an equalizer, and once again it was play-maker Andrea Pirlo who made the assist as Materazzi made amends for his earlier transgression, heading home Pirlo's curling corner kick.

Zidane rose to prominence on two more occasions prior to the awful head-butting incident. Both were more significant in retrospect than when first seen.

Zidane was injured late in the game when Cannavaro made his presence felt literally, crashing into Zidane's shoulder as the two men contested for a header. As Zidane sat on the field, wincing and clutching his shoulder, he signalled to the French medical team that, yes, he was really hurt. The Italians weren't sure how to respond to this event. Cannavaro appeared to show some gentlemanly concern, but Zidane dismissed him as cynical.

Everyone waited nervously to see if Zidane had dislocated his shoulder, or if Cannavaro had dislocated it for him. The scrupulously even-handed referee allotted extra time for Zidane to be treated on the field, rather than whisked away by the stretcher-bearers. Elizondo shared the trepidations of the fans and the other players. Nobody – with the exception of the eleven Italians on the field – would want the game to resume without Zizou.

When Zidane trotted back into action only minutes later, billions felt relieved: the less-than-gentlemanly Italians would not be able to steal a victory by removing Zidane from the scene. But Zidane himself was clearly out of sorts. His shoulder was painful. Seen in retrospect, the angry look on his face when he re-entered the match might have been a sign that he was plotting revenge.

Having gained a clear ascendancy in the second half, the

French continued to dominate the play in extra time. As the game proceeded, the Italians were increasingly making errant passes, as if they were nervous, whereas the French were stroking the ball between themselves with calm determination. The elegant striker Thierry Henry began to play with more gusto. Whereas it looked as if Italy might be content to hold the fort, hoping to allow their goalkeeper, Buffon, to win the day in a shootout, France appeared more likely to score.

Having enjoyed a clear advantage in ball possession during the first half, Italy withered. Rather than try to score themselves, the Italians were relegated to trying to prevent the storybook ending in which a team of "old guys," including Fabien Barthez, Patrick Vieira, Zinedine Zidane, Lilian Thuram, and David Trezeguet (substituted at one hundred minutes), all of whom had won the World Cup eight years earlier, would amazingly repeat their heroics.

It almost happened. Fabio Cannavaro saved Italy with a last-ditch tackle on Malouda, and Franck Ribéry missed by inches, but the spectacular moment-that-wasn't occurred when Zidane leapt unmarked in the goalmouth, on a beautifully timed run, to head a perfect cross towards the goal. Having scored twice with headers against Brazil in the final in 1998, Zidane must have known, even before he jumped, that this would be his golden chance to make history as possibly the greatest footballer ever to play the game. If Italy's keeper, Buffon, hadn't brilliantly extended his arm and deflected Zidane's superb header clear, Zidane could have gone to his grave more venerated than Pelé.

This time, instead of clutching his shoulder in pain, Zidane clutched his head in disbelief.

It was only minutes later that Materazzi began his harangue, goading Zidane after grabbing his jersey, even pestering him as he walked away, until Zidane turned on the Italian with defiant rage, walked up to him, and, bang, the incident will be forever replayed as the second most infamous occurrence in football history, after Maradona's stupendously deceitful "Hand of God" goal in Mexico.

Zizou was ejected. And there were no further goals.

Prior to the penalty shootout, Barthez and Buffon embraced, genuinely, in a meeting of the minds and the hearts radically different from the coin toss between their two captains. Each man knew he had an opportunity to be the hero, or the goat, but each man also knew whoever won wouldn't be able to celebrate with unrestrained joy. The climax of this match was already marred. The manner in which they embraced and held on to each other said as much as any commentator could say about how the game had unfolded.

Neither Barthez nor Buffon were factors in the shootout. The Italians, led by Andrea Pirlo, were perfect with five goals from Pirlo, Materazzi, Daniele de Rossi, Alessandro Del Piero, and Fabio Grosso. Despite successful shots from Sylvain Wiltord, Patrick Vieira, and Willy Sagnol, David Trezeguet's lone miss, when the ball hit the crossbar, proved fatal.

⚽

For football puritans, Zidane's "moment of madness" must reverberate as a lesson with moralistic underpinnings. While the freedom to do evil, to cheat, to disregard the rules, is always tantalizing, eventually criminality leads to self-destruction.

In literature, this message is revealed in John Milton's epic seventeenth-century poem, *Paradise Lost*, in which Lucifer, a proud angel, refuses to view the other angels as equal to himself. Pride comes before a fall.

Zidane's folly was his indulgence in egocentricity. He allowed his pride to get the best of him. He placed the importance of his own emotions over the importance of his team's fate. His ultimate loyalty to his family honour and to his racial heritage overrode his loyalty to his comrades on the field, and to France. His counterattack on Materazzi, as an act of self-defence, as retribution, might have been justifiable or even praiseworthy in the eyes of some, but for most viewers of this human comedy with a ball it was a horrible way to end a great career. Life is a game of snakes and ladders, and Zidane, nearing the top of the board, rolled the dice and slid on the back of a snake, all the way down to where he started.

By indulging his vengeful and violent side, by failing to turn the other cheek, by reducing himself to Marco Materazzi's level, Zidane, like Lucifer, fell from grace. And his fall was injurious to more than himself. If his goatlike behaviour meant he was merely losing commercial endorsements as a male model, well, so be it. But Zinedine Zidane was the French equivalent to Jackie Robinson in baseball. Intellectuals had marked his ascendancy as the touchstone for a new era. As a player who saw himself primarily as someone of Kabyle Algerian descent, Zidane was fully aware of his importance as a symbol for others. After France's glorious victory over Brazil in 1998, when the Algerian flag was seen hanging alongside the famous tricoloured flag of France on the Champs-Elysées, Zidane knew he had won more than France's first World Cup. "We were a family who had come from nothing," he said, "and now we had respect from French people of all sorts."

Remarkably, as a so-called *beur* (French slang for Arab), Zidane topped a *Journal du Dimanche* poll for "the most popular Frenchman of all time." Although Zidane steadfastly resisted the temptation to make any overtly political state- ments, he fully recognized the responsibility his popularity entailed. "To be recognized by a whole country is incredible," he said. "This is massive. Before it was hard to talk about certain things, especially if like me you came from a difficult area or from an immigrant background. But now it tells you how France has changed and is changing. It's a message to everybody – politicians, the kids I grew up with, ordinary French people – about what can be done."

The team led by Zidane in 1998 was celebrated for being "black, *blanc*, *beur*." One French social critic named Pascal Boniface suggested Zidane's rise to prominence in French society marked the beginning of a new Enlightenment. The novelist Philippe Sollers suggested Zidane should become the French prime minister. After his father, Smail, left his village of Taguemoune in the remote hills of Algeria, endur- ing privation in Paris and settling in the northern suburbs of Marseilles, in La Castellane, an immigrant zone dubbed as a *quartier difficile*, Zinedine Zidane had somehow overcome racial prejudice and poverty to twice become FIFA World Player of the Year (1998 and 2000), and the world's highest- paid footballer (2001), when Real Madrid acquired him for roughly U.S. $66 million.

Having succeeded in elevating the prestige and honour of his fellow Algerian Muslims in France, he was ending his career by providing fresh fodder for the racists in France –

most notably the right-wing zealot Le Pen and his followers – allowing them to say, "Aha! You see! These people can't help themselves! In their hearts, they will always be barbaric!" Once an Algerian, the racists muttered, always an Algerian.

This was a tragedy well beyond the realm of football – and everybody felt it. Certainly the victorious Italians on the field did. One of their players had succeeded in goading the most sublime player in Europe to fall from heaven. It was an unseemly way to claim superiority. The body language of the Italians after the game's resolution showed they knew they were not outright winners. The Ukrainians had celebrated much more exuberantly when they had merely qualified for the quarter-finals. For that matter, the Trinidadians had celebrated more openly when they had gained a single point. Only Trezeguet's volley off the crossbar had separated France and Italy.

When it was over, it was easy to see there were three winners of World Cup 2006.

Germany's surprising team finished third, they scored the most goals (fourteen), and they boasted the winner of the tournament's Best Young Player Award, Lukas Podolski, as well as the winner of the Golden Boot for most goals (five), Miroslav Klose. More importantly, Germany had won friends, overriding the sixty-year-old stigma of Nazism and successfully welcoming the planet to the most widely seen and smoothly run human gathering in history.

France was a winner, beating Brazil and finishing second.

Italy won by becoming only the second nation to win the World Cup as many as four times.

As for Zidane, he could not escape the spotlight. Not only was he photographed with the French team at the Elysée

Palace, where they had lunch with French president Jacques Chirac on the day after the game, he was also filmed for worldwide coverage as he meekly waved from the presidential balcony to thousands of still-adoring French fans. Worse, and more absurdly, Zidane's exit from professional football was made even more problematic and controversial when thousands of journalists awarded him the Golden Ball award as the tournament's outstanding player.

This was an embarrassment for FIFA and for Zidane. To his credit, FIFA president Sepp Blatter suggested Zidane might be stripped of his Golden Ball award by a FIFA committee that investigates all red-card incidents. He told *La República*, "The winner of the award is not decided by FIFA, but by an international commission of journalists. That said, FIFA's executive committee has the right, and the duty, to intervene when faced with behaviour contrary to the ethic of the sport."

Prior to the match, Zidane had been the sentimental choice for the award because he was retiring and because he had not received the award in 1998, when journalists, casting their votes before the final ended, selected Ronaldo. Journalists in 2006 were able to vote for the Golden Ball award up until midnight on game day, but many of them voted before the head-butting incident, preferring to join the partying after the evening match, which ended only shortly before midnight. Traditionally journalists had been required to vote before halftime of the final game. It was not revealed or known how many of them did so, but certainly many did. Had FIFA been less hasty and required all journalists to cast their votes only after the final whistle, Italian captain Fabio Cannavaro would surely have won.

Zidane had an opportunity to make the most dramatic and noble exit in football history, witnessed by an unrivalled number of people, but instead he disappointed his wife and their four sons, his family, his countrymen, and billions of football fans by foolishly losing his head, much as he had done in 1998 and 2001. His ejection from the game marked the fourteenth time in his career that he had been red-carded.

Most famously, during Zidane's final season playing in Italy for Juventus, in 2001, he had received a five-match suspension for head-butting Jochen Kientz during a Champions League game against Hamburg. In 1998, Zidane had missed two World Cup games after he was red-carded at the outset of the tournament for his deliberate attack on the Saudi Arabian captain, Fuad Amin, ostensibly in response to a racial slur against his nomadic Muslim ancestors, the Kabyles.

This time it was quickly rumoured that Materazzi, a much-penalized player, had called Zizou a "dirty terrorist" or "the son of a terrorist whore." A Brazilian TV station engaged a lip-reader, who suggested Materazzi said something insulting about Zidane's sister. Others were fairly certain the Italian had said, "I wish an ugly death to you and your family."

Materazzi was coyly circumspect. He reported that Zidane had objected to Materazzi tugging on his jersey, by sarcastically saying, "If you really want my shirt, I'll give it to you afterwards." Materazzi admitted his retorts were insulting, but he would not repeat their exact wording or nature. Reports soon surfaced that Materazzi had responded, "I'd rather take the shirt off your wife." Or else, "You can keep your shirt for your sister, the prostitute."

The French wanted to make Materazzi into the villain of the piece, but he had not viciously head-butted anyone.

Zidane would not spill the beans, but he wouldn't entirely repent either. He said Materazzi hadn't used the word *terrorist*, but "they were very harsh words. You hear them once and you feel bad. You hear it twice. Then you hear it a third time. . . . I tried not to listen to him, but he kept repeating them. I'm a man, and I'm telling you that I would rather have been punched in the face than have heard those words. . . . I can't regret it, because that would mean he was right to have said what he did. . . . Of course the reaction has to be punished. But if there had been no provocation, there would have been no reaction."

By the time Zidane held his press conference and accused Materazzi of insulting his mother, the stand-up comedians and Internet wits were having a field day, vilifying the prideful French and the sneaky Italians.

Envisioned as a glorious gathering to obviate racism, the 2006 World Cup had culminated in a calamity that encouraged tribalism. After more than 5,800 minutes of mostly superb football, tragically one second of barbarism had prevailed as the dominant memory. It made us all wonder what the hell sport was really all about.

⚽

On the same night as the head-butting incident, we gathered with our wives for a long-planned Spanish-themed party at the home of our sixty-two-year-old left back, Ian Hutchinson, a part-time Hispanophile. Everyone was disappointed with the conclusion to the World Cup, including the two Italian-born Tonys on our team, both of whom expressed mixed emotions about the Italian victory.

As we ate paella and drank sangria under a huge willow tree, seated at outdoor tables covered by red-chequered table-cloths, we were all on our best behaviour. Nobody got drunk. Nobody said anything they shouldn't have said. Even the wives tried to like one another. If we could play football as well as we socialized, we would win every game.

In football, as in life, most of us are destined to go out with a whimper, not a bang. The evidence was undeniable. And yet we all harboured the same childish imaginings that somehow, if fate played into our hands, if the stars were correctly aligned, if the ball bounced our way . . .

But ultimately the downfall of the illustrious Zidane was both sobering and deeply troubling for me and my grey-haired teammates as we looked forward to our own, most memorable football encounter, in Spain.

In a nutshell: If the great Zidane couldn't manage to get things right, what chances did we have for making noble exits? How could we possibly keep from humiliating ourselves in Spain against opposition that was likely going to be formidable?

INTERVIEW WITH A MISTRESS #3

NETTIE: Why the big smile?

ALAN: I just got an email from Kyrgyzstan.

NETTIE: Who do you know in Kyrgyzstan?

ALAN: Our left fullback. He sent a message confirming he can play on Sunday.

NETTIE: Today is Friday.

ALAN: Correct.

NETTIE: So this guy is halfway around the world and he's planning on playing over-fifties soccer two days from now,
even though there are twelve time zones in-between.

ALAN: It's eleven or thirteen time zones.

NETTIE: How can that be?

ALAN: Depending on which way he flies back.

NETTIE: And this makes you happy.

ALAN: It does. Max is a terrific tackler. If we take into account
his speed and his stamina and his grit, he's our fourth
or fifth most valuable player. He used to be an engineer
in the military. Now he's a consultant.

NETTIE: What kind of consultant?

ALAN: Mining, I think. I'm not really sure. We have another
guy who works as the head engineer of the TRIUMF
nuclear research facility at the university. I don't know
exactly what his job entails. Another fullback, Brian,
was just in Ottawa negotiating some kind of national
public safety pact on behalf of British Columbia, but I
don't know exactly what he does for a living. We don't
talk about stuff like that.

NETTIE: Since you took over as manager, how is the season
going?

ALAN: Seven wins and one loss.

NETTIE: How did you lose one?

ALAN: We were playing against a team called Ben United,
and we didn't adjust to their offside trap. Our substitute
keeper let two shots go through his hands. We outplayed them, possession-wise, but we lost by one goal.
The longer we play, the more I agree with Tony Waiters,

the manager of Canada's national team, that one time
we reached the World Cup. He says the goalkeeper is
the most important player on the pitch. That was our
biggest problem area last year. The first thing I did
when I took over as manager was get us a goalie. It
changes the confidence level of the team. Fidel has
scored seven times for us in the past three games, but
if our keeper, Tony, doesn't show up, if he's twisted his
ankle or something, I'm worried sick.

NETTIE: It doesn't sound like being the manager is a whole lot
of fun.

ALAN: Keeping track of lineups, handling substitutions, strategizing, dealing with personalities and egos, it becomes
like a part-time job, only you don't get paid. Often it's a
pain in the ass. But ultimately it's a lot better than *not*
doing it.

NETTIE: You're a control freak.

ALAN: I'm a winning freak. The more you win, the more you
can't stand the idea of losing. Pretty soon you discover
the pressure to maintain your winning streak is as bad
as the pressure of being on a losing team, just struggling to win one game. They say money doesn't bring
happiness, but at least you can park your yacht right
next to it. It's much the same with winning. It doesn't
guarantee happiness. But you get to stay within close
proximity.

NETTIE: So winning can turn into an addiction.

ALAN: Something like that. No matter how much they're paid,
I'd guess it's never much fun being Alf Ramsey. Or
Matt Busby. Or José Mourinho. Somebody is always
second-guessing you. If you're the managerial type, you

start to look for things to worry about, even when
things are going well. You can't help yourself.

NETTIE: So with eight months to go before Spain, are you
getting nervous?

ALAN: Yes. You'd think eight months would allow plenty of
time for boyish dreams. We ought to be able to sit
happily in the Wolf and Hound and savour the anticipation of our greatest game ever, without the stress of
worrying about winning or losing, but already I foresee
problems, mainly administrative, and I want to fix
them before anybody else gets a chance to fix them.

NETTIE: Pray tell.

ALAN: I worry there could be too many players making the
trip, accompanied by too many wives, so the notion of
being on one team is going to evaporate, both on and
off the field.

NETTIE: You fear a fiasco.

ALAN: As far as I can see, it would be dumb to arrive in Spain
with enough players for two teams. It's hard enough to
form a cohesive team with fifteen guys, let alone thirty.

NETTIE: If it turns into a schmozzle, that just becomes part of
the story. For all we know, you guys could all be wiped
out on the team bus. If we could predict the future, it
wouldn't be worth living. You should go with the flow.

ALAN: I absolutely disagree. Somebody has to worry about
details. We didn't change from being a losing team into
a winning team by going with the flow. We had a
regime change. I wrote a memorandum at the outset of
our season, and all twenty guys signed off on it, agree-
ing we would have four half-fee players who could be
rested whenever we had too many guys. Now I make a

lineup several days in advance and let people know where they're going to be playing.

NETTIE: Stalin would approve. Do you make them salute when they show up at the park?

ALAN: I don't have to. It turns out nearly all of them like winning a lot better than they like losing.

NETTIE: That's why you're smiling?

ALAN: Yes and no. I have some good news and some bad news.

NETTIE: What's the good news?

ALAN: Tara and I are going to be grandparents.

NETTIE: What's the bad news?

ALAN: The due date is June 15.

NETTIE: The day you're arriving in Granada.

ALAN: It's a bizarre coincidence.

NETTIE: Now you've got a managerial decision on your hands.

ALAN: I already have the tickets.

NETTIE: You could still cancel.

ALAN: I've signed a contract to write a book.

NETTIE: Pshaw. You're going to miss the birth of your first grandchild, and all because you want to chase a ball around the way you did when you were six years old.

ALAN: I'll have dozens of years ahead to be with my grand-children.

NETTIE: Is Tara going or staying?

ALAN: Staying.

NETTIE: Hmmm. I see.

ALAN: She might come later, after the baby is born. It's the compromise solution.

NETTIE: This way you get to have your cake and eat it too.

ALAN: It's like the set-up for a movie. I could be transformed into a grandfather just as I'm scoring the winning goal.

It reminds me of an old film called *Damn Yankees*. This guy makes a deal with the Devil to beat the New York Yankees, so the Devil agrees to turn him into a young athlete who plays centre field for the Washington Senators. On the final play of the game, as he's running back towards the outfield fence, about to make the final out, about to secure the win for the underdogs, he starts to stumble and he turns grey. I remember that movie like it was yesterday. I saw it around the time I started playing soccer. In 1958.

NETTIE: It obviously made a big impression on you. The tragic hero. Making the ultimate sacrifice.

ALAN: There was a temptress in that movie named Lola. She sang this song . . . [Singing] "Whatever Lola wants . . . Lola gets."

NETTIE: I guess I'm your Lola.

ALAN: There goes our PG rating.

NETTIE: You are a typical baby boomer. Greedy beyond words. You want to become a granddaddy just as you're scoring the winning goal against the Granada Veterans, like that guy in *Damn Yankees*. That's where your imagination goes. You *enjoy* the added complexity of the first grandchild and the final game. I know men. I know what makes them tick. Ideally you will get injured during the game and you will continue to hobble around the pitch in pain until your moment of glory arrives. That's the way your childish brain works.

ALAN: If I'm a typical, unevolved baby boomer, why do you even bother with me?

NETTIE: It's never boring.

IN PRAISE OF STANLEY MATTHEWS

Football is an extraordinary education for life. – Michel Platini

Once a week, on Thursday nights, we put the cork back into
the wine bottle and drag ourselves away from our television
sets to congregate in a smelly gymnasium in a former school
for the blind. Here Ken Falk divides us into teams for indoor
football. Some of us, as we head out the door, remind our
partners that they could have married gamblers, or drug
addicts.

For two hours, we huff and puff our way through a mini-
tournament of frantic, three-minute games. I loathe it. This
is not soccer. Indoor football is not about anticipation and
passing and decision-making, and it's not about using open
spaces; it's only about quickness, like a video game. If I had
wanted to learn how to play racquetball or squash, I would
have become a stockbroker or a lawyer.

When the volleyball we use bounces off the walls and ric-
ochets off the rafters like a pinball, I feel like a rat in a maze.
Dave Naphtali's eldest son, Kevan, dribbles around us like we
are scarecrows in a field. He is so much faster than the rest
of us that it is more fun to watch Kevan play than to try and
play against him.

During one of our five-a-side games that winter, my teammate Ned appeared to have touched the ball with his hand,
whereupon an opposing player shouted, "Handball!" Everyone stopped playing, except Ned. Innocent as a newborn,
Ned was much aggrieved to be accused of an infraction. Like
a poker player challenging others to match his ante, he was

signalling to everyone that he was going to take this matter seriously – and see if he could bluff his way through.

"It was a handball," I announced flatly.

Ned was irate. How could a player on his own side be a traitor? He hurled some abuse in my direction and stormed out of the gym. It was an embarrassing blowup, but I did not regret voicing my opinion. It was for the public good. If someone calls a foul on the playground, or in the gym, it's common etiquette to respect that person's decision, then quickly resume the game. We were just a bunch of old guys in a neighbourhood gym at ten o'clock at night, for God's sake. My loyalties were to the collective, to the concept of fair play, not to a temporary teammate.

Whether it is a case of old guys in a gym on Thursday nights, playing five-a-side, or English youngsters on a side street in Stoke-on-Trent in the 1920s, using coats piled up as their goalposts for a twenty-a-side "kickabout," soccer games played without referees can be the best games of all. As Stanley Matthews recalled in his autobiography:

> These games helped all those lads to become better citizens later in life. All such kickabout football games do. My reasoning behind this is quite simple. We had no referee or linesman, yet sometimes up to 40 boys would play football for two hours, adhering to the rules as we knew them. When there was a foul, there would be a free kick. When a goal was scored, the ball would be returned to the centre of the waste ground for the game to restart. We didn't need a referee; we accepted the rules of the game and stuck by them.
>
> For us not to have done so, would have spoilt the game for everyone. It taught us that you can't go about doing what you

want because there are others to think of and if you don't stick to the rules, you spoil it for everyone else. Of course, that was not a conscious thought at the time, but looking back, those kickabout games on the waste ground did prepare us for life.

Sir Stanley Matthews had an innate regard for the sanctity of the game. He knew the value of sportsmanship.

Stanley Matthews left school and joined the grounds-keeping staff of Stoke City at age fifteen and made his professional debut in 1932 at age seventeen. During his thirty-three-year career he made 697 League appearances and represented England fifty-four times, in an era when there were far fewer international games, until 1957. He became the first-ever Footballer of the Year (1948), the first European Footballer of the Year (1956), and the first footballer to be knighted (1965).

A self-disciplined fitness fanatic ever since boyhood, Matthews became the oldest player to appear in the top division of English football, playing his last League game at age fifty, and he played his final competitive game in Brazil at age seventy – and injured his cartilage. (These days, Teddy Sheringham is considered remarkable for playing in the Premiership at age forty-one.) As a highly skilled winger, dribbling around large fullbacks, Matthews was always a target for the tough guys who had earned their reputations for fierceness, but somehow he persevered. Amazingly, during more than eighteen hundred matches, Stanley Matthews was never cautioned by the referee or sent off the pitch.

Surely *that* constitutes greatness.

Pelé, to his credit, once said Matthews was "the man who taught us the way football should be played."

In a game as passionate and violent as football, it takes considerable aplomb *never* to have a serious altercation with a rival player or an official. One would assume that Matthews was unusually passive, or cool-headed, but that was not the case. Matthews never learned how to approach the game of football with the Zen-filled equilibrium of Roberto Baggio. To the contrary, he viewed football as a celebration of life, and he approached each contest with quivering anticipation.

> In the immediate build-up to a really big game, your mind can play tricks on you. You become aware of every little thing about you. You play around with your socks to get them just so. Having tied your tie-ups, you feel they are not sitting comfortably about the leg, so undo them and tie them again. Then it's the boots, the studs are checked and re-checked to make sure there are no worn edges and that they are hammered well into the sole. The laces are tied and re-tied until you feel they are not too slack or too tight around your boot.

Far from being calm, Stanley Matthews vomited before most of his big games. A Stoke City teammate referred to Matthews's chronic upchucking as "Stan's technicolour yawn." Intensely competitive and high-strung, Matthews also had a plethora of nervous tics and pre-game jitters, and yet he never unduly lost his temper or played recklessly. The more we play football and strain to emulate Stanley Matthews – hoping to be lucky enough to injure our cartilage at age seventy – the more Matthews's remarkable record of self-control seems out of keeping with our times.

Nowadays television cameras routinely display showboating dances in end zones, somersaults after goals, and outrageous basketball dunks. Top-notch athletes are glamour-ized for their lives of conspicuous excess amid private swimming pools and antique cars. Not surprisingly, temper tantrums have become a normal part of sport, and top-ranked athletes are often preening egotists, rattling their jewellery.

I'm fairly certain, had God or my parents granted me the body and opportunity to play professionally, I would have been ejected from at least one game. I have often earned angry reactions from my opponents, and I have frequently signalled my disrespect for weak referees. I understand Ned's theatrics in the gymnasium, because we live in a world that reveres Maradona more than Matthews.

Even some non–soccer fans know about Maradona. In the aftermath of the Falklands War, in the same game, the stocky forward scored two of the most memorable goals in soccer history, only four minutes apart, enabling Argentina to beat England in Mexico – and he later boasted that God had enabled him to cheat.

From the outset of that famous match, Tunisian referee Ali Bennaceur tended to favour the Latins, allotting a yellow card to England's Terry Fenwick early in the game. After a scoreless first half, about ten minutes into the second half, after a flurry at the edge of the English box, English defender Steve Hodge hooked the ball backwards, in the air, towards the ever reliable English keeper, Peter Shilton.

You can easily view this turning point in soccer history on the Internet. The much taller Shilton had the descending ball in his sights, and Maradona raced towards him, hoping to intercede. As Shilton raised his arm to punch it away, the diminutive Maradona leapt high and raised his left hand, deflecting the ball into the English net.

This was the infamous "Hand of God" goal. Incensed by Maradona's audacity, the normally cool-headed Shilton hurried to the referee to plead his case. "I actually saw Maradona's hand go up and punch the ball," England's Glenn Hoddle later recalled in his autobiography. "I must admit he tried to disguise it very well, flicking his head at the same time as he handled. But it hadn't fooled me. I have seen that done in Sunday morning matches at the local park, and the players there have never got away with it."

If your country has just lost a war with the country of your opponent, all's fair in love and war, and in professional football. Maradona celebrated joyously, without hesitation, encouraging his teammates to do the same. Mr. Ali Bennaceur either didn't see the incident or he was fooled by Maradona's sleight of hand. Maradona later justified his fakery by claiming that if a goalkeeper such as Shilton had an opportunity to disguise the fact that the ball had gone over the goal line, he certainly would do so – therefore cheating is a natural part of the game.

"I was instantly aware that he'd handled it and for a couple of seconds I didn't panic," English coach Bobby Robson recalled in 1995. "Then I realized that everyone was rushing back to the halfway line, including the referee and the linesman, and my instant reaction was, 'Hell, they haven't seen it,' and then suddenly it all dawned on me. This was a goal."

Soon afterwards, Maradona scored a scintillating goal, dribbling his way from the centre line. After his performance at the World Cup in Mexico, Maradona was touted as the most talented player in the history of the game, eclipsing Pelé. It was another rags-to-riches story. Maradona was the illegitimate son of a Guarani Indian from a tiny village near the Paraguayan border. His mother was a devoutly religious daughter of dirt-poor Italian immigrants. Having grown up in squalor, without running water or electricity, with minimal education, Maradona became the youngest player in football history to play in a premier division match when, on October 20, 1976, just ten days shy of his sixteenth birthday, he appeared in a match between Argentinos Juniors and Talleres of Córdoba.

By the time he was twenty-one, the five foot four Messiah had led his Boca team to the Argentinian championship. Then he captained his country to two World Cup finals. But Diego Maradona was no Stanley Matthews. He was not equipped to manage fame or fortune or serious setbacks. When he failed a drug test at the World Cup in the United States, Maradona was forced to leave the tournament in disgrace. But in a world in which they can make a Broadway musical about Eva Perón, perhaps it only stands to reason that a narcissist such as Maradona can reinvent himself as a political folk hero, even leading street protests against George Bush Jr. Overweight, dependent on drugs, mixed up with the Mafia and routinely manipulated by politicians, Maradona has persevered and somehow regained his fame.

"Years ago," writes Jimmy Burns in *The Hand of God*, "Maradona might have simply passed into history as just one more self-possessed and not very intelligent footballer who was nevertheless the best player the game has produced. But he has become a myth in his own time, carrying millions of people with him."

Then there's Freddy Adu. When the youngest player ever to play for the U.S. national team made his first international appearance at age sixteen, in San Diego, having chosen not to play for his native Ghana, the outcome of the nil–nil draw with Canada was forgettable, but his debut was not: entering at the eighty-first minute as a substitute, Adu pretended to be fouled in the penalty area two minutes later. The Mexican referee, Benito Archundia, didn't buy the fakery, and Freddy Adu received a yellow card.

"It's no big deal," Adu said. "You go down, and it could go for you or it could go against you. It's one of those things where you put the referee in a tough position." The coach of the American team, Bruce Arena, believed Adu did just fine. "It's always good for a young kid to get a taste of competition." Freddy Adu tried to cheat, but that day God was not on his side.

There is the Maradona path to glory and the Matthews path to glory, and each player, at some gut level, gets to choose.

PUSKAS AND VANCOUVER

If there is no friendship, there's no football. – Ferenc Puskas

Every time you lace up your boots, you are part of a grand continuum, like those illustrations in school texts that show hunchbacked hairy apes evolving into Neanderthal Man and Cro-Magnon Man, gradually morphing into an upright, standing human. The more you play, the more important it becomes to catch a whiff of the eternal spirit of football and learn a little bit about your ancestry, venerating the game with your teammates.

Ferenc Puskas's death was a case in point. As soon as Fidel

heard the news on Friday, November 17, 2006, he sent me an email. "Ferenc Puskas died at age 79 in Budapest this morning . . . Pelé of his time . . . Maestro."

Indeed. Ferenc Puskas was a brilliant orchestrator, an ingenious conductor who revolutionized how the game could be played. Once voted the sixth best player of the twentieth century, behind Pelé, Johan Cruyff, Franz Beckenbauer, Alfredo Di Stéfano, and Diego Maradona, Puskas was more durable and valuable than any of them. Although comparisons between players from different eras are always suspect, I believe that, more than anyone, he was both a superlative goal scorer and an exemplary leader.

Born as Ferenc Purczeld on April 2, 1927, he grew up in a working-class district of Budapest, kicking stones more often than footballs. Nicknamed Osci ("little brother"), Puskas honed his talents as a youth by endlessly juggling a tennis ball with his feet. In his adult career, he scored eighty-three goals for his country in eighty-four appearances, a scoring rate only barely eclipsed by Pelé, and he led his team to an Olympic gold medal in Helsinki in 1952.

In November 1953, Puskas and his pals became the first foreign team to beat England at Wembley Stadium, thrashing the English 6–3. The first "foreign" team to win on English soil were the Irish, who bested England at Goodison Park in 1949, but it's that first trouncing by Puskas and his pals, the first thrashing from a "continental" opponent, that most Englishmen remember as a watershed moment. "Their game" had been taken away from them.

Even before the game, Puskas silenced the crowd by performing hitherto unimaginable tricks with the ball, rolling it off his shoulder and down the length of his body, flicking it backwards, catching it on his arched back, grinning with the aplomb of a circus seal balancing a beach ball on its nose. When the game began, it soon became apparent that the English had overestimated their own abilities. The roly-poly Puskas was anything but a pushover. A reporter for the *London Times* described how Puskas deftly outwitted the English captain, Billy Wright, cleverly pulling the ball backward with the sole of his boot, sending Wright rushing past him, "like a fire engine going to the wrong fire."

That Wembley result was no fluke. The following May, England travelled to Hungary for a return match, and were whipped 7–1.

Hungary was expected to waltz to victory at the World Cup held in Switzerland in 1954, where they humiliated Korea 9–nil and annihilated Germany 8–3, in the opening round. But Puskas was forced to miss several games after he was roughly kicked from behind by the West German centre half, Werner Liebrich. That was perhaps the most notorious and influential foul in the history of the World Cup to that time.

Not fully fit, Puskas returned to action for the World Cup final, and promptly scored the game's first goal. The West Germans rallied to take a 3–2 lead with six minutes remaining, then Puskas scored what appeared to sixty thousand spectators at Wankdorf Stadium in Berne to be the equalizer with two minutes remaining – only to have the English referee, Bill Ling, uphold a perplexing offside call made by Welsh lineman Mervyn Griffiths.

The so-called Magical Magyars have long been considered the best team never to have won the World Cup. Two years later, on tour with his army club, Honvéd, the pudgy Puskas, and several of his teammates defected in response to Russian tanks crushing the Hungarian revolution. After Puskas refused to play for Hungary while it was occupied by the Soviet army, FIFA sided with the forces of tyranny and banned Puskas from competition for eighteen months. Unbelievably, the English Football Association subsequently refused to allow him to sign with Manchester United.

Ex-Hungarians Sandor Kocsis and Zoltan Czibor went to play for Barcelona, and Puskas began his storied career with Real Madrid in 1958, partnering with the Argentine-born Alfredo Di Stéfano. When their team pulverized Eintracht Frankfurt 7–3, to win the European Cup in 1960, Di Stéfano scored a hat trick, and Puskas tallied four times. Both Puskas and Di Stéfano became Spanish citizens.

Despite his increasingly chunky frame, Puskas, "The Booming Cannon," led the Spanish league in scoring four times and Real Madrid won five successive Spanish league titles, from 1961 to 1965, during his ascendancy. He once scored five goals in one game against Holland's Feyenoord. Collectively Puskas scored 952 times in 966 games for Honvéd, Real Madrid, and Hungary's national team, a scoring efficiency rating of 0.995 (better than Pelé). In 1995 the German-based International Federation of Football History and Statistics recognized him as the top scorer of the twentieth century.

Oddly, the nadir of Puskas's career occurred in my hometown. After he was hired to coach the Golden Gate Gales in San Francisco in 1967, Puskas rolled into Vancouver in 1968 to serve as the coach for the Vancouver Canadians. His coaching role on the West Coast is a little-known footnote in Canadian soccer history. The original professional Vancouver soccer franchise in 1967, known as the Vancouver Canadians,

The Magnificent Magyar, Ferenc Puskas, revered by soccer purists as the greatest footballer ever, served as the coach for the Vancouver Royals, a short-lived professional team.

played within a FIFA-sanctioned United Soccer Association (USA) that was the brainchild of Jack Kent Cooke, owner of the Los Angeles Lakers (basketball), the Los Angeles Kings (hockey), and the Washington Redskins (American football). Cooke spearheaded a twelve-city league that provided a calibre of play better than most North American fans deserved.

The Golden Gate Gales were really the Dutch team ADO Den Haag from The Hague. The Wolverhampton Wanderers served as the Los Angeles Wolves. Hibernian from Scotland became Toronto City. Cerro from Uruguay were renamed the New York Skyliners. Northern Ireland's Glentoran team was imported to serve as the Detroit Cougars. And so on.

Prior to Puskas's arrival in Vancouver, the Vancouver Canadians – really Sunderland from the English Premier

Division – won their home opener on June 7, 1967, before 10,053 fans by beating Scotland's Dundee United, a.k.a. the Dallas Tornado, 4–1. They ended their season on July 8 by beating Stoke City, a.k.a. the Cleveland Stokers, 3–1. Their cumulative 3–5–4 record had placed them fifth in their six-team division, out of the playoffs. Led by Puskas, the Dutchmen known as the Golden Gate Gales fared slightly better, finishing second in their division, with five wins, four losses, and three ties.

In December 1967, when seventeen franchises from the two competing professional soccer leagues in North America – the United Soccer Association and the North American Soccer League (NASL) – were forced to merge into one league, the owner of the San Francisco Golden Gate Gales yielded to the Oakland Clippers franchise and left the Bay area, preferring to purchase controlling interest in the Vancouver Canadians north of the border.

Trouble was, the Vancouver Canadians had arranged to hire a high-profile coach – the great English footballer Bobby Robson. When Robson was offered the position of assistant coach in order to make way for Puskas, he refused to co-operate and resigned. He later described his Hungarian rival as "an old player masquerading as a coach." This Puskas–Robson schism was the first of many conflicts between the two ownership factions.

The Vancouver Canadians became the Vancouver Royals partly because "Royals" had been a nickname for Real Madrid when Puskas was rescued from soccer oblivion at age thirty, hired to play by his former Honvéd manager, Emil Oestreicher, during those dark days of unemployment when he was being dismissed by others as an overweight has-been.

Although Vancouver had the third best NASL attendance figures in 1968, they finished at the bottom of their four-team Pacific Division, behind San Diego, Oakland, and Los Angeles, with a 12–5–15 record. The apocryphal story arose that Puskas had demoralized the goalkeepers on Vancouver's team with the power of his left-footed blasts during practice.

In 1969, when the league folded, Puskas fled the football Siberia that was Canada to coach Panathinaikos of Athens. After taking them to the European Cup final of 1971, losing to Ajax, Puskas left Panathinaikos in 1974 to coach at Real Murcia, Colo Colo in Chile, AEK Athens, Al-Masri in Egypt, Club Sol de América, Cerro Porteño, and South Melbourne Hellas, winning an Australian title in 1991. All the while he feared an army court martial if he set foot in Hungary.

He finally came home in 1992. Ten years later the national team stadium in Hungary was renamed Ferenc Puskas Stadium. When he was seriously ill, in August 2005, Real Madrid came to Budapest to play against Hungary as a fundraiser to help pay for his hospital treatments.

"Everyone knows he was a great player and an even better person," Di Stéfano said, learning of his friend's death. "He was a phenomenon, a very generous man." Alzheimer's disease took Puskas's memory, but he will never be forgotten.

⚽

Two days after Fidel's email, blessed with an opportunity to play on one of only two pitches in the city that were declared playable after a deluge of rain for a week, our squad arrived on a windswept field in Richmond in good spirits, eager for combat, a trifle giddy with the absurdity of our good fortune.

We were further blessed by the arrival of a conspicuously cheerful ex-Brit referee who took the same boyish delight in our bizarre circumstance.

Prior to the opening whistle, when I gathered the boys together for our customary one-minute mind-meld, I dedicated our game to the memory of Ferenc Puskas. This idea prompted Fidel to ask our referee, a knobby-kneed and physically fit man in his seventies, if we could observe one minute of silence to honour the Galloping Major. The referee was so completely in accord with this notion that he almost danced a jig in response. It was as if we had just given him a surprise gift. "I know I'm a Brit," he blubbered, embracing me in the middle of the pitch, "but I believe Puskas was the greatest player to ever play the game!"

As I blurted similar platitudes, with our faces almost touching, it was as if we were two characters in a romantic comedy. (Note to self: Small wonder he later excused your blatant slide tackle in the second half that sent one of their better players limping to the sidelines, unable to continue.)

We weren't certain if all players for the opposing team, Giant Panda – hospitable Chinese-Canadian guys – were fully apprised of the significance of standing still amid the slanting rain for sixty uninterrupted seconds of silence, but they all respectfully bowed their heads. Eight days after Remembrance Day, we were honouring a fallen hero in a way that felt natural. As I stood near the centre line, gazing at my boots, I knew that if we ever considered the top ten moments in our season, this would be one of them.

It was so windy that if you miskicked the ball, it would blow backwards towards you like a poorly thrown Frisbee. We won handily. We played with a superior diligence from the opening whistle. For once, we were not reliant on Fidel for our creativity. We shared the ball, making lots of short passes, avoiding high balls into the wind, so that the number of touches that each player had was more equal than ever before. In defence everyone was taking responsibility for picking up the nearest man, limiting passing opportunities, smothering our opponents with self-discipline.

It was a breakthrough performance. With an impregnable backline of Hans, Bill, Gord, and Max, we dominated play with relative ease, winning almost all the balls in the air. For once, our defensive aggressiveness and cohesiveness was even more intimidating than Fidel's fancy footwork. Panda did get one goal towards the end of the game, on a long ball that danced and swerved fortuitously in the wind, falling miraculously just beneath the bar, as if someone on the sidelines had a joystick that was navigating its downward flight by remote control, but they were outmuscled and outrun for ninety minutes, and the result was never in serious doubt.

Thereafter it became known as the Puskas Game.

GENTLEMEN, START YOUR ENGINES

There has to be thought behind every touch of the ball.
– Dennis Bergkamp

The debut of our Spanish contingent was forgettable. On April Fool's Day 2007, a bitterly cold Sunday morning, against Cliff Avenue United, fourteen of our Spain-bound enlistees lost our first exhibition game 4–3 at Jericho Park. The score didn't look pathetic, and therein was the danger. Winning and losing can be contagious. If you start to learn how to tolerate losing, you won't get around to mastering the art of winning. They scored four unanswered goals in the first forty minutes. Our keeper, Tony Arimare, had allowed an average of only 0.5 goals per game during our winter season, so this deluge of goals in a short time span was bizarre.

The failure of several players to demonstrate any grit didn't bode well for Spain. Who was going to show some leadership? Gimped from a serious groin injury, relegated to managing the team, I vowed that we mustn't lose twice in a row. I knew I wasn't alone with that attitude. Hans, our most competitive fullback, was furious at the defensive miscues.

On a purely selfish level, for me our 4–3 loss was reassuring. Every team needs someone to challenge for every header, to compete for every loose ball, and to punish the opposition in the centre of the pitch, where fouls can't hurt you. For the Italian side that won the 2006 World Cup, that player was Gennaro Gattuso. While I am not our most talented or fastest player, I know I can serve as the competitive barometer, forcing everyone to play harder, like a Gattuso, so I knew at least I was needed.

At halftime I pointed out to the team that we had committed only one foul. This was far too mild-mannered for any team, even guys our age. We had seven guys from one team, nine guys from another one, and three guys from yet another team, and half of them were avoiding contact at close quarters. How could we possibly expect to gel as a team if we hadn't learned one another's moves? And if too many guys were afraid to get hurt?

Having failed to warm up adequately, we were asleep for the first half-hour until Fidel finally scored, making it 4–1 just before the interval. We stormed back, scoring two more unanswered goals in the second half, but even Fidel – our Andrea Pirlo – looked listless, out of sorts. Maybe he missed his Gattuso. Or maybe it was his neck injury. "There were seven goals scored in this game," I said at the end, "and we were responsible for six of them." That drew a laugh, but they knew I wasn't kidding.

That opening Battle of Jericho was a classic chemistry lesson in how not to approach the game. More concerned with socializing than with beating the other guys, we were sloppy from the get-go. I decided we had to win our second exhibition game one week later in Richmond against the Pioneers. Two of our key players who had missed the Jericho encounter, Dave Naphtali and Bruce Fleming, would raise our intensity level considerably, and we would add two skilled players, Alex and Arthur, who had both grown up in Scotland. Arthur, my designated replacement in the middle, is a smooth player who uses open spaces beautifully, always moving, always making the most efficient pass. Alex, in contrast, can be mouthy and cynical in his challenges, but he can confidently bring the ball up from the back instead of randomly booting it forward. Alex is the sort of character you hate to play against. When I had approached him about playing, he had replied that he had the flu, and it would be a good thing if he played so he could get rid of it.

I set the carpool time earlier than necessary. That way, everyone would arrive at the Pioneers' pitch at least a half-hour early. We were all on the field, warming up, before the Pioneers starting drifting by, seeing that we were ready for action. Even in our league, you can't discount the fear factor. It's there in every game, and you have to swallow it or spit it out. Never swill it around in your mouth, tasting it. One way to win the fear contest at the start is simple: always make the other team think you are keener to win than they are.

Our confidence level was apparent from the kickoff. We distributed the ball backwards, allowing half of our players to get touches on it before any of the opposition could get into the game. We exhibited trust among ourselves, and the opposition could sense it. Their keeper was forced to make several exceptional saves before Fidel deftly slid the ball past him before halftime.

It was still anybody's game. The Pioneers were skilled, well-organized, and eager to win. And they could be physical. A cynical tackle on Bruce left him writhing in agony, furious at what he saw as a deliberate attempt to injure him. A foul was called, but the indignity of the attack upset him as much as the pain it caused. He left the park at halftime to get treatment.

With Bruce's departure from the midfield, April Fool's Day came a week late for me. Having already told myself I mustn't play for at least another two weeks, I opened the back of my station wagon and changed into my strip in the parking lot of Richmond High. At the outset of the second half, we counted our players and confirmed that without Bruce we were one man short, so I ran onto the field without hesitation.

I sent Fidel to play forward and took over the midfield with Arthur. After Alex committed a foul near the top of the box, the Pioneers converted on the free kick due to a rare goal-keeper's error. Nobody panicked. Tony had already made one astonishing save in the first half, tipping the ball over the bar, so we had him to thank for our one-goal margin.

We increasingly took control of the game, and then Fidel notched his second goal, cheekily pushing the ball between the goalkeeper's legs. We outfought them the rest of the way, winning 2–1. Hans was particularly defiant, blocking a powerful shot. Alex and Dave and Ken and Nick were invincible at the back.

We deserved to win. Although I could barely walk afterwards, I told myself it was worth it. If we had lost, *not* playing in the second half and losing would have bothered me more than the pain. I didn't want to be the coach of any team that had a losing record of 0 and 2, so I had taken a calculated risk, not a reckless one, even though I had probably set back my recovery time by a few weeks. Fidel understood why I had played in the second half. We didn't have to talk about it. He would have done the same thing.

When we eventually competed against the Spaniards, the inevitable distractions of family and foreign surroundings would be considerable, so it was easier – more efficient – to set the standard of intensity before we left.

Our third exhibition game was on the artificial turf field at Kerrisdale. Instead of having a rematch against the Pioneers, Alan Cook and I had opted for an easier contest against a newly formed team to boost our confidence. I volunteered to act as the referee to avoid the temptation of playing.

It was a sorry contest. The pace was slow, and the style was sloppy. It looked like old man's soccer. We won 4–1 but the giveaways were rampant. There was precious little playmaking in the midfield. Fidel and Tony, our keeper, were absent and I was glad Fidel wasn't there to see it. He might have threatened to quit. The difference between the intense competition against the Pioneers and this "run in the park" was extreme, but at least we could tell ourselves we had a winning record. It was better than the alternative. When the Magnificent Magyars practised for international competitions, Puskas and his mates often played against industrial sides, hammering them 10–nil. There is much to be said for this approach.

For our fourth warm-up match, Alan and I decided to have an inter-squad match during which the guys who were going to Spain would play against the guys who weren't. Fidel and I, accompanied by Tonko, his son, brought along two sets of jerseys to a rain-soaked park on the eastern side of town. Although Fidel always maintains one should never keep track of the score in practice situations, and one must never take notice of who scores, I wanted the Spanish contingent to get addicted to winning, and expecting to win. The Spanish-bound Mangos (in our weird light orange strip) out-lasted the non–Spanish-bound Whites 5–3.

I refereed that game in rubber boots, because I knew if I wore galoshes I would resist the temptation to run. Referee-ing two games in a row had an odd effect on me. I found I enjoyed being outside the game, looking in, and I began to glimpse a possible future as an ex-player. As I tromped and squished my way back and forth at Rupert Park, wearing rubber gumboots in April, watching Fidel continually trying to set up his teammates rather than score himself, blowing my whistle as little as possible, and encouraging the players who made good passes, I understood once more the essen-tial, civilizing role of the referee.

It is only human nature to resent the authority of the referee, any referee, but as I gathered up the rain-soaked uniforms after the game, two of my teammates thanked me. Three others offered good-natured jibes. I had called about ten offsides, but none were disputed.

The following morning, when I was taking the white and mango jerseys out of the clothes dryer in the basement, doing a half-assed job of folding them and dividing them into two piles, storing them in two separate containers behind the furnace, I was struck by how much I had enjoyed the game.

Despite the slippery conditions, our inter-squad game had not been blemished by even a single foul. Statistically this was extraordinary. For ninety minutes, everyone had behaved in an exemplary manner. Nobody had spoken in anger or frustration. A spirit of camaraderie and laughter had prevailed. The soccer was forgettable, but somehow a spirit of communion had percolated into our busy lives.

INTERVIEW WITH A MISTRESS #4

NETTIE: Why so glum, chum?

ALAN: Not glum, just pensive.

NETTIE: It must be the groin. I can tell by the way you wobble when you walk, like an old cowpoke.

ALAN: And here I thought I was doing a good job of concealing it.

NETTIE: It's a dead giveaway when you lift your left thigh with both hands in order to get your leg out of the car. And you shout "Ow!" when you sneeze.

ALAN: Before this happened to me, I wasn't even certain what a groin was. Now I wince in pain if I have to hurry across the street. It's awful.

NETTIE: Do you want me to feel sorry for you?

ALAN: That would make it worse. We've got only two months left before we go to Spain, and here I am on the side-lines. Pretty much the same thing happened to me when we went to France two years ago. I can't believe it! I feel like I'm in a foot race against Father Time and he's catching up on me all because I'm a cripple.

NETTIE: The correct term is physically handicapped.

ALAN: Whatever. The physiotherapist said I'm not allowed to run until I can hop on one leg without pain. So I can't even kick the ball. Instead I get to torture myself with stretching exercises and swimming. I *hate* swimming. I especially dislike public swimming pools. And stretch-ing exercises remind me of Nazi youth rallies or mil-lions of Chinese doing tai chi in Tiananmen Square.

NETTIE: Thousands of years of evolution and this is what we get.

ALAN: I'll take a rational approach to paying my taxes or buying a house and I'll take a rational approach to making sure my kids get enough food to eat and own a decent pair of shoes, but I don't want to take a rational approach to playing soccer. I want to continue to take my body for granted.

NETTIE: Denial only works until age forty. You should be doing your stretching exercises at least three times per day.

ALAN: I just paid a physiotherapist eighty bucks to tell me the same thing. I *hate* talking about being injured. I feel like I'm an old car that is turning into a bucket of bolts.

But instead of a garage, I've been going to the acupuncturist once a week.

NETTIE: It's your own fault. You shouldn't have tried to play in the second half against the Pioneers.

ALAN: That was the only way I could convince myself I was seriously injured.

NETTIE: I beg your pardon? That doesn't make any sense.

ALAN: You heard me. I had to make it worse before I could get better. I had to scare myself. I knew if I was able to let myself continue to believe I might be getting better by doing nothing, I would have continued to go that route, so I had to ratchet up the pain level in order to force myself to take this situation more seriously.

NETTIE: I can't believe you just said that. I can't believe you think that statement might be coherent.

ALAN: I'm not taking pride in being stupid. I'm a creature of habit. Denial has worked just fine for me for fifty years. It's hard to deny denial. It's hard to go through that change.

NETTIE: You're not a bucket of bolts, you're a nutcase. Let me get this straight. You're telling me you're going through some sort of Male Athlete Menopause thing? Are you getting hot flashes?

ALAN: Just shooting pains.

NETTIE: Does anyone on your team know about this?

ALAN: Of course not.

NETTIE: Men really are hopeless.

ALAN: True.

NETTIE: Look, I know you honestly resent time spent with medical types instead of fooling around with me, having strangers touching your body, and pretending to do some stretching exercises, but I think there's more to this than you're letting on. You can't fool me. This is all part of your underdog agenda. Right now you're relishing the drama of an uphill struggle so you can resurrect yourself in Spain. That'll make for a storybook ending to your playing career.

ALAN: It's possible.

NETTIE: Is there something else you're not telling me?

ALAN: As a matter of fact, yes. The groin injury is a minor problem. Today it's barely on the radar. Yesterday my mother got hit by a taxi in a crosswalk. She's in the hospital.

NETTIE: Good God!

ALAN: If only God had something to do with it.

NETTIE: What happened?

ALAN: The taxi driver was parked on the side of the road, on his cellphone. My mother got about halfway across the crosswalk, and bang, I guess he took off in a hurry without looking. Someone called for an ambulance. There's a police report, but I haven't seen it yet. She's about to turn eighty, same age as the Pope and Queen Elizabeth. She's not going to die, but I expect she's never going to fully recover. These events put things into perspective.

NETTIE: And there you were, worrying about a silly groin injury.

ALAN: Precisely. They operated on her last night. That's why I don't look so hot. But the glass is always half full, not half empty. She could have been killed. Or this could have happened one week before Spain.

NETTIE: So the game goes on.

ALAN: My mother watched me play on Saturday mornings. I think she liked to get away from Dad. Nearly every morning, rain or shine, she was there. She also bought me my first typewriter. When she was forced to leave the house, when I was about twelve or thirteen, and she didn't have any money, she somehow managed to buy me a typewriter. So, yes, the game is still on, Nettie.

NETTIE: If you were a professional athlete, you could dedicate your game to her.

ALAN: That would be absurdly pretentious.

NETTIE: Now you've got your wife and you've got your mother and you've got me. I guess I just got knocked down a notch.

ALAN: True, our romance has fallen from the top of the agenda. Sport is an illusory universe, like television. A groin injury barely registers on the radar of things to worry about. There are times when I even wonder why I bother playing soccer at all. As the English captain Eddie Hapgood said in 1939, "Football is like the dilemma of a love affair. If you don't take it seriously, you get no pleasure from it. If you do take it seriously, and as a player you have to, somewhere along the line it will break your heart."

CAPTAIN COURAGEOUS

I play every game as if it might be my last. – Hans Hart

Boyishly eager to show off the new team jerseys he has purchased for our trip, Hans drops by my backyard office at eight on Sunday morning, two hours before kickoff, hard-wired for another contest. As we're driving to the field, Hans asks if I have heard of Goji juice, and I tell him I have not. Ever since he stopped self-injecting interferon, Hans has been drinking Goji juice as a miracle cure to combat his hepatitis C. He says Goji juice is from the Himalayas. I nod. The guy selling it to him was the best man at his wedding. Goji juice is expensive, but Hans can afford it as the hands-on owner of Doormaster, a successful company that supplies and installs garage doors.

It often occurs to me that possibly Hans, Fidel, and I are friends because we have the least formal education of the guys on the team.

Two days later, I see a CBC documentary exposing Goji juice as a scam, and I mention this exposé to Hans. He shrugs. He has seen the same documentary, and his partner has always been skeptical about the miracle drug, but he buys Goji juice anyway. He's reluctant to hurt his friend's feelings by not reordering it. "It can't do any harm," he says, cheerfully. True enough. Goji juice has lots of vitamin C. Trouble is, as the CBC has revealed, the remarkable qualities of the Goji berry are not replicated in Goji juice.

For Hans this amounts to one more darkly comic situation: he can't afford not to try it. He's one of those people whose laugh is distinctive because you hear it so often. Extremely bright, but simultaneously wary of intellectualism, Hans tends to articulate his opinions on weighty matters through wisecracks or swearing. Often he makes light of his terminal illness, because there is no better way to handle it. An amateur psychologist might wonder if Hans's aloof father, a retired professor in Holland, has never fully approved of him. Hans has not mentioned his Indonesian mother much, but then I've never seen fit to ask.

It's never easy to figure out what really makes Hans tick. He lives in the present tense more than most people, possibly because he's not keen on the past or the future. And he plays right fullback with a vengeance.

Sometimes, when your adrenalin is pumping and all the pistons are firing, when the opposition is your enemy instead of your atrophying self, there are moments of bliss, moments of carefree athleticism, and you can have the illusion that you and your body are symbiotic twins, dancing like characters depicted on an ancient Greek vase. Teammates become action figures for the ages, immortals, and soccer becomes an alternate universe in which mortality does not exist.

Hans probably thinks about these things too, but he would never risk comparing himself to an ancient Greek or describe soccer as immortality in motion. He understands all too well that his body can also be an oppressive cage. For him soccer is strictly a battle in which other human beings conveniently take the place of oneself as the primary adversary.

⊛

At first I thought Hans might be Cree or Blackfoot or Iroquois, a First Nations Canadian, because his skin was so dark. I didn't know about the hepatitis. Later on, when Hans began his second round of chemo treatments at age fifty-four, as a last-ditch effort to combat the disease, we all marvelled at this bizarre twist of fate: they say lightning isn't supposed to strike twice in the same spot, but Hans began self-injecting only one week after Ken Falk returned to the team after his four months of chemotherapy. What were the odds that two fullbacks would be forced out of the lineup that

Frances Metcalf

Despite a leg injury, Hans Hart contributed his inspirational presence as our captain, chief partygoer, and the guy who bought the team jerseys.

way, one after the other? The timing was disturbing, as if God was playing chess against us. By rallying around Ken, we had somehow removed one piece from jeopardy; now He was going after another.

Of course Hans, being Hans, refused to stop playing. After a life of difficulty with authority figures, Hans rejected his doctors' advice to quit playing soccer in the same stubborn way he had rejected their advice to quit drinking. Hans was unstoppable. He and Frances were building their dream home on Carriacou, a tiny island near Grenada in the Caribbean, where they liked to take long vacations. If Hans conceded an inch, he would have to stop being Hans.

Hans usually defends territory like a pit bull. You don't want to go near him, so he comes as close as he can, almost leaning on the attacker he is marking. Although he can sometimes appear awkward, his refusal to show weakness makes him an excellent defender. He is cleverly physical, an expert at almost committing fouls. Quicker than he looks, he is seldom penalized, and is a clever dribbler. But after only two weeks of interferon, Hans was noticeably weaker. After three weeks, he was noticeably slower. After four weeks, his efforts to remain part of the team were making us all feel uncomfortable. He was running out of steam before our eyes, barely able to move towards the end of a match. He had lost weight quickly. Even though he couldn't keep his food down, he continued to behave like he was Horatio at the bridge.

The sicker Hans got, the more we started to worry that we were being irresponsible for letting him play. One game, when we had a two-goal lead going into the last five minutes, I begged him to stay off. "Hans," I said. "We're ahead by two goals. Come back on if they score." So he stayed off. After that, it was easier.

When we were slated to play in a two-day tournament, I wrote to him:

Dear Hans,

Remember when we were all in France? Playing in that tournament? And my leg was so completely buggered that I literally could not run? And I tried to play anyway?

Towards the end of that one game, when I was unable to even kick the ball, I moved myself over to the left midfield position. I was hobbling around and you hollered over to me from your right back position, "Alan, get off the field!"

If I was crazy enough to keep playing and injure myself further, I really needed someone to say, hey, that's not good for you! You did that for me and I really appreciated your intervention. For the rest of that tourney, I ended up being the coach. I hated it, but it was the way I could best contribute to the team.

So you know what's coming.

You are one of the best, most-liked and respected players on the team. Even at half-strength, you're valuable. So lots of people care a great deal about your present situation and some of us – well, Fidel, Alan Cook and Ken, to name names – are wondering if you would be willing to accept a promotion.

We know it's impossible to tell you to do anything that you don't want to do, so the brain trust, such as it is, would like me to invite you to lead us into battle this weekend as our head coach. We've got too many players, so it's going to be a schmozzle, getting everyone onto the same page. We need someone to take control. That would really help the team, even more than you playing.

But mostly this offer is being made because we really want you to get better, as fast as possible, and playing your heart out for us, right now, for a relatively meaningless tourney in Aldergrove, might not be the best way for you to get better.

Screw Aldergrove; think Spain.

– Alan T.

Hans agreed to act as coach. He gave us a pep talk about winning that first game, but as soon as I looked at the roster, I knew the odds were next to hopeless. The other teams had bolstered their squads with invited players, while we entered the tournament with a different philosophy. Anyone who wanted to participate was welcome, regardless of their skill level. The cold drizzle added to our misery. My right calf gave out in the second half of the second game, so I was knackered for the third contest. I floundered like a fool, but if I had asked Hans to coach, surely that meant it was my job to play.

We were out of our element, without a proper goalie. By the time we were losing our third game in a row, it had turned into one of those matches where you are just waiting for it to end. When soccer is really dismal, you forsake the fantasy of a comeback and your substitutes huddle on the sidelines under heavy winter coats, not hankering to return to the pitch. Towards the end of the second half, I approached the referee and asked him to blow the whistle to end it. He obliged.

I had brought a cooler full of beer, but the host team informed us that there were strict regulations against drinking in public. The blue Coleman cooler was heavy, filled with ice and unopened beers, too heavy to carry all the way to the parking lot alone. Hans was closest to me. Without thinking, I bent down, picked up one of the handles, and motioned for him to do the same. Then I thought, if he was too weak to play soccer, should he be carrying a cooler full of beer?

"Are you sure it's okay?" I asked.

"I'm not dead yet."

Walking to the parking lot, with the cooler between us, Hans told me he had lost fifteen pounds. One of the few foods he didn't vomit was yogourt.

"I'm shrinking. The worst part of it is, I've got wrinkles everywhere. Even my hands. I'm wrinkling up. I feel like a snake."

It was one of those weird, unsettling comments that don't go away.

After the tournaments, everybody went to the White Spot diner, where Hans took it upon himself to pick up the tab for all of us. This was Hans's way of doing things, and the logic of his gesture was not to be debated. We didn't even make a gentlemanly show of protest. Even if he wasn't on the field, he was still going to be a force.

You think you play to beat the other team, to score the winning goal in the final seconds, but there is always more at stake than just the score. There is dignity; there is pride. Nobody on our team would vote for Hans as our most skilled player. Like Ken, he doesn't have much of a left foot, but he has always been a leader. If you were stuck in a trench during the First World War, you would want a guy like Hans next to you, someone who would refuse to be beaten, someone who would risk his neck for you.

After Hans told his doctors that he had decided to quit his chemotherapy treatments, he began to make arrangements for his son Kyle to share ownership of his company, just in case he kicked the bucket sooner rather than later. About a month later, Hans showed up at one of our games in Richmond, distressed. Four computers had been stolen from his office during a break-in. Then, on the way to the game, he was in a car accident. "This guy runs into me and takes off," he said. "I followed him. I cornered him in a cul-de-sac. But then when I contacted the cops, they said they couldn't classify it as a hit and run because I caught the guy!"

That evening we played against some Yugoslavian guys who didn't appreciate losing 6–nil. The usual chippy stuff ensued. Hans took offence, and he got thrown off the pitch. That night, he wrote to me and Fidel:

I guess I was a bit of a head case on the pitch but afterwards I went to the pub with Brian, Franco and Ollie and ran into the guy who got tossed from the game with me. He is from Bosnia and we are good friends now. (Well not quite.) I find as you go through life there are new and interesting ways to meet people and make new friends. Are you sure you want another head case (ME) on your team?

I wrote him back to say he was a heart case, not a head case. Fidel responded:

That guy is Serbian, not Bosnian. They don't know what they are anyways or not so sure. Also during the game several times he was saying that he will start elbowing you, good for him he didn't try to come on me despite approaching me at the half-time. Therefore he can't be your friend . . . He call me PAESANO but since I thank God I live my life in Canada I did not answer on his false effort. Otherwise I would tell him that POTATOES are his Paesanos. You know Hansi that we all love you the way you are and that's that.

Hans is no stranger to friction. After his divorce, he got into a fight with his ex-wife's new boyfriend on the sidelines during one of Kyle's soccer games when Kyle was about nine or ten years old. Hans recalls what happened and laughs. "The kids were saying, 'Hey, there's a fight. Hey, Kyle, it's your Dad!'" Then Hans imitates his son's nine-year-old groan. He doesn't recall the incident with pride, but it's clear he's not ashamed of it either.

⚽

On the Italian squad that won the 2006 World Cup, defensive midfielder Gennaro Gattuso was impressive with his tournament-leading total of forty-seven successful tackles; their playmaker, Andrea Pirlo, was man of the match three times, and the world's highest-paid goalkeeper, Gigi Buffon, was only beaten by an own goal and a penalty kick, but most people who followed soccer seriously agreed their fullback and captain, Fabio Cannavaro, was the most valuable player. "Cannavaro was the man of the tournament," said Maradona.

A former ball boy in Italia 1990 in Napoli, Cannavaro was no spring chicken, yet he shared the honour of spending the most time on the pitch 690 minutes – with Buffon and German defender Philipp Lahm. With his outrageous head-butt, Zidane did not deserve his Golden Ball trophy nearly as much as Cannavaro, who gained his one hundredth cap during the final game against France.

As well, Cannavaro's stalwart performance best reflected the style of play that had dominated the tournament. In terms of World Cups, with sixty-four goals overall, it was the lowest-scoring tournament. The winner of the Golden Boot in 2006, Miroslav Klose, only netted five goals. Cannavaro's presence, if measured statistically, in terms of his success as a defender for the minutes he played, was much more significant than Klose's, but defenders like Cannavaro – or Hans – seldom get the attention they deserve. Mouthy field marshals like me in the middle, or talented players like Fidel up front, get twice as many touches on the ball, and therefore they more easily find the spotlight, but fullbacks are often the heart of a team. As Spain approached, I came to realize that Hans was at the heart of our expedition, our Cannavaro. Having played together the longest, Ken, Hans, and Dave Naphtali, as a defensive trio, would provide the character our team was going to need, like ballast for a ship.

The distance from Holland to Spain is relatively short, but Hans, typically, hadn't taken the easy route to get there.

⚽

"I was born in Amsterdam. I didn't start speaking until I was four years old, and I haven't stopped talking since. I left Holland when I was six. I never played soccer there. I didn't start playing until I was thirty-nine.

"The minute I finished high school in Calgary, I moved out of the house. I lived in the streets for a while. The streets in Calgary, the streets in Vancouver. I lived on freight trains. For about two years, I lived all over the place. Between the ages of seventeen and nineteen, I was doing drugs, stealing shit, and going to jail. I went to jail a few times.

"I got in about six fights in jail, so I like to say I took up boxing in jail. [Laughter] I was a punching bag! One guy beat me up three times. It happened after I got transferred from a medium security prison in Calgary to a minimum security facility in the Rocky Mountains between Banff and Jasper. It was a bunch of trailers. There were two inmate trailers, the guard trailer, the cooking trailer, and the recreational trailer. I was the smallest guy there. And there was Big Ed, the biggest guy there. He's huge. He's a monster.

"So one night we're sitting in the recreational trailer playing a game called bid whist, which is like bridge. And at the end of the hand that he won, Big Ed says, 'That's ten points.' But it's only supposed to be five points. It's kind of like if you score a goal in soccer and you say, 'Okay, that's two goals.' I say, 'Look, Ed, you won the hand. You're taking five points.'

"This went on a couple of times. He says, 'If you don't like it, you can just quit.' I put the cards down. I quit. Ed took the cards, threw them in my face, and proceeded to beat me up.

"Ed is in one trailer with twelve bunks, and I'm in another trailer with twelve bunks. Later that same night, in my trailer, the guys say, 'Hey, Ed just beat you up. We're going to teach you how to fight.' I said, 'Okay, fine.' It's something I need to know, right? [Laughter] So they took the pillows and held them up. They told me to hit the pillows. That was the boxing lesson.

"So I go back into Ed's trailer. I say, 'Fuck you.' And Big Ed gets up, he looms over me, and I go – one, two, three – right into his stomach with my fists. It has no effect whatsoever. So he pounds me several times until I'm down on the ground. I'm lying flat on my back and Ed is just about to take his size-sixteen foot and put it into my face, and the guard opens up the door and he says, 'What's going on?' And we both look up and we both go, 'Nothing.' And so the fight broke up.

"I fought him one more time after that. I can't remember the third fight. I just remember it was the worst. I couldn't eat for a couple of weeks. But I had to fight. If you don't fight, everybody beats you up. I was the smallest guy in the camp. Big Ed was the biggest guy in the camp. After that, people said, 'Well, if he's dumb enough to fight Ed, you don't want to fuck with this guy.' It worked. Sort of.

"You find out who you are in jail, real quick. There's no illusion, right? Wherever you go, you have to somehow turn it into something positive. You gotta keep going. You have a choice of either having a positive attitude, no matter what, or a negative attitude. A negative attitude does nothing for you, whatsoever.

"It was the same when I was living in the Okanagan. I lost my business on the same day my son Aaron was born mentally retarded and physically handicapped. To this day he's got the brain of a six-month-old. That was in 1984. You gotta keep going anyway. You can't erase these things from your memory.

"A lot of people can always find someone else to blame for their troubles, but I know I didn't have to go to jail. I brought that upon myself. I created my own little tragedy. I dug my own hole. It wasn't society's fault that I ended up where I was. You have to accept responsibility for who you are.

"For me the change occurred when I was in Penticton. I was on probation. I wasn't supposed to be in British Columbia, but I got caught stealing some shit in Penticton and I went before this judge. I was in for about the sixth or seventh time in Penticton, and I had decided that I was probably going to be a lifer. I wasn't a mean person or anything like that, but I wasn't a very good person either.

"I declined having a lawyer. The judge says, 'So what's going on?' The Crown prosecutor says he wants to give me two years, less a day, indefinite, and six months indeterminate. The judge says, 'Whaddya got to say for yourself?' At first I told him I had nothing to say for myself. Finally, after some encouragement, I got up and I spoke for half an hour. I gave him the Broken Home Hans story. I basically told him what had been going on in my life.

"And at the end of it, the judge looked at me and he says, 'You know, after that story, I'd just like to put you on probation. But you're already on probation and you're in British Columbia, and you're not supposed to be in British Columbia . . .' So he gave me only a month in Kamloops Regional prison. He did me a big favour. I really should go back and thank that man.

"I didn't have a lot of self-respect at the time, compared to how I feel now. That experience taught me that if you actually learn to speak for yourself, you don't have to be this rotten person. After that I said, 'That's the last time.' After that I wouldn't even jaywalk. I did nothing wrong, absolutely nothing wrong.

"Looking back, I was lucky. I was born with a pretty good brain. And no physical or mental handicaps. Just on that alone, I should be happy, right? I see a lot of people that are less fortunate. Some of my childhood was rough, but you compare it with some of the other people, it's nuttin'. It's a walk in the park, right?

"Kyle was born four years before Aaron. When the marriage broke down, we had two children. I moved to Vancouver with Kyle when he was four years old. Kyle started his soccer career when he was six years old. That first year, he didn't like to play because he wasn't the superstar. My wife said, 'Well, he doesn't like to play.' And I said, 'Well, at six, they don't know what the fuck they want. He's playing . . . and he's going to be a right fullback.' And he was. Now he loves the game. [Laughter]

"Kyle's first coach was Rhonda Bridgewater, and I was her assistant. That's how I met Dave Naphtali. He gave a coaches' clinic at Queen Mary school. I would have been thirty-six years old at the time. I still wasn't on a team. I was just learning. I played two or three scrub games a week. Eventually Ken Falk took notice of me and said, 'Hey, why don't you come and play with Dave and me for Point Grey over-forties?' I was thirty-nine. I know I'm not the world's best player, and I know I'm not the world's worst player. But I'm tenacious. I like to think I'm relatively easy to get along with, except when someone tries to get the ball off me.

"I remember this one time, me and Dave Naphtali, we're playing against this guy who was really fast, and physically fit, and highly skilled. He was busting through our defence all the time. So he squirts between Dave and me, but we catch him, right? Well, the next thing we know, he goes down. He plays for about another five minutes, then he goes and sits in a chair in the sidelines.

"Bruce goes up to him, looks him over, and decides he should go to the hospital. Well, the poor guy has a collapsed lung. It was a fullback move. [Laughter] I mean, I didn't get a penalty. It was just one of those things. I'm trying to do my job, right? So at the end of the game, I know the guy is in the hospital, but I don't know what he's got. I don't know what I've done to him.

"So I think, okay, I better go see this guy at the hospital, right? So I go to the hospital, and I find the guy sitting in a wheelchair. He sees me coming and looks up at me, and he covers his face with his hands, cowering. He thinks I've come to finish him off or something! [Laughter]

"Did I ever tell you about the gun incident? We were playing against Dutch Masters, and they had this Yugoslavian player. He has a short fuse, right? And Thomas, our guy, he has a short fuse. So they threatened each other. The Yugoslavian says, 'That's fine. I have a gun.' Thomas gets on the phone and calls the cops. The next thing we know, the cops arrive at the schoolyard. It turns out this guy doesn't have a gun. And he doesn't admit to saying he had a gun. So everybody looks at each other. Should we continue to play? [Laughter] So we continued to play!

"Another time we had a goalie who got knocked out in the box, right? And so Bruce looks at the guy and says we have to call an ambulance. So we wait around until the ambulance comes onto the field and takes the guy away. When the ambulance goes, we're all left standing there. So we all decide to start playing again! [Laughter] No mercy!

"Because he works in the emergency ward, Bruce has a different perspective than the rest of us. Some guy goes down on the pitch and all of us go, 'Holy smokes.' Bruce knows it's nothing! He's just seen some guy who fell off a truck going thirty miles per hour. [Laughter]

"Bruce will give you the shirt off his back if you ask for it. You know when I was on chemo the second time, I didn't want to bug Bruce about it, because I've seen games where eighteen guys show up to play and seven of them are waiting in line to talk to Bruce. And Bruce is unselfish and he just stands there, but you can see it in his face. When I come to soccer, do I want everybody to talk to me about installing garage doors?

"Because I didn't want to bug Bruce, I went over to see Kenny instead. Misery loves company. I needed someone to talk to, and Kenny had just recently gone through his chemo treatments. About a day or so later, Bruce phoned me. I guess Kenny put a bug in Bruce's ear. That's the way it works, right? I explained the situation to Bruce. He says, 'Hans, anytime you want to know something, and if I can help you out, it's no problem.' So I said, 'Well, anytime I can fix your door for you . . .' [Laughter]

"When I wanted to quit taking the chemo the second time, Bruce was a good listening post. Basically he said, 'Hans, it's your life. It's your body.' It was a tough decision to make. I hated it, I absolutely hated it. I have nothing good to say about chemo. Out of all these experiences I've had in my life, I can't say nothing good about chemo. It's just awful.

"What happens is, you do the injection and you start to feel good at about day six, and on day seven you've got to take another one. Then I missed one because I developed an infection. I didn't know what was happening to me. I thought it was all just part of the punishment for being a shithead when I was young.

"After I decided to go off it, I was driving across the Lions Gate Bridge after playing soccer again. I had been off the chemo for about two weeks. It was rush hour traffic and there was a stall. No traffic was moving. Everybody was fuming, just sitting there on the bridge. And I was the only person smiling."

⊛

During our soccer trip to France in 2005, Bruce presented Hans with an honorary doctorate at a public dinner, in front of one of the French teams, and everyone applauded heartily. If Bruce had felt it necessary to make an accompanying speech, he might have said: "Outwardly, Hans, we know you have chosen the role of party guy, but we know that's not the whole ball of wax, not by any stretch. Hans, in many ways, you are our most charismatic player. You do the most with the least, you are a terrific right fullback, we love you, and don't go changing." When Hans rose to accept the makeshift degree, he was speechless.

Since then, when I think about Hans, I think about my own problematic body. My body, my enemy. You are an insatiable master. You makest me lie down in green pastures. You makest me sleep, eat, shit, pee, and fornicate. Most of the time I am at your mercy. Sometimes I fear you. You are a machine without sentiment. You lull me into a false sense of security only to show me who's really the boss. I can go jogging, I can eat well, I can pretend to take control, I can abstain from sex or I can indulge in sex, but I might as well be a felon doing push-ups inside a prison. You alter my appetites and my desires without notice. I can never fully trust you to conform to my hopes. But sometimes, for ninety minutes at a time, we are meant for each other, we are one, and you make me gloriously happy.

In early May I informed Bruce and Alan Cook that I planned to nominate Hans as our captain for Spain. "He's the only one of us with hep C," I said, "and that C could stand for courageous." They concurred.

Subsequently I sent the following email to the team:

Rather than carry two complete sets of uniforms to Spain by himself, our intrepid right fullback and inspirational leader Hans would like to distribute them to everybody on Saturday, May 26th, during an all-male team meeting and BBQ, commencing at 6 pm. Copious amounts of red wine and humdrum food shall be provided on my back porch. I promise I will not try to make paella.

BBQ

Life gets complicated when you love one woman and worship eleven men.
– Nick Hornby

When Dante wrote *The Divine Comedy* in a new language he called Italian, he described the various levels of Hell in "The Inferno," but somehow failed to include the level of purgatory to which husbands are relegated during the twenty-four-hour period preceding any party or dinner at one's home. This is the mind-chilling phase in which appearances count for *everything*. Fresh flowers must be displayed. Fresh towels must be provided. It is also necessary to remove the toaster from view. It is absolutely essential to go through one's fridge and vengefully toss out yogourt that might be a bit off, half jars of pickles, and perfectly good slices of leftover pizza.

It is a military situation. It is suddenly necessary for the male to remain on full alert, like a skittish cat afraid of being kicked. To make one's home presentable, a myriad of tasks must be invented, and these must inexplicably consume most of the morning and much of the afternoon. The sequence of errands must never be divulged to the errand runner in advance. Errands must never be combined efficiently into one trip.

A tablecloth must be ironed. Decks must be washed. The trusty red wheelbarrow must be hidden beneath the deck so the view of the garden is ideal. Even if the male's solicited opinions are automatically considered worthless, the menu must be discussed. It is important that any baking or cooking must be perfectly timed to raise the tension level. Ideally, everything must be taken out of the oven as the first guests are arriving so maximum hospitality points are scored.

Dante and his wife were relatively well-to-do. They must have entertained a great deal. Dante wrote beautiful poems for his beloved Beatrice, but not a word about his wife, Gemma. Literary scholars should check out the theory that possibly his reticence to describe his marital life was a sly form of revenge for his being just another domesticated male during the majority of his life when he was not otherwise engaged earning his reputation as The Supreme Poet. He could have included Hospitality Hell in "The Inferno," but he almost certainly feared his wife's wrath if he pointed out how women, who mostly rule the roost anyway, tend to abuse their powers whenever company is coming.

Hans wanted a pre-game event. I had agreed to host a barbecue to distribute our new uniforms on one condition: *guys only*. The couples had mingled at Ian's paella and sangria party eleven months before, coinciding with the final game of the World Cup. It wasn't necessary to reintroduce our significant others. Been there, done that. Fidel and I would supply guy food (sausages, kebabs), and I had a case of homemade red wine. Volunteers could bring salads, desserts, appetizers. That way we just might be able to talk about soccer – rather than real estate, restaurants, offspring, or movies.

I wanted everything *simple*. My email invitation suggested we might raise a glass to Owen Hargreaves, who had just been transferred on May 20, 2007, to Manchester United from Bayern Munich for 25 million Euros, after being named England's best performer in the World Cup. According to Tony Nardi, who invariably knows somebody who knows somebody who knows somebody, Owen Hargreaves' father in Calgary told Tony's friend the real reason behind the Canadian's transfer.

"Owen was not entirely happy in Bayern with the tone in the locker room," Tony told us. "It appears that Oliver Kahn, especially, made it very difficult on the non-Germans." Tony was of the opinion that Owen Hargreaves would make a great replacement for Paul Scholes in the Manchester midfield. Tony was often right about soccer and wine, and he could be a deft passer. For the party, he would show up with a bottle of Prosecco, one of Tara's favourites. Not only was he a shrewd playmaker, he could always be counted on to decipher where the real power lies.

Even though the guests were only a bunch of soccer players, Tara whipped up a Spanish dish and a cake for dessert. I put a poster of Stanley Matthews on the fridge and hung one of Hans's spiffy new jerseys on an ornamental tree in the front yard.

As expected, there was far too much food. Alan Cook arrived first, with two bottles of wine, a huge salad, and cookies made by his wife, Linda. Ken brought olives, reminding everyone that Spain was the world's leading producer of them. Ian, always civilized, brought a Spanish fish dish and talked to Tara about her garden. Tony and Bruce took over the barbecue. Bruce had brought his own barbecue utensils.

There was a lot of laughter. During a conversation about why women generally outlive men, Hans asked, "Do you know why men usually die before women?" There was only a short pause. "Because they want to." Alan confided that he had bought a motorcycle at age sixty to preserve his sense of adventure. Ian and I nodded: it was important to live experimentally. That's what Spain was all about. A story with an ending that couldn't be foretold. An experiment.

Fidel mostly sat in a corner of the deck and watched. I knew he was casting his mind forward, wondering how our far from formidable group might fare in Spain. "We should talk about the lineup," he said to me at one point. Ours was far from being an all-star team. If we could have hand-picked the best players from our two Point Grey over-fifties clubs, at least half of the volunteers for Spain wouldn't be there.

As a way of thanking Hans for purchasing the uniforms, Dave Naphtali had brought a team pennant that everyone signed. As Alan and I had prearranged, after Dave made the presentation I nominated Hans to be our captain. "Italy just won the World Cup with a fullback as their captain," I said, "and we know you won't embarrass us by trying to speak any bad Spanish."

Alan read aloud a letter from the mayor of Vancouver, Sam Sullivan, to be given to our Spanish hosts, and he read aloud a progress report from Myles, our man in Granada, who lived near the centre of town, one block from Bodegas Espadafor, the bar run by Miguel, the organizer for the Granada Veterans club:

> Things are starting to shape up pretty good for games. I was in Miguel's bar two nights ago and we went over a few things. Considering the number of players we have, he is going to try and gather up enough players from the Veterans Club to make up two teams and therefore have two games. We'll see how it goes. The first game will likely be on Saturday. Weekend games will be during the day. Weekday games will be at night.

I stood on a bench and assembled everyone for a team photo. As I pressed the camera button, I noted the unusual eagerness with which everyone came together and posed, which made the occasion seem special. Ross Mitchell, an accountant, insisted on my being included in a second photo, so he stood on the bench and I replaced him. Giddy with our new-found sense of camaraderie, as if we were being called upon to sacrifice ourselves for some higher purpose, we were a little like a group of young men going off eagerly to fight in the First World War. All of us had escaped warfare in our lives, so on some subliminal level Spain was going to be a replacement of that adventure.

As we all smiled for the camera, I understood why young men leap out of trenches and get themselves shot to death, lodged on barbed wire. The shared adrenalin was like a beautiful drug. We were being swallowed by a false sense of unity. The French have a phrase, esprit de corps, and it fits. Our joint fearlessness was a bodily sensation.

The next morning Dave Naphtali wrote to everyone:

Last night we bestowed titles on various individuals. Here is the equivalent Spanish terminology for the trip. Hans: Captain – *El Capitán*. Alan Twigg: Coach – *El Entrenador*. Alan Cook: General Manager – *El Director General*.

Alan suggested I circulate lineups in advance. I did so by applying some basic math. Twenty guys and four games. With fifteen-per-side rosters, everyone could be rested for one game each. We hoped the first game would be a seniors-only clash. Any games after that, during the week, would

*Fidel, Alan, France,
Victory, 2005.*

have looser parameters, possibly incorporating the sons of several players, who were bringing along their boots.

I wrote:

> For some of us, this could be our last kick at the can, so let's make it a memorable adventure, win or lose. There will be some injuries, hangovers, and sunstroke. If you're feeling unusually old, generous, or injured, or any combination of all three, you can consider donating some or all of your playing time during weekday games to someone younger (if our weekday opponents are amenable). Should anyone need to get hold of me in Spain, I'll be staying at our Balzain soccer boot camp, working on my inspirational pre-game speeches and long-winded post-game excuses.

Alan Cook sent me a private note:

Nice job Alan. This seems very straightforward and fair. One possible wrinkle is that, in some cases, fathers have asked to be given playing time WITH their sons. I imagine this has come about in family negotiations where wives have "suggested" that the father take the son along and son has agreed on the basis they would get to play some soccer.

Clearly the likes of Sir Alex Ferguson and Rafa Benítez didn't have these problems. When I gave Fidel the lay of the land, he responded, "Complicated this Canadian soccer it is . . ."

"You're as Canadian as me," I replied.

INTERVIEW WITH A MISTRESS #5

ALAN: Only a month to go.

NETTIE: Got the tickets?

ALAN: Yup.

NETTIE: Confirmed the reservations?

ALAN: I have the printouts.

NETTIE: Got some Euros?

ALAN: Yup.

NETTIE: So let's get this party started.

ALAN: I wish.

NETTIE: Don't tell me you're afraid of flying.

ALAN: No. I'm just nervous about all this drama that is getting

built up around me. Lately it feels like I've been building a sandcastle and the tide is about to turn.

NETTIE: Are you afraid of losing?

ALAN: No, it's all the action off the field that is preying on my
mind.

NETTIE: The first grandchild? Your mom?

ALAN: It's like I'm playing a poker game against Fate and it's
not going very well. My mom was three-quarters of the
way across that crosswalk before she got hit. Now I've
spent the last six weeks visiting the hospital each day,
dealing with medical politics and insurance hassles. I
don't feel I'm in control.

NETTIE: But the grandchild will be a good thing. That ought to
even the score.

ALAN: Except there are only four weeks left to prepare for
Spain and I can't friggin' run! This is a plot twist that I
could definitely do without. Now I know how real athletes feel when they get injured and they have to worry
about missing the big game. You start to feel like a
loser even though it's not your fault. If I can't play, I'll
be letting down the team.

NETTIE: You don't have to pretend to be noble with me. I know
you better than you know yourself. It's not just about
the team. Being injured in Spain will kibosh your
storyline.

ALAN: It's true. If I'm injured, I'll be relegated to being a mere
playwright instead of an actor. I'll be like one of those
mountain climbers who doesn't quite make it to the top
of Everest. He gets frostbite, so he has to stay in one of
the base camps, lower down the mountain, and listen
on the radio as his buddies reach the summit.

NETTIE: You still have some time to recuperate. Maybe you're overdramatizing the situation just to give yourself the impetus to do something about it. Haven't you just gone to the gym two days in a row? That's a record for you.

ALAN: Drugs. I think drugs could be the answer.

NETTIE: I worry that you're not kidding.

ALAN: For the first time in my life, I feel some sympathy for all those athletes who take drugs. Once you can't perform at your top level, you quickly lose your identity and you'll do whatever it takes to get back to where you were, once you know you've fallen below your optimal level. Like that baseball player, José Canseco, who appears on reality TV shows.

NETTIE: Never heard of him.

ALAN: Lots of women have plastic surgery as they get older. It's pretty much the same phenomenon.

NETTIE: So taking steroids is not really about cheating. It's about staying in the game.

ALAN: Something like that. When you get injured, your body starts to fill up with fear. Self-doubt starts to spread inside you like an infection. You worry you'll never be the same again.

NETTIE: Like a hooker who loses her looks. Useless. Ready for the scrap heap.

ALAN: Precisely. This week I had a camera pushed up my bum so they could look through my intestines for bowel cancer. Then I had an MRI for forty minutes to see if my brain tumour has paid a return visit. Then I went to a Chinese acupuncturist to learn my pelvis is out of alignment. Guess which one was most upsetting?

NETTIE: If this is supposed to turn into a joke, I think it's not going to be funny.

ALAN: The first two appointments were a piece of cake. They were merely concerned with matters of life and death. My third appointment, with Dr. He, the Chinese healer, proved that my body is out of alignment.

NETTIE: Well, that beats the hell out of bum cancer.

ALAN: I'm pretty sure just about everybody has got a pelvis that is slightly out of alignment and everybody's got one leg longer than the other, but the trouble is you end up believing this guy because he can prove how your strength is unevenly distributed. You walk out of that office believing you're off-kilter. You are like a car that has been in a bad accident and the frame is bent. Its resale value goes way, way down. The idea gets stuck inside your head. Every time you experience some pain in your groin when you sneeze, you have to say to yourself, "Aha! I'm chronically out of alignment."

NETTIE: You should be glad you don't have to worry about menopause.

ALAN: That's like saying I should be glad I don't live on the moon.

NETTIE: You're not being entirely reasonable about this.

ALAN: I don't want to be reasonable about soccer.

NETTIE: I've noticed.

ALAN: If I could play in pain, it would be fine. But I'm at this terrifying stage where I can't even do that!

NETTIE: You need to relax, look around you, and tell yourself not to panic. If you are angry at your body for turning against you, just think what it must be like to be in Hans's cleats.

ALAN: I've been thinking about Hans a lot.

NETTIE: Maybe you should talk to him. He might help you more than a brain surgeon or a proctologist or an acupuncturist.

ALAN: Hans would tell me to suck it up, get on with life. Make the best of it. I already know that. It would make more sense to talk to Bruce.

DR. BRUCE

I arrived on the planet on 11/11/51. Still kicking.
— Bruce Fleming (a memo)

Fidel and I have had an abiding interest in Dr. Bruce for several years. We like him as a soccer player, we admire him as a friend, and we remain curious about his character.

After one summer game at Strathcona – I remember it well, because it was the only time I have been responsible for an own goal – we were drinking cans of beer from a cooler under a tree when two elderly Chinese-Canadian women approached. They were competing with each other, in a less than friendly way, to see which of them could gather the most beer cans to return for deposit money. Although their invasive empty can–collecting technique was off-putting, nobody was certain whether the behaviour of these two women was pathetic or admirable. While we all politely tolerated their hovering, Bruce made a stiff ceremony of donating his beer can to one of them, extending his hand with all the decorum of a Governor General bestowing an honorary citation. Then he walked over to Fidel and whispered, "She reminds me of my mother."

The incident was one more indication that Dr. Bruce might have a pain-riddled inner life that remains beyond our comprehension. We could not tell whether he felt sorry for her or not.

Two or three times over a three-year period, Fidel and I have watched Bruce grab his head with both of his hands during a game, as if he has been paralyzed by torment, as if his head has been zapped by lightning bolts. Each time, he has stopped running to grasp his head, as if he is afraid it could explode. This gesture is the soccer equivalent of *The Scream*, that classic expression of disbelief and anguish. Usually there is an element of physical harm or danger involved. A dastardly opponent has made a flagrant attempt to injure Bruce, whereupon Bruce has pleaded with the referee – or God – for justice, but to no avail.

This meltdown is intriguing because it is so contrary to Bruce's cucumber-cool persona. In the same way that we automatically feel compassion if a teammate falls to the ground, writhing in agony, we cannot fail to worry about Bruce's condition when he feels there has been some gross trespass against him. When this reaction occurs, I am again struck by how little I know Bruce, and how much I would like to know him better.

Bruce Fleming, after all, is the soccer player I have known the longest – since I was six years old – and yet he remains an enigma. We like each other a lot, but mutual respect and affection does not necessarily constitute intimacy.

When Bruce and I were growing up in West Vancouver, back in the days when it was still a middle-class enclave with vacant lots and chicken coops, Bruce's father ran Fleming's Hardware across from the funeral home, Harrington's Florists, and Bernie's Billiard Hall. Our bonds were sociological as much as personal. We eventually became soccer players instead of hockey players because our families weren't rich enough to join the Capilano Winter Club, the only facility with an ice rink. We had some mutual friends, but we never did anything together, just the two of us.

Now Bruce is a self-described journeyman soccer player and an attending physician in the emergency ward of the largest hospital in Western Canada. He and I were coincidentally reunited in the 1990s after a guest at our house keeled over suddenly, choking, delirious, after a dinner party. We somehow kept him from dropping into a coma before the ambulance arrived. The physician at the emergency ward turned out to be Bruce. After Bruce took control of the crisis, joking to put us at ease, he took his coffee break with us. It was a normal night at work for him.

In 2001 I had a seizure after a Sunday soccer game. Tara drove me, unable to talk, to the emergency ward the following morning, and Bruce showed up a few hours later, having seen my name on a list of emergency ward inductees. It was a terrific pleasure to see him. He calmly discussed my brain tumour with Tara as I listened. I don't recall that he offered any particular advice, but he contributed his reassuring concern, which was a sublime gift.

So Bruce and I have inexplicably kept reconverging. After meeting in grade one at Pauline Johnson Elementary School, we have fortuitously ended up on the same over-fifties soccer team about a half-century later. Our friendship has been unintentional, and yet it has endured while thousands of other more active relationships have withered.

Ever since those visits to the emergency ward, I've come to appreciate the challenging role of the emergency ward physician. He is someone who voluntarily ventures onto the front lines, not unlike a war correspondent. In the same way that the foreign correspondent chooses to visit war zones, refugee camps, and natural disasters, the emergency ward doctor goes to work knowing that strife, anguish, and pain are on the menu.

If Fidel scores, I don't hesitate to embrace him, but when Bruce plays on the right side of me, in the midfield, we battle side by side, with occasional hints of brotherly affection, but we never touch. I enjoy passing the ball to him. I know he will always make the best of it. He won't perform miracles, but he will take the responsibility of ball control with great seriousness. He is someone who is deeply determined never to let our side down.

Bruce's steady dependability is the main feature of his game, but on those rare occasions when there has been an unfair tackle against him and the referee fails to make a swift and appropriate decision, Bruce's face becomes twisted with a rare expression of helplessness, exposing the boy beneath the man, and I glimpse the young person I met many years ago, before we learned to conceal our passions, and I am struck by a fraternal closeness that feels quite odd. I am estranged from my own brother much of the time, so I wonder if Bruce is a substitute brother.

The nakedness of Bruce's despair in disturbing situations serves as a mirror for the rest of us. We know that Bruce and

Richard, our two physicians, daily endure the most intense professional responsibilities in their jobs, putting them among the most respected and admired components of our team. So if Bruce's demeanour on the soccer pitch can sometimes lay open his soul to us, we have to wonder how much our own flawed and tormented characters are revealed by the way we play.

When he's at the emergency ward and they start to shuttle in the bleeding bodies from the latest carnage on the highway, we're fairly certain Dr. Bruce doesn't respond to the crisis by grabbing his head, contorting his face, and yelling the wordless screaming equivalent of "Woe is me." So the fact that he allows himself to be glimpsed so clearly through the window of soccer is a privilege for us.

Soccer, for Bruce, is clearly an outlet. He is among the first to admit it. "In my darkest moments in the emergency department," he says, "when there are lots of people waiting and we're way behind, and it feels like we're never going to catch up, I sometimes remind myself I have a game in the next day or two. And that gets me through. I often visualize a June evening when the grass is long, and the sun is an hour from setting, and we're running up and down the field as fast as we can, chasing the ball. I love those magical evenings when it's warm, but not too hot."

Instead of confessing his sins in a church, Bruce – and the rest of us – expiate our frustrations on the field. Soccer isn't just sport. It can be an exciting form of therapy. When other players lose their cool during a contest, it's usually not a pretty sight. You want to turn away. But on those few occasions when Fidel and I have spotted Bruce in turmoil, our responses are the opposite. We feel compassion.

Frances Metcalf

Bruce Fleming cheerfully doctored all our Spanish wounds, except our pride.

Over the years, watching Bruce make his thrilling runs down the wing, overpowering defenders with his burst of speed and determination, making a perfect cross or drilling a decisive blast at the goal, I've come to wonder if Dr. Bruce might be one of those habitually conformist types who might respond more comfortably in a formal interview than in a confidential conversation. That's why I asked him to lunch at the New India restaurant near the hospital, only a few days before we left for Spain. Even before I turned on the tape recorder, he was eager to speak openly. "I've spent my whole life trying to be good," he said.

It wasn't a statement of regret, merely an indication that he was willing and able to speak the truth.

ALAN: When did you start playing organized soccer?

BRUCE: Not until I was about thirty. We moved back from New Zealand, where I did medical training, and got our first house across from Douglas Park. One morning in October, I saw a bunch of guys playing soccer, so I wandered over and asked if I could play. They were a bunch of post-office workers. My son Andrew and I still go back to Douglas Park sometimes to play seven-a-side soccer. No referees. No offsides. No penalty kicks.

ALAN: What's your family background?

BRUCE: My mom came from a farming family in the prairies. There was a very strong religious undertone to life there. It was either feast or famine. Her brothers remained very devout Christians in the Baptist faith, but she turned her back on it. Subsequently I turned my back on it too. I remember showing up for Scouts one night, when we were living in West Van, and everybody was upset because one of the Scouts, a guy named Terry, had been shot by his mother. She was mentally ill. Then she shot herself with a hunting rifle. It was one of several things that got me thinking about the fact that we're all going to die.

ALAN: And now you're seeing the fragility of life every day in the emergency ward. What's the attraction?

BRUCE: I'm not an adrenalin junkie. I'm not a typical person in that environment. I'm convinced that I'm there largely because I fear it. I'm challenging that fear. I'm known, I think, as a calming influence, but mostly I'm trying to

calm my inner turmoil. I can put on a calm exterior,
but it's not what's going on inside.

ALAN: That still doesn't explain why you do it.

BRUCE: There is no sameness. Every day, every hour, is different, and there's a constant parade of people. From the
most successful people in our society to the most
unfortunate, everybody has got a story if you have time
for it. Probably if I wasn't doing this [work], I would be
a family doctor.

ALAN: You get to be a family doctor every time you show up
for soccer.

BRUCE: [Laughter] Yeah, I suppose.

ALAN: I can remember playing some baseball with you at
Pauline Johnson school when we were about ten or
eleven. Do you remember we sometimes played with
Nigel Hart?

BRUCE: Don't get me going on Nigel. I have this terrible guilt.

ALAN: He killed himself, right? Just like my friend Don Sharp,
another gifted athlete. I played with both of them on the
same soccer team that won a provincial championship.

BRUCE: It's very strange. Nigel Hart was one of these guys who
would rummage through a box and find a ball. You
could throw it to Nigel and he would hold it. And he
would instantly know what to do with it.

ALAN: I clearly remember Nigel Hart's father drove a Jaguar.
That was a very unacceptable thing to do in West
Vancouver, to be that ostentatious. It was always noted
by the other parents with disdain.

BRUCE: I got to know the Hart family really well. Something
ripped them apart. I won't go into the gory details. One
brother was a Canadian national team cricket player.

Another was a very gifted rugby player. Nigel went to India. I didn't hear from him for months and months and months. I had been his sidekick growing up. He beat me at everything we did. He was just a natural, easy-playing, goofy kid.

ALAN: Are you talking thirteen or fourteen years old?

BRUCE: Yes. Later too. I remember when I just got my driver's licence, I was sixteen and looked like I was twelve. Nigel and I were in my mom's Austin Cambridge. A couple of kids drove up beside us at a stoplight. One of the guys said, "Aren't you guys too young to be in a car?" We freaked out. We drove off as fast as we could go. They were laughing, trying to catch us. We made it back to our neighbourhood and went zooming into Nigel's driveway. These guys got out of the car, maybe to check our licences. Nigel's Dad had been a professional boxer. He was only five foot eight, but I remember the way he confronted them. "I'd like you to leave," he said. It was impressive. The tone of voice he used.

ALAN: There was an underlying militarism in his manner. Didn't he spend time in India? In the British military?

BRUCE: Well, eventually Nigel went to India and got hooked up with this Guru Maharaji. He becomes a total convert. He comes back and I remember talking to him. He wasn't the same. He was probably in an early stage of psychosis. I can remember asking him what was going on in his life. "You cannot understand the place that I have come to," he said. About ten months later, his mom phones to say he's been admitted to Crease Clinic.

ALAN: The loonie bin. That's where my friend Don Sharp went too.

BRUCE: I didn't visit him. I was not brave enough to go and talk to him. The next thing I knew, he'd gone missing. Within about twenty-four hours, he was found under the Port Mann Bridge. He had jumped. He'd left a note. He said, "Mom, I can't continue living like this." Within a year, his mom was dead and his dad was dead. I never went over there. I was busy at university. Their son was dead, and I never had the courtesy to go over and see his mom and dad to wish them well.

ALAN: Much the same thing happened with Don Sharp. He got involved with taking some bad drugs, LSD laced with strychnine, or so we heard. I did go and visit him in Crease Clinic once, but there was nothing you could do. He ended up killing himself too. Nigel, Don, and I had won the provincial championship together on a team called the Spuraways, but both those guys imploded.

BRUCE: My daughter Julia played at the university level back east for Concordia. She went way further than I did. She was living the life. On her team, when she played at the Metro level, there were at least five of her teammates with depression, and a few were hospitalized.

ALAN: The casualty rate of people taking sports too seriously is huge.

BRUCE: Yes, like Nigel. I think Nigel was in his early twenties when he killed himself. Whenever Nigel was caught by somebody doing something wrong, they'd say, "Who are you? What's your name?" and he was clever enough to have a whole alter ego. His name was Leroy Solar. I've often thought if I ever have to give someone the wrong name, that's the name I'm going to use.

ALAN: Both Nigel Hart's father and Don Sharp's father struck me as being ex-Brit soldier types.

BRUCE: Yes. Now we live in this amazing part of the world, relatively untouched by war. We've been so fortunate. Just to the south of us is a whole nation that's been to Vietnam and now Iraq. There are households filled with Daddy Harts and Daddy Sharps. In Canada we've been mostly untouched since 1945. But in the United States, there's a whole generation of young people growing up in those troubled, pressure cooker environments. They grow up with demons.

ALAN: Our little excursion to Spain is like a military expedition. It's like we're playing at going to war.

BRUCE: Except the casualty rate is zero.

ALAN: But we're developing a pack mentality.

BRUCE: Totally. Our little games on the weekend are mini-conflicts. It's us against them. They're the enemy. And these are my colleagues, and they're going to stand up for me.

ALAN: During our last game against the Chinese guys, Giant Panda, it became horribly palpable. The racial difference accentuated that imperative to depersonalize the opposition.

BRUCE: It's very basic, very tribal.

ALAN: The barbarism of sport can be hateful.

BRUCE: But it's all contained. We can make it acceptable.

ALAN: When we collectively decided we wanted to turn ourselves into a winning team last year, nobody stood up and said we should not do that.

BRUCE: You know the only person who did? Kate, my daughter.

She said we were taking it way too seriously. She said, "You should just go out and have fun."

ALAN: The trouble is we're having a lot more fun winning than losing.

BRUCE: Yes, there's something to be said for winning. One of my favourite expressions is "A tie is akin to kissing your sister."

ALAN: Do you think Ken Falk worries about winning and losing the way we do?

BRUCE: He is from a superior perspective. In the evolutionary scale of things, he's up there, and I'm down here as a primate. He'll kick the ball in his own net and laugh and giggle. He was like that before he got sick, but now he's even more so. If I kicked the ball into my own net, I would be totally pissed.

ALAN: The price we have paid for not losing any games so far this year has been interesting. The desire to win is a drug. Nothing will satisfy you until you get another hit of this drug.

BRUCE: Yes, it can get ugly.

ALAN: How do you feel about this trip to Spain?

BRUCE: I wonder about the skill level of the opposition. I think we all fear that they will be quite gifted, whereas we mostly play soccer for laughs. We've got a few good players, but this is not a soccer culture. I don't necessarily want to win, but I don't want to be embarrassed.

A MERCIFULLY BRIEF HISTORY
OF SOCCER IN CANADA

A national football team represents a way of being, a culture.
– Michel Platini

If we go to Spain with CANADA on our chests, it helps to know that Canadians were not always soccer patsies. The earliest recorded game was played in 1876 in Toronto, and the Dominion Football Association was formed in Montreal the following year. By 1880 there were nineteen clubs playing in Berlin, Ontario, a town that was renamed Kitchener during the First World War. (In a park in downtown Saskatoon, a memorial to that war is topped by a statue of a soccer player, his foot on a ball, representing the thousands of players who joined up and died in Europe.)

Canada won its first international match, against the United States, in Newark, New Jersey, in 1884, by a score of 1–nil. Four years later an Ontario team toured Britain, recording nine wins, nine losses, and five ties. Then – believe it or not – a Canadian team won the second Olympic gold medal for soccer.

Back in 1900, when soccer was first included as an Olympic sport, almost any amateur team that could afford to show up for a round-robin tournament was welcome. Four years later, when the Olympics were staged in St. Louis, Missouri, the cost of travel for most European athletes was prohibitive. Only three teams entered the soccer competition. Two were from St. Louis, and one was from Galt, Ontario, a town located ninety kilometres from Toronto.

Rival Ontario teams knew they couldn't hope to defeat the

mighty men of Galt, so they decided not to take the expensive train ride to Missouri. Guaranteed a medal just for lacing on their boots, Galt had been a venerable powerhouse since 1882. It had won the Ontario Cup in 1901, 1902, and 1903, as well as Western Football Association championships in 1886, 1887, 1888, 1893, 1901, 1902, 1903, and 1904.

After Galt easily won its two Olympic matches, defeating Christian Brothers College of St. Louis 7–1, and St. Rose Parish School of St. Louis 4–1, the mayor of Galt was on hand to present each member of Canada's winning squad with a personally inscribed gold medal.

Anyone who doesn't believe this happened can visit the Canadian Soccer Hall of Fame and Museum in Vaughan, Ontario, and see the gold medal won by forward Fred William Steep, a machinist who died in 1956.

On their train trip back to Canada, Galt FC stopped in Chicago and whipped an American all-star team 4–2, for good measure. Arriving in Galt (since renamed Cambridge), the team was mobbed by three thousand well-wishers who staged a torchlight parade to the opera house. In 1905, when Galt FC hosted a touring British team of amateurs named the Pilgrims, the contest was billed as the Championship of the World. Almost four thousand fans cheered as the home side tied the British 3–3.

⚽

Among the Olympic heroes in Galt in 1904, few were more celebrated than Alexander Noble Hall, the centre forward who scored a hat trick during Canada's first game against Christian Brothers College. After the 1904 Olympics, the

Scottish-born marble cutter packed his bags for Scotland, where he played soccer for St. Bernard's of Edinburgh. Then he made his debut for the English First Division champions, Newcastle United, against Sheffield Wednesday on September 7, 1907. Hall scored twice in six games for Newcastle before he was transferred in March 1908 to Dundee in the Scottish First Division, where he appeared in thirty-three games for the club. He was on the bench when his team won the Scottish Cup in 1910. Alexander Noble Hall later captained the Toronto Scots and worked at the Toronto Incinerator. He died in 1943, even more obscure than the Olympic gold medal he had helped win.

The first Canadian to make his mark in English football was Edward Hagarty Parry, who played for Oxford University and the Old Carthusians, and represented England for two matches against Wales (1879, 1882) and one against Scotland (1882). His career marked the beginning of a continual trickle of Canadian soccer players who have advanced to play professionally in Europe.

With difficulty, you can find information on the Internet about the likes of Robert Logan "Whitey" McDonald, who signed with Glasgow Rangers in 1928 after the Rangers officials saw him play during their North American tour, and goalkeeper Joe Kennaway, who was similarly elevated into Scottish professional ranks after he impressed a touring side. Kennaway performed solidly for Celtic from 1931 to 1939, winning three Scottish FA Cups and two Scottish League championship medals. He recorded eighty-three shutouts for "the Bhoys" during his 295 appearances.

A rare "double international," Kennaway made an international appearance for Scotland against Austria at Hampden

Park in 1933, having previously represented Canada during a match against the United States in Brooklyn in 1926. Kennaway might have played more games for Scotland, but the English formally protested his involvement as a Canadian. Despite his impressive statistics, Kennaway's claim to fame will always be associated with one of the greatest on-field tragedies in soccer history. He gained his big break in Scottish soccer after a much-admired goalkeeper for Glasgow Celtic died shortly after a goalmouth collision.

Born in Calgary in 1930, John Little played fullback for Glasgow Rangers and once represented Scotland against Sweden in 1953. Born in Hamilton in 1956, but raised mainly in Belfast, Jimmy Nicholl played for various teams, including Manchester United, and made seventy-three international appearances for Northern Ireland. He helped Manchester United win the FA Cup in 1977.

Born in Trinidad and Tobago in 1963, defender Randy Samuel played for various teams in Europe and has represented Canada in more international matches than any other player, earning eighty-two caps between his international debut in 1983 and his retirement in 1993. He now runs a soccer coaching service in Richmond, B.C.

Born in Guyana in 1967, Canadian striker Alex Bunbury was once named the Most Valuable Player in the Portuguese SuperLiga (Premier League), and he established a team record of 59 goals during his 165 games for Marítimo. Bunbury, who ended his career with the Kansas City Wizards, remains the third-highest scorer for Canada in international competition, with 16 goals during his 65 appearances.

Hockey buffs might know John van 't Schip, born in Fort St. John, B.C., in 1963, as a cousin to NHLers Joe Nieuwendyk and Jeff Beukeboom, but he's famous in Europe as a former captain of Holland's perennial powerhouse, Ajax. After earning forty-one caps for Holland internationally, spending eleven seasons with Ajax as a player, Johannes Nicolaas "John" van 't Schip became an assistant coach for the Dutch national team.

Vancouver-born John Catliff scored nineteen goals for Canada in forty-three appearances from 1984 to 1994, tying Dale Mitchell for all-time top spot, but he spent most of his playing career in North America. Having won the Canadian Soccer League (CSL) scoring championship in 1990, he accumulated sixty-nine goals in his five CSL seasons, the second-highest tally in league history.

Also Vancouver-born, Dale Mitchell was appointed head coach of Canada's senior team in May 2007, one month before the poor performance of his Under-20 squad at the World Cup. He scored nineteen times in fifty-five appearances for Canada. Although he was the Major Indoor Soccer League's third-highest all-time scorer, with 406 goals in nine indoor seasons, he never played professionally beyond North America.

Born in Poznań, Poland, in 1973, striker Tomasz Radzinski immigrated first to Germany, at age thirteen, then on to Canada. After Radzinski proved himself as the top scorer in the Belgium league, he played for Everton and Fulham. At Everton he scored twenty-five times in ninety-one games, but he reportedly rankled the team's ownership by urging Wayne Rooney to quit the squad. Fulham released him in 2006, leading to rumours that Radzinski might be added to the roster of Toronto FC as a designated player with the advent of the so-called Beckham Rule, which enables each team to sign one player beyond their salary cap.

Born in Etobicoke, Ontario, in 1977, Paul Stalteri, a defender for Tottenham Hotspur, has accumulated more than fifty caps playing for Canada, the most of any active player. He became the first Canadian to score in the Bundesliga while making his professional debut for Werder Bremen in 2000.

Prior to returning to Canada as the co-captain for Toronto FC, Jim Brennan played professionally for thirteen years for Bristol City, Nottingham Forest, Norwich City, and Southampton.

After a coach in Marseilles advised him to quit the game, Toronto-raised Julian de Guzman Jr., the son of a Jamaican-born mother, persevered and gained a spot with the Bundesliga team in Hanover. After joining Deportivo de la Coruña, he became the first Canadian to play in the Spanish First Division in a game against Real Betis in September 2005. On October 26, 2005, he scored the winning goal against Spain's World Cup goalkeeper, Iker Casillas, when Deportivo defeated the world's richest club, Real Madrid, 3–1.

Jonathan de Guzman, six years younger than his brother, has signed a contract extension with the Dutch First Division team Feyenoord Rotterdam through 2010. Like his brother, Jonathan was trained by his father, Bobby de Guzman – the Walter Gretzky of Canadian soccer dads – on the snow-covered fields in Scarborough, but Jonathan's future is generally acknowledged to be much brighter. The big question is not whether Jonathan de Guzman will excel; it's whether he will choose to play internationally for Holland, Jamaica, or Canada.

At only age twenty-four, Burnaby native Christine Sinclair was the highest-scoring Canadian player in international soccer, with eighty-one goals in ninety-nine international "A" appearances prior to the 2007 Women's World Cup in China. She contributed to Canada's best-ever World Cup showing when Canada's women placed fourth in 2003.

Calgary-born and -raised Owen Hargreaves is by far the most successful Canadian soccer player to date. The son of an English father and a Welsh mother, Hargreaves chose to play for England instead of Wales, having been passed over by Canada's national team program when he was eligible to play for Canada at age seventeen. He has twice played for England in the World Cup, and his pro team in Germany won the Champions League, the World Club title, the German league championship (three times), the German Cup (twice), and the German League Cup.

An avid basketball player in his youth, Hargreaves was encouraged to pursue soccer by his father, a former striker for the youth team of Bolton Wanderers in the United Kingdom. Owen Hargreaves was scouted by Bayern Munich at age sixteen, and moved to Germany in 1997, keeping his spirits up in the team's youth hostel with a poster of David Beckham. "I couldn't speak a word of German," he told the *Guardian* in 2004, "and I ate nothing but schnitzel for the first six months. Life was pretty hard and lonely but I had Beckham on my wall."

Hargreaves eventually made his debut with Bayern Munich at age nineteen in 2001, soon contributing to his team's double victory as Bundesliga and UEFA Cup champions. As one of Bayern Munich's top players, he made the transition from midfielder to left back. Although Owen

When Pelé arrived at the Vancouver airport in 1972, a Portuguese-speaking historian named Roderick Barman and his family served as the city's unofficial welcoming committee – and Pelé chatted amicably. Only four people showed up to see him. That's the extent to which Vancouver was at the edge of the soccer universe when I was playing in the 1960s.

Hargreaves has never resided in England, he earned his first cap for the English squad against Holland in August 2001, soon after Sven-Goran Eriksson became England's manager.

Despite some early controversy (hostile reporters called him "Mountie Boy," a disparaging reference to his Canadian roots), Hargreaves has continued to play for England, earning more than thirty caps, and rising to prominence in 2006 when he was voted England's best player in the World Cup. In 2007 he transferred to Manchester United.

Between 1980, when the United Nations began comparing living standards of its member nations, and 2005, Canada was selected as the best place on the planet ten times out of eighteen. Fortunately for Canada, when the Pakistani economist Mahbub ul Haq developed the United Nations Human Development Index (UNHDI) to measure the social progress of nations, he failed to include soccer prowess in his list of indicators.

Canada has more than 33 million citizens and its most played sport is soccer. But since Canada joined FIFA in 1914, the country's record in international competition has failed to match its rankings on the UNHDI, to put it mildly. Never mind socialized medicine and good sewer systems, what is *wrong* with Canada?

If there's a World War to fight, give us a call. Canadian troops, acting as the "spearhead to victory" in the final months of 1918, liberating Holland in the Second World War, and providing some of the staunchest opposition to the Nazis on several occasions, have repeatedly proven themselves as tough as they come.

We can still kick the crap out of the Americans and the Russians at hockey, so why did Holger Osieck, former technical director for Canada's World Cup team, describe Canada as soccer's "land of the lost?" And why can't Canadian men score goals?

In 1986, competing in the World Cup for the first and only time, Canada notoriously never scored a goal and finished last in that tournament, losing to France 1–nil, to Hungary 2–nil, and to the Soviet Union 2–nil. Canada's Under-20 squad beat Brazil in Edmonton 2–1, in front of fourteen thousand fans, on May 19, 2006, but during our only other World Cup appearance, when we hosted the U-20 version in 2007, we distinguished ourselves by becoming the first host country to fail to score even once, losing to Chile 4–nil, to Austria 1–nil, and to Congo 2–nil.

Canada's women's team, on the other hand, has consistently ranked in the world's top ten, and they finished fourth at the 2003 Women's World Cup in the United States. Christine Sinclair and Kara Lang are widely acknowledged as two of the best female soccer players in the world. When the first FIFA World U-19 tournament for women was held in Edmonton, Victoria, and Vancouver in 2002, more than fifty-five thousand fans gathered in Edmonton's Commonwealth Stadium to watch Canada lose the final match to the United States on a golden goal.

This big, cold country is too vast, and the population is too small, for Canada to warrant a professional soccer league of its own, so essentially the best excuse we can give ourselves and the world is geography. Because Canada's most gifted players must seek work in Europe or the United States, it has become extremely difficult for any national coach to gather players to practise or play exhibition games.

On the West Coast, the first professional league soccer game in Canada was played in 1910, in Vancouver. In the inaugural match of the British Columbia Professional Football League on March 25, 1910, at Recreation Park, the Vancouver Callies beat the Rovers 3–nil. For reasons of climate – the mild winters allow year-round play – Vancouver and Victoria have remained hotbeds of Canadian soccer ever since.

Of the twenty-two players on Canada's only World Cup squad – the most successful men's team to date – fourteen were born in British Columbia or played soccer within the B.C. soccer system: Dale Mitchell, George Pakos, David Norman, Mike Sweeney, Randy Ragan, Jamie Lowery, Greg Ion, Bob Lenarduzzi, Bruce Wilson, Randy Samuel, Ian Bridge, Colin Miller, Paul Dolan, and Sven Habermann.

By 1978 the Vancouver Whitecaps were drawing crowds of more than thirty-two thousand per game, and young Vancouver native Bob Lenarduzzi was named North American Soccer Player of the Year. The following season the Whitecaps won their division, stunned the New York Cosmos in the semifinal, and beat Tampa Bay to bring home the NASL championship. A victory parade attracted one hundred thousand cheering fans.

Now the focus for soccer in Canada has switched to a professional franchise in Toronto, complete with a new stadium, corporate sponsors, and network television affiliations. If Canadians see Toronto FC represented in the sports highlights of American television stations, perhaps we will gradually allow ourselves to believe we belong back on the international soccer map, where we briefly claimed supremacy in 1904. We play the game – a lot – we just don't know how to watch it.

Although our side fizzled in the FIFA U-20 World Cup held in Canada, there is no shortage of promising, homegrown talent. Like his father Eddie Edgar before him, David Edgar has earned a spot as a defender for Newcastle United. Other Canadian-born players on European rosters include Marcus Haber (FC Groningen, Holland), Jaime Peters (Ipswich Town, England), Jonathan Beaulieu-Bourgault (FC St. Pauli, Germany), Keegan Ayre (Hibernian, Scotland), and the 2006 U-20 captain Will Johnson (Heerenveen, Holland).

PART THREE

SPANISH LESSONS

Flanked by Granada organizer Myles Ellis (holding his child) and other teammates, Serge Guilbaut read the Spanish version of a letter to the mayor of Las Gabias from Mayor Sam Sullivan of Vancouver.

BOOT CAMP

I want to play sexy football. – Ruud Gullit

In June, with Tara awaiting our first grandchild back in Vancouver, I was assigned to the only all-male cabin at the Balzain ski resort about ten minutes southeast of Granada. Farther up the mountain road, beneath the Sierra Nevada, were fancy houses for rich European ski enthusiasts, but our six cabins at Balzain were comfortably rustic, surrounded by terraced hillsides that were covered in olive trees.

We were the only guests, making our compound seem like an exclusive training camp. Our regiment of thirty-seven invaders included Bruce's daughter, Kate; Hans's son, Kyle; Nick's son, Andrew; and Ed's son, William. Familial and marital connections mostly determined the sleeping arrangements. Tony Nardi also brought along his son, Rob, so they bunked together in one room of my cabin; Serge and Christian, both raised in France, shared another room that was quickly dubbed the French Quarter. That left me in the third room, alone.

The concept of sharing a cabin in Spain with four other guys for seven days gave me the heebie-jeebies, but I have learned to cope with my lonerism the way someone with agoraphobia learns to deal with open spaces, or someone who is afraid of heights tends to avoid staring over cliffs. In our cabin, my room was the smallest, with the least light, but I much preferred privacy to comfort. If I were placed in solitary confinement as a prisoner, I just might prefer it. I skulked in the corners, worrying about being anti-social, while Tony and Serge took charge of groceries and conversation. Tony and Serge were talkers, and Christian and I were listeners, so there was at least some balance.

On our first night, there was a delightful meal at which Serge and Christian laughingly recalled their roles in the Paris student riots of 1968. Christian described how he was the only student protester to erect a street blockade – in a cul-de-sac. Serge was part of a contingent that triumphantly occupied a government building and boldly placed a long-distance call to Cuba, but didn't know what to say to his fellow revolutionaries – so he asked them what the weather was like.

If Fidel is Mozart, Bruce is Penicillin, and Hans is Captain Courageous, I could be Garbo because I usually *vant* to be alone. On the second night, Christian and I opted out of the group dinner at a swanky restaurant up the hill, La Guitarra, in favour of finding the only cyberstore for Internet connections in the nearby suburb of La Zubia.

A former tennis pro who grew up in Paris, Christian once sailed across the Atlantic with his wife in a homemade boat and another time started a tennis camp in Whistler with Bjorn Borg. After three years of producing *Hobo*, "Canada's

Tony Nardi

Roommates Christian Doigment, a magazine publisher, and Serge Guilbaut, an art historian, regaled me with their exploits during the Paris student riots of 1968.

only international arts magazine," Christian confided that he and his son had yet to make any money from it. Eating tapas in an outdoor bar, we discussed the potential advantages of formulating a non-profit society to operate his magazine. Ironically, by opting for non-profit status, he might be able to access enough federal funding to start paying himself.

Coaching can be contagious. Evidently it is often much easier to manage other people's lives than to manage your own. I am uncertain whether coaching the soccer team fell into my hands because I am a control freak or because I am motivated by the need to make myself useful, to serve the public good. It's likely some combination of the two.

Managing a soccer team, as Alan Cook and I have learned, is mostly thankless. The major consolation is that you can sometimes tell yourself that things are less screwed up than if someone else had been in charge. People in the business world often accept unwanted promotions for precisely this reason. Even though I had spelled out the logistics to everyone beforehand, I hadn't yet revealed the particulars of who was going to play where in the first game, and I was nervous about it. I could not finalize our lineup until I knew who had arrived on time at Balzàin. This meant I didn't know whether Christian would be playing in the first game or not. We chatted amicably, but in the back of my mind I was hoping he wouldn't ask me about the lineup.

Serge made a show of referring to me as the Big Chief, mainly because, as the former head of the fine arts department at Western Canada's largest university, he has become unaccustomed to being told what to do. So when he said he preferred not to play in the first game, it was good news, because I might not have to inform Christian that he was not playing in the first game.

We were scheduled to eat breakfast collectively at eight-thirty in the morning. The first game would be at eleven. I planned to explain the logistics of getting to the La Chana stadium and the details of the lineup at that breakfast. Around midnight on Friday, I began to rehearse what I might say.

When I woke up at five-thirty that morning, I started drinking copious amounts of water. Driving too much, drinking too much, failing to stretch adequately, I had aggravated my groin injuries, but as soon as I put on my white soccer socks and my black soccer shorts, I started to persuade myself I was feeling better. Ibuprofen and adrenalin would get me through the first game, and I would see how I felt afterwards. At breakfast, I posted the starting lineup on a pillar beside the long table. Midway through the gathering, with the wives present, I rose to speak.

"Everyone can figure out for themselves what this game means, so I'll resist the temptation to make a rah-rah speech. You guys are all smart, so I'm not going to insult your intelligence by telling you how I think we should approach this game or what it means. But it is entirely necessary to go over some logistics.

"Driving in Granada can be a nightmare. We have allocated considerable time and money to get here, so I don't want anyone to miss one of our games by taking a wrong turn and getting lost in a maze. Some of us made a reconnaissance trip yesterday to La Chana stadium, so I have some written instructions. You would be wise to copy them down. If you take a wrong turn in Granada, getting to the game could turn out to be even more problematic than playing it."

I proceeded to give everyone precise directions. Turn here, take this exit, look for this sign. "Most people in Granada don't speak English. If you get lost and you have to stop and ask someone for help, tell them La Chana." The women were busily taking notes. I knew the minds of the players were mostly a blur. They were waiting for me to tell them who was playing, and who was not, but I felt more like a schoolteacher than a coach as I gave the complicated instructions.

The lineups for the next four games, by comparison, were easy. I explained our system in less than sixty seconds. Each of our twenty players would miss one game of the four games. So that nobody could feel overly slighted, I had divided the team into four quintets. Tony Arimare, Fidel, Dave Naphtali, Hans, and I were Apples. Ken, Bruce, Trevor, Myles, and Alan Cook were Oranges. Nick, Tony Nardi, Ian, Ed, and Christian were Bananas. Ross, Dave Turner, Richard, Randey, and Serge were Pears. They would collectively miss game one. Bananas would miss game two. Apples would miss game three. Oranges would miss game four.

It sounded like an egalitarian system, but playing times could vary. I particularly wanted the Apples to play against the Granada Veterans. By midnight the previous night, Dave Turner, Richard, and Randey had failed to arrive, so it didn't make much sense to add any of them as starters, given jet lag and fatigue. The big loss was Hans, who, with minimal self-pity, had told me he couldn't run. A soccer injury sustained two weeks before his departure would mean he could only make a token appearance. We would miss his fiery temper at the back. In his place we elevated Trevor, our stout-hearted seventy-year-old.

I wanted to call the first game Canada versus Granada – because I like the way those two words fit together – but it didn't seem prudent to raise the stakes higher than they already were. We had asked for one game against Spanish guys our own age, and we expected this game would be it. I had seen the field, and there was nothing grandiose about it. Better to take a businesslike approach. Better to be calm. No oratory. I didn't want to make our guys any more nervous than they already were.

Driving to that first game, I was surprised by how distracted I felt. My mind was not on soccer at all. Circumventing Granada on the Ronda Sur, I found myself thinking about the Moors and how they might have felt when they took over Granada ten centuries earlier. Geographically, Granada was an anomaly: a defensible position, in an arid climate, that was well irrigated by rivers flowing from the Sierra Nevada. I'd read somewhere that Granada means pomegranate in Spanish, but the city more likely derived its name from the Moorish word *Karnattah* (or *Gharnatah*), meaning "hill of strangers." The Moors established their reign in the eleventh century, and built the Alhambra about two centuries later.

I was more charmed by Granada itself than the Alhambra, another glorified fort once occupied by the ruling class. In Granada they weren't accepting American dollars, and the vast majority of people didn't speak English. Driving to the game, as much as I wanted to pretend I was an athlete, I was reminded that I was mostly a tourist trying not to get lost, beset by my own stupidities. In Spain, where the shower taps are marked C and F, my North American brain leapt to conclude those initials for Caliente and Frio might somehow signify Cold and Hot. Similarly, on the Gran Colon, when I saw everyone waiting at the crosswalk for a green light even though there wasn't any traffic and it was easy to cross, I presumed the fines for jaywalking must be severe. It took me several days to realize that people in Granada are simply much less keen to rush.

Instead of worrying about the big game, I found myself thinking about how the Europeans are ahead of North Americans in so many ways. Several times I had patronized a little coffee shop at the Plaza de Triunfo at the edge of the Albayzín district, "the Moorish Casbah," managed by a calm Algerian. They didn't have any plastic cups for takeout. None of their clientele would dream of hurrying off with a coffee in their hand. What would be the point of having your morning coffee if you couldn't sit in the public square and watch the world go by? Why would anybody want to quickly grab a Starbucks coffee in a throwaway cup in order to drive around in traffic talking on their cellphone? The Spanish, like the

French, had had more than a few centuries to figure out how best to live.

But that didn't qualify them as friendly. If we were a Canadian hockey team and a Spanish team arrived to play our game, how might we respond? With that thought, I started to wonder what Fidel might be thinking and feeling as he was heading to the game. Normally we would compare soccer notes once or twice during the week, before the game. It didn't feel right, taking separate paths.

MAD DOGS AND CANADIANS

Football is a simple game made complicated by people
who should know better. – Bill Shankly

A year earlier, when plans for our trip began, we were told we would be playing our big game against the Granada Veterans in a converted bullring. That turned out to be misguided advance hype or else wishful thinking. La Chana is a neighbourhood on the southwest outskirts of Granada that is not shown on the tourist maps. Its playing field is surrounded by a high wire-mesh fence. It looks like a prison compound.

We arrived more than forty minutes before the kickoff. We had not known whether La Chana would have dressing rooms, so we emerged from our flotilla of rental cars ready to play, resplendent in our white jerseys with red maple leaves.

There was nobody at La Chana to greet us. Our first challenge was to negotiate our way onto the artificial turf. Although the athletic complex comprised two square blocks, there was only one entrance, which proved to be located about a ten-minute walk from the parking lot. Lugging our gear in the late-afternoon sun along cement sidewalks was an athletic undertaking unto itself. We soon learned that La Chana lacked two essentials: toilet paper and shade.

We had yet to learn that teams in southern Spain rarely appear on the pitch until ten minutes before the game. Instead they remain sheltered in their cement dressing rooms, possibly stretching, certainly conserving their energy. We, on the other hand, instinctively replicated our habits from North America, as if running around like geriatric gazelles in thirty degrees Celsius for half an hour might be a good form of preparation for a game.

We had only two balls to kick around between us. One was a black-and-white beach ball, an imitation soccer ball that I had purchased on a whim in Nerja, the Spanish seaside town in which Tony Arimare and Alina had passed some idyllic days more than twenty years ago. I was able to forewarn Tony that it had been transformed into another post EC gulag of cement hotels and condominiums, even though it was still advertised as a "sleepy fishing village" on the Internet. It would only occur to me after the game that if a team from Spain had travelled all the way to Canada to play against us, and we saw them warming up with a beach ball, we would have introduced ourselves and lent them one of our balls to practise with before the game.

When they emerged from the dressing room, en masse, like a military unit, none of the Spaniards came to our side of the field. After Serge had announced that he would serve as a photographer for the game, I asked him if he would take a photograph of both teams together before the kickoff. We

Our acrobatic goalkeeper Tony Arimare was by far our most effective player, making superb saves in every game. He exchanged gloves with one of the Granada goalies.

both assumed this could be easily arranged because Serge spoke fluent Spanish, but when none of our opponents showed any signs of friendliness, the notion of a shared photo was discarded.

For a sense of an opening ceremony, our team posed by ourselves. Most of us were aware of how lucky we were to have flown across the Atlantic Ocean to play soccer, and this sense of good fortune made us cheerful rather than nervous.

Somebody suggested the players in the back row fold their arms, like a real team. The guys in the front row all knelt on one knee. "At least this is something we know we're good at," I said. We could at least organize ourselves well off the field.

I knelt between Fidel and Tony, our goalkeeper. I could feel Fidel's impatience for the game to begin. After about thirty seconds of posing, he rose and announced, "Thanks." By the way he said it, he really meant, "That's it. That's enough." Following Fidel's lead, everyone disbanded from the group photo. I assumed he didn't fully approve of posing like that, as if it was somehow tempting the soccer gods. We were acting like a soccer team before we had proved ourselves as one. It was possible he was interpreting the collective photo op as an outward sign of vanity, and vanity was a sign of inner weakness. I knew that whereas most of us saw our soccer expedition as boyishly pretentious, Fidel considered himself to be a serious player. The difference in attitudes and abilities was exacerbated somewhat by Fidel's decision to stay outside Granada, in Orgiva, rather than with the group.

Later Fidel told me that during the warm-up he had approached Miguel, the bar owner who had organized the game, and jokingly told him not to beat us by more than 3–nil. Months earlier Fidel had predicted to me that the Spanish would not behave in the congenial manner of the French, whom we had played two years earlier. He remembered an important game that was played between Yugoslavia and Spain more than twenty-five years earlier, a game that had generated serious bad feelings between the two countries. So Fidel was testing Miguel's character, his level of friendliness. By the stiff way that Miguel responded, Fidel confirmed his pre-game suspicions that our Spanish hosts were not inclined to be gracious.

Miguel took his soccer as seriously as Fidel did. Three nights earlier, in Granada, when I was staying in the Albayzín district, waiting for the rest of the team to arrive, I visited Miguel's tapas bar. It was immediately apparent that he was the guy in the soccer jersey, rushing about the place, telling his employees what to do. His bar was a bohemian hangout, not far from the university, but he himself was clearly not an intellectual. He had the energy of a hustler, a fixer, someone who is socially active but simultaneously all business. I judged, by the hyper-efficient way that he treated his patrons, that he would not wish to give me the time of day, that I would be a mere nuisance. My lack of Spanish and his lack of English would make any interaction between us a waste of time.

So the aloofness of the Spanish soccer players at La Chana did not surprise me – but their age did. For about six months, Alan Cook and I had urged Myles to impress upon the Spaniards that we wanted to have at least one game with a so-called level playing field. To stress to our Spanish hosts the nature of their competition, I had contacted our players and calculated our median age – fifty-seven – and passed this information along to Myles, who in turn had given the information to Miguel, but it was evident that Miguel had failed to honour our request for a fair game between veteran teams. More than a few of the opponents he had lined up for us were about half our age.

Either Miguel had not bothered to accept the information about our age level, or the Spaniards were simply unable to field a team that was anywhere near our median age, or they didn't care. It was apparent, even before the kickoff, that we would be playing against guys who were, in some cases, young enough to be our sons. Whereas nearly every one of them was an ex-professional, one of our fullbacks was seventy years old and lots of our players were in their sixties. How could these guys possibly take us seriously as opponents? It was a ridiculous mismatch.

I called our players into the centre of the field, away from the wives and relatives on the sidelines, in the hope that we could gain some strength by recognizing the situation. I don't recall saying anything profound. It was the act of coming together in a circle that mattered.

Every player in our starting lineup of fifteen guys seemed to grasp the situation without any explanation. This was an international match. We would behave as best we could. Given the failure of the Granada Veterans club to lower their age level to the occasion, we could not realistically hope to win this game, but we could give our best effort.

Nobody felt any self-pity. On the contrary, we felt privileged. We were alive and well and playing soccer in Spain with CANADA on our jerseys. Although this game wasn't precisely what we had asked for or imagined, nobody wanted to leave La Chana. We had no grounds for complaints. We had enlisted.

When the Spanish took the kickoff and began to pass the ball strategically in their half, we didn't bite. If anything, we enjoyed the semi-arrogant way they wanted to toy with us, like a cat taunting a mouse, or a matador taunting a bull. We didn't rush madly after them, but we did provide some intelligent pursuit. We understood that soccer can be like a chess match: patience can be a virtue. The Spanish were able to control the ball, but they were stymied from making any meaningful penetration. We were playing more intelligently than usual, rising to the occasion.

After several minutes, it became apparent to me that the Spanish were overestimating our capabilities. That was all to the good. We could not steal the ball, or control it, but neither could they run circles around us. Our starting lineup was adequately anticipating where the ball would go. We were running to fill the holes. It wasn't pretty, but we were not being foolish.

Dave Naphtali quickly established himself as a fast and formidable defender on our back line. Best of all, Tony swiftly and confidently controlled his box. The manner in which he hollered instructions and pounced, catlike, when the ball came near, made us appear respectable as a team.

I did my best in midfield, sprinting hither and yon, coming close to intercepting some passes that might otherwise have been routine. Only Fidel showed signs of creativity, although he could not generate any offence in their area. We had less than 35 per cent of the play, but our tenacity level held firm. Instead of teamwork, we had gumption and energy. The longer we held them at bay, the more the Spanish team could not automatically assume that we would be easily beaten.

The longer we persisted, the better we felt. The hard surface of La Chana made the ball move extremely fast along the ground, giving our younger opponents a tremendous home-field advantage, as they expertly kept the ball on the ground rather than resort to long balls in the air, but they were slightly taken aback by our grit.

The Granada Veterans had so many highly skilled players that it wasn't possible for us to identify one or two major threats. We were too busy reacting, defending all out, hoping for a lucky break. During one of our rare excursions near their penalty box, I was able to challenge for a ball in the air and hook it high into the box, where Ed got his head on it. For a few seconds, the Spanish were under pressure. The score remained nil–nil, but we had showed that we could threaten them if they became over-confident.

One of their older players, who had played in La Liga, was superior as a playmaker, and I tried to keep track of him for the first fifteen or twenty minutes, forcing him to distribute the ball harmlessly, not allowing him time or space, but I could feel that my legs and groin would not be able to endure the pace for ninety minutes.

Even before the game, I had imagined that our most realistic chance to score would be, in a word, Fidel. I had suggested to him that he ought to play forward instead of attacking midfielder. I was concerned that he would soon run out of steam if he had to chase the ball with me in the middle. It was better for him to preserve his strength so the team might benefit from a flash of his brilliance. But he had chosen to retain his usual position as an attacking mid-fielder, and I wasn't about to tell him what he ought to do.

During four exhibition matches in Vancouver, I had observed the inability of Ed and Fidel to combine their talents. I rarely saw them pass the ball to each other. It was happening again at La Chana. I wanted to push either one of them forward to obviate this chemistry problem, but I decided I should wait until halftime before making any move of that kind. After all, by some miracle we weren't losing.

Fidel would later claim the turning point in the match occurred around the twenty-minute mark, when I was fouled. Or, rather, I assumed I was fouled and Fidel believed

I was fouled too. But shortly after the whistle blew, one of the Spanish players took the ball and executed a short free kick, passing to a nearby opponent, to resume play, and the referee did not interfere. I had been prepared to take the free kick, but I didn't know how to object to the referee in Spanish.

It was a subtle moment in the game, something that only someone like Fidel would recall. After my moment of annoyed surprise, I had rejoined the play as quickly as possible, but Fidel was deeply irked by this degree of gamesmanship and subterfuge. Not only were we playing on a foreign surface, in unusual heat, against better-organized, younger, and more talented players, we had a referee who could not be trusted.

This incident reinforced Fidel's worst suspicions about the Spanish approach to the game. The cynicism of the referee infuriated Fidel. I could see it in his face. He knew better than the rest of us that the Spanish didn't give a fig about international courtesy. They wanted only victory. If he had been playing against them on a team with his brother and other Croatians, they would have played sharply ("with a knife," as he put it) to send a message of aggression, but instead Fidel found himself playing with a very loose consortium of relatively civilized and naive Canadians.

We had decided in advance to share playing time among fifteen players per game, regardless of the score. Before this game, I had asked one of our guys on the sidelines to tell me when we reached the halfway mark of the first half. As the playing coach, it was important for me to set an example. I called upon Alan Cook to replace me. Ian and Christian were also added.

I regretted leaving the game, but I was relieved that my groin injury had allowed me to run as much as I had. I was hoping our luck would hold, Tony would continue his heroics, and we could miraculously retain our nil–nil draw to halftime. Our opponents were methodical in their attacking patterns, but now I sensed hints of frustration in their voices as they called to one another.

But disaster struck for us when the Spanish took a corner kick. As a high ball went into the penalty area, the referee blew his whistle. Tony and the rest of our players responded to the whistle, presuming the referee had noted an infraction. We all stopped to watch the ball sailing harmlessly through the air as one of their players easily headed it into the net. We waited for the referee to indicate what the infraction was – but instead he allowed the goal.

We were flabbergasted. Aghast. A goal! It was too bizarre to comprehend. He had blown his whistle when the ball was in the air. Surely our Spanish opponents were not going to accept this travesty. Surely one of their senior players would come forward and agree to overrule the gross ineptitude of the referee. For the Spaniards to accept that goal would be to accept their team's complicity in a charade.

Our opponents trotted back towards the centre line with the insouciance of Maradona after his notorious Hand of God goal. We didn't have a Hand of God goal, we had a Whistle of God goal, but it amounted to much the same thing. Even worse, we now had grounds for believing we were being victimized by a conspiracy of injustice. In this case, the referee had not missed calling a hand ball; instead he was aiding and abetting a soccer crime against us.

Most of could not speak Spanish sufficiently to register
our astonishment and disgust, but Fidel protested in the best
Spanish he could muster and Tony Arimare chased the
referee all the way back to the centre of the pitch, where he
was able to engage him in a few words of conversation.

"You blew the whistle after that ball was kicked!" Tony said.

The referee's reply told us everything we might want to
know about his character.

"Did I?" he said.

Just as the English were unable to recover from the
Hand of God goal in Mexico City, we began to crumble
almost immediately. Less than two minutes later, one of their
younger players rifled a shot from thirty metres. Tony read
the blast and timed his save perfectly, raising his hands to
stop the ball, only to have it squirt through his grasp and into
the net. It was 2–nil.

And it was game over.

Now comfortably assuming that the twenty-five-minute
nil–nil draw had been an aberration, the Spanish team
scored twice more before the half ended. Whether our hard-
fought respectability was a fluke or not quickly became irrelevant as I watched helplessly from the sidelines.

We had entered a different contest, a contest with ourselves. We were going to lose the game, but we could lose
well or we could lose badly. The remainder of the game
would be a test of our character, not our pre-geriatric soccer
skills or our minimal strategizing. As chasing the ball took
its toll on our legs and our hearts, we would slide towards
humiliation and be found guilty of overreaching ambition.

We all felt we were being placed on trial together. We
became imprisoned in our own half. Even Fidel was unable

to outmanoeuvre them. I put through two decent balls for him in the second half, but each time he was unable to shake himself free. Our opponents had quickly deduced that he was our only viable scoring threat, so he was smothered whenever we passed him the ball. I could sense his mounting anxiety about our collective predicament and the soccer cell into which we had unwittingly placed him. His wife, Ivana, rarely, if ever, had watched him play, and she had travelled across the Atlantic Ocean with Tonko to see this. Our ineptitude and the unfair advantages taken by the opposition must have been deeply distressing for him.

For an objective observer, most of their goals must have been pleasant to see. It was possible to appreciate their first touches on the ball, the way they always kept at least two men moving into open spaces for the ball carrier, the way they frequently swung the ball to the opposite side of the field, the way they conserved energy at the back by always having at least one defender wide, ready for an easy outlet pass.

The final score was 8–nil. Kenny joked, "They were getting dispirited towards the end."

After the game, Myles gave me a quick rundown of some of their players and their former professional connections. It was daunting. The speedster Roberto Valverde had recently played for two years with Real Madrid, with stints at Jaén, Granada, and Valladolid. Castellanos had played for Valencia, Granada, and Sabadell. Santi had played for Hercules, Granada, Jaén, and Murcia. Aquilena had played for Burgos, Cordoba, and Granada. The bar owner Miguel Espejo had played for Granada, Lerida, Pontevedra, Jaén, and Aviles. And so on.

Driving home with our goalkeeper and his Colombian-born wife, Alina, we mused about the Latin character and

Speedster Roberto Valverde, recently retired from Real Madrid, was half as young and twice as fast as some of our players.

Alan Cook

agreed the Spanish attitude was different from what many of us had anticipated. With their own Latin origins, Tony and Alina surmised that maybe the Spanish believed the world had too many soccer players already, so we should be discouraged from trying to play the game, so the Spaniards were doing us a favour by trying to humiliate us.

The Monty Python fans among us inevitably joked that nobody expected the Spanish Inquisition, but to the Granada Veterans we were no laughing matter. In a way, we were infidels. We were obviously not *real* soccer players. We needed to be banished. Even though the European Union had wrought prosperity for Spain, maybe they still resented outsiders, as they had done for centuries. As invading tourists, maybe we were the new Moors.

Only two anecdotes remained with me after the game. Both told me more than I wanted to know.

When the outcome of the game was obvious, and the Spaniards continued to press for more goals, possibly hoping to make this contest memorable by scoring in double figures, Fidel found some space and made a dash with the ball, threatening very little, but gamely operating at their skill level. As he was predictably disarmed by the converging opposition, one of their players sneered at him, "*Puta!*"

After the game, one of their players approached Christian and asked him, in Spanish, whereabouts in Australia we were from. Beyond the fact that the word CANADA was clearly evident on our jerseys, the question was deeply disturbing. It revealed how little the Spanish players knew about who we were.

COLD MOUNTAIN

The missing of chances is one of the mysteries of life. – Alf Ramsey

At the communal breakfast on Sunday, first-comers left a chair for me in the middle of a long table that accommodated up to forty people. Apparently I was expected to give another orientation address. Having relayed instructions on how to participate in the 8–nil loss the previous morning, I felt I ought to be relieved of my duties as a tour guide. Couldn't somebody else explain the directions to Montefrío?

I looked over at Alan Cook, asking him if perhaps someone else could speak, but he confirmed that the group was expecting to hear from me. It was one of those situations to which one literally doesn't wish to rise.

I felt apologetic. It was illogical to feel that way, but logic and sports don't always coincide. If I had led the team into battle as a coach, I was necessarily responsible. Someone has to take responsibility when things go wrong, even if they are not directly culpable.

I didn't wish to talk about soccer. It would have been absurd to attempt a rallying cry, or some General Patton–like tirade. Talking about playing soccer and playing soccer are as different as Venus and Mars, and there was nothing I could say that everyone didn't already know. Instead I used the opportunity to apologize to our female companions for not acknowledging their attendance during a difficult defeat. As the words spilled out, I felt they were true, and there was a slight quiver to my voice.

"I would just like to say that it meant a great deal to all of us to be able to look over and see you," I said. "We were more than a little bit distracted, and that's why we neglected to thank you for being there. Your support means a great deal to us."

Nobody had expected our Significant Others to act like cheerleaders, but their presence was comforting and generous. Acknowledging the partnership of our wives made me inwardly aware of Tara's absence. I was glad she had not witnessed the crushing defeat. Was an 8–nil loss in Spain really worth missing the birth of a grandchild?

In the process of analyzing and accepting our defeat, I stumbled upon the realization that our group was extraordinary for a reason that I had completely failed to notice. Never mind that there were twenty men trying to play competitive soccer in our fifties and sixties; we were extraordinary because nineteen of our twenty players had never been divorced. Unless you happened to live in an Amish community, surely that ratio of prolonged compatibility was statistically bizarre.

Because our soccer campaign was so multi-levelled, it was easy to overlook the roles of the wives. I prepared a mental list of our agendas: We were on a cultural exchange. We were a quasi-military exercise. It was a holiday. It was a social experiment. It was our last chance for glory. And it was sport.

No wonder so many coaches forbid wives and girlfriends from connubial relations before important games. It wasn't that the sexual activity was draining; it was the complex nature of sport that demanded so much concentration.

At the 2002 World Cup, for example, the favoured Brazilians were instructed by their coach, Luiz Felipe Scolari, to practise abstinence in order to retain their testosterone at maximum levels. "Any individual who cannot control this aspect of his life," Scolari said, "is not a human being but an irrational animal." Ronaldo reportedly didn't have sex for forty days and forty nights. The Brazilian dissolved into laughter when asked "What is more rewarding, winning the World Cup or having sex after going without it for forty days?" He replied, "Winning the World Cup is more important. I will have sex in a few moments, but the World Cup only happens every four years. But I have to say, sex feels like every four years for me at the moment!"

Scolari's replacement for 2006, Carlos Alberto Parreira, took a very different approach. "I don't think that sex one day before the game will have any harm on the player," he told *Maxim* magazine. "Just sex, no problem. The problem is, they don't eat, they don't sleep, they smoke, and they drink. That is the problem. Sex? No, sex is always very good – always welcome." Rather than impose a no-sex edict, Parreira supplied his players with musical instruments to ensure they were not high-strung or anxious. Ronaldinho was an avid player of the samba drums. "Psychologists say it is very important in the dressing room and coming from the hotel to the stadium that you do something with your hands, with your mouth," said Parreira. "If you just sit there worrying? Clutching your hands? That does not help. If you play something it helps relax. That is why we give them the drums and things. Since 1970 we have done this. We buy instruments for them, and they play on the bus – instead of saying, 'Oh my God, we are going to play Germany or England in a World Cup game.' That does not help."

The Republic of Ireland's Tony Cascarino was almost sent home by his manager, Jack Charlton, when it was discovered he'd smuggled a woman into his room during the buildup to the 1990 World Cup. Similarly, George Best was once caught by the Manchester United physiotherapist having sex with a girlfriend on the afternoon of an FA Cup semifinal against Leeds United. Best was nearly sent home.

Sex bans at the 2006 World Cup remained common. The Japanese team rigorously segregated its players from any liaisons with women prior to major contests. Nigeria's manager, Festus Onigbinde, announced, "My players must get themselves prepared spiritually, and this can be best achieved through total abstinence from women. . . . They [the players] must be pure and forget earthly affairs." Polish coach Jerzy Engel took a softer approach than the Nigerians, saying that fornication was fine as long as the players paid for it. "Nobody said that sex at the right place and the right time could do anyone any harm," he announced. This was before he added that any players wishing to bring their wives would have to pay for their flights, and their wives would have to stay in a hotel 120 kilometres away from the players.

Italian boss Trapattoni banned sex, declaring, "On the whole it is better to abstain. I've been away training for big matches myself in the past and I know what goes on. I know what footballers think about. But there have to be rules and regulations even if it comes to a matter as delicate as this." He later relented slightly by allowing the players limited access to their partners after the first round, but only "providing they exercise moderation. They can make up for lost time when they return to Italy."

In 1999 Italian researchers at the University of L'Aquila were claiming that sex before games was good. They discovered that testosterone levels in men rise after an increase in sexual activity. "If a sportsman needs to be more aggressive, it's better to have sex," said Dr. Emmanuele Jannini. For my morning address, I toyed with the notion of giving a professorial lecture on sex and soccer, using a pointer and a blackboard, as if I was explaining the theory of relativity. I would ask the women if they had had sex with their partners prior to the Granada Veterans game. If anyone responded affirmatively, I would ask them to discontinue the practice, and if anyone responded negatively, I would ask them to please give it a try.

Discretion proved the better part of valour. I avoided the subject entirely and, to change our luck, announced we would switch to our snazzier red uniforms. We were supposed to give one set of uniforms to an opposing team. If we wore both sets of jerseys, instead of keeping one set clean for gifts, that might complicate matters, but surely it was more important to try and win a game, or at least score one goddamn goal.

I repeated Myles's directions about how to get to Montefrío, a.k.a. Cold Mountain, the focal point for the olive industry. It would soon become apparent during the course of our excursion that Myles had never been there himself. He didn't provide any information about the team we would be playing, mainly because he didn't know much. Miguel's ineptitude had placed him in a very difficult position, having to organize games for us at the last minute, so it seemed unfair to pester him for details.

Our cavalcade to Montefrío gradually coalesced into a caravan outside the city limits of Granada. Several times along the way we stopped to take photographs or compare conundrums about where to turn next, and each time the sight of our gaggle of rental cars on the edge of the highway was comical.

As we climbed into the picturesque mountainous terrain, our spirits rose with the altitude. Possibly our opponents in this remote town would be more accommodating. Myles had said the dirt soccer pitch in Montefrío would be easy to find, but we had to get directions from the locals, most of whom were more than willing to help. In the dawning era of Google Earth, it was reassuring to know that a conversation with a gap-toothed old man outside a gas station was still necessary.

My black Volkswagen Punta arrived at the Montefrío stadium first. Pepe, the local soccer contact, was waiting for us in the parking lot. I asked Tony Arimare if he would help me say hello to Pepe upon our arrival. I felt it was important to initiate friendliness, having learned from our experiences at La Chana. To my great relief, there were big smiles all around when I approached the Montefrío contingent.

We were giddy with relief. We knew immediately, regardless of the score, that this game would not be a replay of the preceding match. This was more like it. Pepe and his team were genuinely happy to see us. A medieval church or watchtower was perched above the town, about a kilometre away, making the scene ideal for the cover of a jigsaw puzzle box. Even the stadium was more pleasing. The changing rooms had toilet paper, there were bleachers for spectators, and our opponents had sprayed the dirt pitch with water to eradicate dust.

As we donned our uniforms in the dressing room, seated along a bench, Alan Cook, to his everlasting credit, jauntily started singing a simple soccer song with a one-phrase lyric, "Here we go." Everyone joined him. It was a lovely way of celebrating our good fortune together.

Ian led us into a rousing version of "It's a Long Way to Tipperary" by substituting the word Montefrío for Tipperary. We had never sung together like this. "So long, Kitsilano," we roared. "Farewell, Stanley Park. It's a long, long way to Montefrío, but my heart's still there!" It was nonsensical but fun. Even as we were singing, I realized this slightly daft moment could end up being the highlight of our trip.

The singing helped me come to terms with the fact that our soccer adventures were not limited to ninety minutes between two sets of goalposts. Serge, sidelined with a painful eye ailment, had been visited several times by Dr. Bruce, who gave advice and medicines. Whereas the more avid players such as Fidel and me tended to focus on the soccer itself, dismissing peripheral matters, our adventures were happening

24-7 for Bruce, and the soccer was only one component. Clearly Bruce had the saner perspective.

I asked Tony Arimare to ask Pepe if we could take team photos before the game, and Pepe was eager to oblige. The Montefrío All-Stars seemed to expect that we would want to mark the occasion by linking arms in the middle of the pitch and grinning foolishly at a lineup of ten Canadian women with cameras, all grinning back at us, so there was a fine spirit of camaraderie preceding the game.

Once again it was evident that nearly all of their players were going to be younger than nearly all of our players. This time we weren't surprised or taken aback. The Montefrío All-Stars were quick and talented, but none of them had played professionally in the Spanish First Division. And this time we were adding Hans's son, Kyle, and Tony Nardi's son, Rob, to our lineup, to give ourselves a sporting chance.

We were accustomed to playing once a week. Our game at La Chana ended around eight o'clock the previous evening. The referee blew his whistle to start the Montefrío game at 10:20 a.m. From the outset, as we tried to run off all our aches and pains, Montefrío dominated with much superior ball control, but we frequently penetrated their zone. Once again the foreignness of the hard pitch would adversely affect us, and the heat would inevitably drain our stamina, but we knew this time we would likely have some good scoring chances.

Montefrío scored first and early, but we were not deflated. They lofted an atypical long ball over the head of Kyle – who would prove himself unbeatable for the rest of the match – and their forward artfully lifted the ball over Tony's head as he rushed out to cut down the angle. It was a good goal.

Again, we felt that having a highly capable goalkeeper would force the opposition to be creative in order to score. We were not going to lose 8–nil. Beyond Tony, however, few of us were able to distinguish ourselves in the rising heat. For the second game in a row, Fidel was encountering players as capable as, or better than, him. For three years he had been accustomed to being the best player on the field, dribbling past opponents at will, but suddenly his overt superiority had vanished against the Spanish teams.

To his disgust, Fidel found that now he was merely one of us. As the game progressed, he grew understandably frustrated by our inability to provide assistance. He wanted to blame his own errant passes on teammates who didn't move and who didn't understand the game properly, but at the same time everyone could see that his own competence level had slipped. Once, in a fit of pique, he even deliberately kicked the ball off the pitch, claiming he had had nobody to pass to. I knew Fidel would quickly regret this breach of soccer etiquette, but I also felt helpless to reach him, verbally or athletically, because I had my own challenges, on and off the field. If our best player couldn't get himself untracked, how could we expect to win?

Tony's son, Rob, hadn't played for three years, so he was clearly rusty. Another recent arrival, David Turner, had played very little soccer in recent years. Randey Brophy, a dogged midfielder and former boxer, was an admirable and valuable grinder, but our opponents were too quick to allow themselves to be ground down. The onset of recent parenthood had adversely affected Myles's fitness level. He showed spurts of skill, but he hadn't played regularly since he left Canada several years ago.

I substituted myself into the game at the twenty-minute mark, after our opponents had scored their first goal. Soon afterwards, I didn't like the way I was playing, either. Normally in the course of a game I would head the ball about thirty times. In Montefrío I headed the ball less than ten times. The Spaniards were trained to keep the ball on the ground. I found myself in constant chase mode. My groin injury adversely affected both my attitude and stamina. It was frustrating to realize I couldn't make much of a difference for my team.

At about the twenty-two-minute mark, after taking off Trevor, Bruce, Richard, and Randey, I noticed there was a discernible gap in the midfield, more than usual. Where was Fidel? I shouted to Tony Nardi, who wasn't playing, "Tony, count our players!" Sure enough, Tony confirmed we were down to ten men. Fidel had become so discouraged and embittered by our failures that he had removed himself from the pitch without telling me, or anyone else. Fidel is my closest friend on the team. I wanted to be sympathetic to his plight, but he would agree that you don't jeopardize your team by leaving the game unannounced. I was miffed at Fidel, but letting him know wasn't going to help our cause. I was confident he would try to make amends in the second half.

About forty minutes into the game, Tony Arimare gallantly charged out to a loose ball near the outside edge of his box. It looked like one of the Montefrío players would reach the ball and gain a clear shot on goal, so Tony gambled and slid to reach the ball ahead of him, or at the same time. He succeeded. But after both players collided and lay on the pitch, the undemonstrative referee quietly pointed to the penalty shot.

Only twenty-four hours earlier Tony had felt aggrieved by the Whistle of God goal. Now this. I tried to calm him down, knowing we simply could not afford another temperamental breakdown from another key player. Whether Tony had fouled the attacker or not could be discussed after the game; right now it was crucial to keep his head in the game.

Tony delayed the penalty shot procedure by dallying, fidgeting, moving here and there. Then he set himself squarely in the middle of the net, glaring confidently at the shooter, and dived to his right, guessing correctly where the shot would go. The ball was misstruck, low, going wide of the net, so Tony was able to get one of his hands on the ball and make the appearance of a save. Tony was lucky, but he was also good. He knew precisely how to behave in the penalty kick situation, how to think, and some of that confidence was going to permeate our team.

We desperately needed something to cheer about. This could be a turning point. We all felt it. Penalty shots are often missed, but invariably the failure of the shooter provides a boost to the goalkeeper's side.

By halftime we were still only down 1–nil. But as our players made their way slowly off the pitch, looking for some shade, I could see we were in danger of wilting. In a voice that was probably overly strident, I announced, "You have to take responsibility for your fitness in the second half. Run like hell, then come off and take a five-minute breather."

Fidel was giving as much as he could give, and I felt bad that I was not able to adequately support him as I had done six months earlier, when I was fit, and we were winning all our games in Vancouver. We still had a chance to win. A goal would give us a huge psychological lift. I decided to push for the equalizer by putting Rob and Fidel as forwards. I started the strongest lineup I could.

Invariably, when skilled sides get the ball from the kickoff, they work it backwards, establishing dominance. Ours was not a skilled side. What would be the point of trying to pretend that we were? It might be better to attack unpretentiously and hope to take them by surprise. With that aim, I told Fidel I would make a run for goal. As soon as the referee blew his whistle to start the second half, Rob gave the ball to Fidel, and Fidel sent a long pass to me as I went sprinting downfield. It was a very naive play, akin to a Hail Mary pass in football. No self-respecting Spanish team would try anything so gauche – and that's why I figured it just might work. Somehow, I gained a modicum of control of the ball and lunged to shoot from outside their box. It was too difficult to realistically expect to score, but at least we were signalling some ambition.

On the sidelines someone had suggested that my grand-child would be born precisely at the moment when we scored our first goal. The idea stuck. And a new idea lodged in my head: perhaps I was destined to score our first goal. The baby was already overdue. If I could score, that would help Glencora go into labour. If life were like a novel by Gabriel García Márquez, that sort of thing would surely happen.

Our comeback remained in full swing for about five minutes, until they scored on a counterattack. Our best defender, Dave, who always played with the heart of a lion, failed to make a clearance, so after our brief stint of domina-tion, the ball was inexplicably in our net.

But we didn't submit. I ran like a maniac and took myself off the pitch for a five-minute breather, hoping others would follow suit. Kyle made a nice run down the right side and grazed the top of their net with a blast. Then Fidel raced down the same side, spotting Dave, who was making a spirited run down the left side, unmarked. He tried to cross the ball to Dave for a header, but he miskicked in such a fortuitous way that it sailed towards the top of their net. The goalie was beaten – but not the crossbar. The crowd, such as it was, let out a collective "Ooooh."

When would we finally catch a break?

Around the sixty-minute mark, there was the possibility of a handball infraction inside their penalty area. Naturally we howled our complaints. When I ran over to take a corner kick, I did my best Hamlet-like, tortured-soul impression. The referee was near me at the edge of the pitch. As I pleaded our case with a pained expression of grief and indignation, he consoled me, pointing to his eye and indicating – not without regret – that he had simply failed to see it.

Less than one minute later, Rob bumped into one of their players in their penalty area and fell. If there was a foul, it had occurred near the outside line of their box. Normally when there's a slight foul in that situation, the referee will claim the event occurred just beyond the penalty area. But this time he ruled in our favour and, yes, pointed to their penalty spot! After more than 140 minutes of gruelling defensive soccer, we finally had some good fortune.

I wanted Fidel to take the penalty shot. It only made sense. If Fidel scored, he could rekindle his spirits and ignite ours in the process. Hans, our designated captain, was injured and unable to play, so I didn't hesitate to make the choice. In terms of skill, Fidel was our finesse leader. Everyone heard me say, "Fidel, you take it." I felt that I was doing my job, and making things clear.

Whenever a penalty must be taken, it's important to stamp out any doubt or indecision. Players mustn't squabble. There are always a few players on the field who feel they deserve the privilege of taking the penalty shot, and often they will insert themselves into the situation with an unnecessary remark, upsetting their teammate with a stab of jealousy. This mustn't be allowed to happen. When a player is taking a penalty kick, it is essential for him never to allow his eyes and ears to get the best of him, and always to feel that his teammates are entirely behind him. The opposing goalkeeper must be made to feel that he is the victim, that he is a lamb being led to slaughter.

I was taken aback by Fidel's response.

"No, you take it."

Much of the time Fidel is an unselfish player. That is, he continually passes the ball to weaker players near the goalmouth, giving them an opportunity to score, even though dribbling his way forward would result in a higher percentage of goals. Because he's too advanced for us, some fits of frustration are inevitable. At that moment, I didn't have time to decipher whether he was erring on the side of generosity once again, wanting me to score, or if, after complaining about the play of his teammates, he was reticent to step forward in case he missed. Just as likely, he was simply feeling out of sorts, rankled, and he judged himself to be unfit to make the most of the opportunity, and therefore he was opting out, responsibly – in his mind – for the sake of the team.

I was immediately placed in a complex position. As much as I wanted to force Fidel to take the penalty for us, because I believed he *should* take it, I knew I could ruin a friendship if I insisted upon it, behaving with the presumption that I was his soccer boss. I was a mere organizer of names on a piece of paper. How could I pretend to be a real coach? In a matter of seconds, I decided it was simpler to relieve him of the burden of responsibility than to insist upon him taking the penalty for us.

Now the soccer gods were playing with my head. They had me in their clutches. Why shouldn't I score? I was a prolific goal scorer in my youth. I had converted countless penalties. I had taken hundreds of corner kicks in the preceding three years, and absolutely none of them had gone awry for goal kicks. Instead of soberly considering what to do next, surveying the pitch for confident volunteers, my mind detoured to that comment about the baby being born as soon as we scored.

I never looked at the goalie. If I met him on the street that afternoon, I wouldn't have recognized him. My teammates behind me became invisible. As I stepped up to the ball, I was high on anticipation and drunk on fatigue. Earlier in the game, when I wasn't exhausted, my brain would have worked better and I would have been an excellent candidate to do the job. I would have calmed myself. Instead I fell afoul of wishful thinking. I imagined how the ball would fly into the top right corner, rather than concentrating on making it happen. If the goalie was lucky, it might hit him in the head; otherwise he wouldn't be able to catch it with his hands.

I wasn't even nervous. I told myself I could rely on the power and swiftness of the kick, rather than aim it too much. In my mind, I had the ability of a talented sixteen-year-old, but I neglected to fully consider that I was trapped within a fifty-five-year-old body. As I ran forward, telling myself to keep my head down, I lost my athletic concentration and watched in horror as the ball sailed harmlessly wide, about two feet away from the post. I screamed.

I don't remember much after that. There was a dazed period of horrified grief. Somehow the game resumed. I knew my anguish shouldn't be advertised. I worried that my sense of failure could infect the team, so I took myself off the pitch soon afterwards. I was too crippled inside to play properly.

Hans took over the substitutions for me and insisted I return to play. Even as I was running again, waiting for the final whistle, I knew the missed penalty was going to be a defining moment for me, a memory that would never leave.

FIDELITY

As much as you can love soccer, you can hate it too. – Fidel Bacelic

"I feel terrible."

It was the only sentence I could muster. I said it to Hans. I said it to Fidel. I wasn't seeking consolation. It was more like I was confessing my guilt to the Spanish Inquisition. Okay, hang me. Okay, burn me at the stake. Let's just get it over with.

Walking alone across the field to get my belongings, I imagined how my mother must have felt after being struck by that taxi in the crosswalk. It was a stupid exaggeration, of course, but such foolish notions can bubble to the surface of your mind when you are filled with self-loathing.

This is how it ends, I thought, with a whimper and not a bang. The missed penalty was a form of psychic punishment.

In a way, it was worse than being hit by a taxi because, deep down, I was telling myself that somehow I *deserved* to miss that shot. It was hubris; it was the *penalty* for assuming I was still the player I once was.

In the parking lot at Montefrío where I took off my boots, Alan's wife, Linda, kindly expressed some alarm about my bloody knee and my bleeding right foot. When I told her it was nothing, I meant it. Cuts and bruises were welcome. When Alan approached and inquired after my welfare, he was smart enough not to refer to my failure directly. "I've had worse things happen to me," I said. At the time, I just couldn't remember what they were. I was still churning inside, and Alan could see it. His muted neighbourly concern touched me more acutely than he would ever know.

I was the last person to shower and return to our cars. Again our team had fought hard and we had done our best, losing 2–nil. Only I had any reason to hang my head, but I resolved to repress my little operatic torment. I don't care what a psychiatrist might say; some repression is good. For that matter, guilt is underrated too.

In contrast to our previous match, after which the victors wordlessly dispersed, we all adjourned to the nearest bar, where the Montefrío players insisted on paying for our beer. The town of Montefrío had given us what we had bargained for: soccer in a wonderful setting with convivial foreign opponents. If we asked for more, if we yearned for victory against much younger opposition, we were only asking for grief.

The much-appreciated civility of our hosts prompted Fidel to give away his jersey to a boy about the same age as Tonko. I took a picture of Fidel bestowing his Canada jersey with his arm around the grinning recipient, flanked by his grinning father. In France I had taken a similar photo when Fidel met a girl around Tonko's age and asked her if she would be Tonko's pen pal. There is a beautiful side to Fidel's character that always resurfaces.

That night Christian drove me to Orgiva, a small town about one hour's drive south of Granada, where Fidel had taken his lodgings. I was not the only player who was concerned about Fidel's relations with the rest of the team, but I was the one best suited to approach him. I told Fidel he had to be realistic. We could not seriously expect to win games against much younger opponents. More importantly, he knew the calibre of his teammates well in advance of the expedition, and therefore admonishments about their abilities were unwarranted.

Fidel knows how I think, and most of the time I know how he thinks. We didn't need to say a lot. I was mostly concerned about whether or not he would show up to watch the next game.

Fidel and I were Apples. It was our turn to rest. I suspected he was considering using his status as an Apple as an excuse not to bother making the one-hour drive into Granada from Orgiva. I worried that such a decision would be interpreted by others as an expression of contempt, even though I knew his feelings were more complicated than that. I worried that if he did not deign to show his support as a spectator, some members of the team might silently turn against him. It was vital to conform, even if his attendance was merely dutiful.

This wasn't a crisis. It was housekeeping. These things happen on every team. I didn't expect Fidel to say yes or no on the spot. It wasn't an ultimatum. I just wanted to let him know what I thought. It was only a peripheral matter, but if you lose your peripheral vision, you're impaired.

The five of us – Fidel, Ivana, Tonko, Christian, and I – adjourned to watch the climactic game of the Spanish First Division. By a fluke of circumstance, three Spanish teams were playing simultaneously at nine that evening to decide which team would win the championship.

Real Madrid would win La Liga if they beat their opponents, but if they lost their match to lowly Mallorca, either Barcelona or Sevilla could take the championship, if they won their matches. The odds were worst for Sevilla, because both Real Madrid and Barcelona had to lose in order for them to have a chance, but it remained statistically possible.

Even though the underdog, Sevilla, was geographically much closer to Granada than the other contenders, nearly everyone in the Granada area was supporting Real Madrid. This was explained to me in terms of Quebec separatism: Catalans in Barcelona were the equivalent of the Québécois. Granadians resented the disruptive tendencies associated with Barca in the way that many loyalist Canadians resented the Parti Québécois.

Real Madrid was atop the standings, slightly ahead of Barcelona on goal differential. Both teams had two more points than Sevilla. Barcelona was soon crushing their opponents, making the outcome of the Sevilla game irrelevant, but Mallorca shocked the entire country by scoring first against the perennial powerhouse, Real Madrid. Now Real needed to win by at least two goals to win La Liga. If the underdog prevailed, elaborate preparations to celebrate Real Madrid's thirtieth league championship would be annulled and David Beckham's swan song in Spain would be ruined.

The television coverage of the Real Madrid match repeatedly showed Tom Cruise at the game, seated beside his wife and Victoria Beckham. Christian said the trio looked like people from a different planet. This was also the final game in a Real Madrid uniform for Brazilian defender Roberto Carlos.

Mallorca took their 1–nil lead into the dressing room at halftime, but after David Beckham was replaced, Madrid proceeded to score three unanswered goals. The routine skill level was even more enticing to me than Madrid's dramatic comeback. Explosions of fireworks resonated around the country after the final whistle.

I was happy for Fidel. He had brought his family to Spain for a special holiday without knowing their stay would coincide with this memorable evening in Spanish football history. The night of June 18 could serve as a significant road sign for Tonko on his football highway, a magical marker for the development of his soccer ambitions.

We all went to a pizzeria across from the cathedral to watch a two-car cavalcade go back and forth, back and forth, back and forth, along the main street of the village, honking and waving with delight. When we finished our pizza, Fidel told me he had not decided yet whether he would appear at Monday's game. That was fine by me. I had said my piece.

And I already knew what he would do.

⚽

Driving back to Granada with Christian at the wheel, I looked back at my friendship with Fidel and realized I had a tendency to romanticize him as a character. This was entirely my fault, not his.

I could easily imagine the day in Croatia when Ivana ran frantically up the stairs to wake Fidel because he was not responding to the air raid sirens. He was a smoker and a drinker, a lady's man, so it's quite possible he had been out carousing the night before. Often unshaven, with a strong chin, he looked like a character from *Cinema Paradiso*, only on a different coastline, about fifty years later, charismatic, handsome, and perhaps a little dangerous.

In 1992 rumour had it their town on the Dalmatian coast was about to be attacked by the Serbs. Ivana's father was the town's chief medical officer, which meant that he was privy to inside information, along with the mayor and the priest. She knew this time it was for real. She reached the top of the stairs, found Fidel, and shook him. Fidel rolled over and said he didn't want to go down to the shelter. There had been too many false alarms. (That would be our Fidel: someone who never likes being told what to do.) He was streetwise, but Ivana was the one with the common sense, a nurse.

The Dalmatians had long felt themselves removed from the political struggles in the north and east. Their dry coast, dotted with a thousand idyllic islands, was an escapist paradise. The nightmarish atrocities of Arkan and Milosevic elsewhere never seemed entirely plausible to them. If everyone did nothing, surely they would be left in peace. But it hadn't worked out that way.

For three days, back in 1991, Ivana and her parents had watched their Serbian neighbours packing up their belongings and leaving town. Even if they had wanted to block the exodus of Serbs, few of the Croatians were armed. When they were told they must go into a bomb shelter, they expected to stay there for twenty minutes. But weeks passed. This prolonged refuge allowed everyone to see the strengths and foibles of their neighbours. When the full-of-himself theatre director was told his thirteenth-century theatre was being destroyed, he yelled that he didn't care. When he and his wife ate together, they turned their backs to everyone and stared at themselves in a big mirror on the wall. His wife had brought plenty of food, but they never shared any of it, while others went hungry. Ivana's mother, on the other hand, made paninis for everyone. She kept insisting the invading Serbs were to be pitied because they were so misguided and deluded in their barbarism. Ivana's father, on the other hand, given half an opportunity, would have stood up to the advancing hordes, unarmed, proudly demanding to be shot rather than surrender.

Some people prayed. Their prayers were answered by luck. For some unfathomable reason, the invading Serbian troops assumed the main bridge leading into town had been rigged with explosives. Not even Ivana's father knew how this ruse was achieved. Whether it was purposeful, or merely the result of a fortunate misunderstanding, either way it was a small miracle.

By the end of 1993, Fidel and Ivana were determined to leave together. They married secretly, using Ivana's sister and cousins as their witnesses, in 1994. Fidel was already a Canadian citizen, having lived in both Toronto and New York during the 1980s.

The Serbia–Croatia debacle appalled Fidel. He understood that if anyone wanted to insist that their ethnic backgrounds or religions rendered them superior, clearly they were not. Not that he was an angel himself. As a boy, less than ten years old, he and his playmates would steal stickers off the bumpers of tourists' cars parked by the cathedral near the sea. Across the square was a four-storey complex. Whenever they were being chased, they would dash into the front door of the building and evade capture by sneaking out the back. They were never caught.

Fidel never had a car, and he never had much money. He lived by his wits from an early age. When he was drafted into the Yugoslavian army, they shaved his head and revoked his passport. They gave him some forms to sign. One of the papers asked if he wished to join the Communist Party. There was a recommendation on the form to join, but Fidel refused to sign.

Most people did as they were told, but Fidel fought back by speaking gibberish for three weeks, faking insanity. At the indoctrination camp, he irritated the authorities by wearing his uniform askew. He knew his garbled slang from the Dalmatian coast would irritate the authorities, so he acted relentlessly stupid, failing to obey orders with brazen consistency. Five weeks later, Fidel was expelled from the army, declared unfit for service.

His father, a sailor, had named him after Fidel Castro. Following stints of casual work in Naples and London, Fidel learned to use the name Philip because his real first name was a disadvantage in the United States. Working in New York City as a waiter, Fidel's favourite customer was Keith Richards. Bony and lithe, Fidel had much the same body type. With his wiry frame, slightly stooped torso, and his sunken eyes in an elongated face, often smoking a cigarette, Fidel might be mistaken for a hoodlum from afar, but up close you could see he was a kind-hearted charmer.

When Fidel/Philip returned to Dalmatia for a visit, he fell for Ivana, ten years younger than him, critical-minded, and the daughter of his favourite schoolteacher. With a baby on the way, they took a chance and flew into Vancouver, where Tonko was born in 1995. Mostly Fidel worked as a house painter, ran a coffee shop, and painted art canvasses. In 2006 he passed the post-office exams, eclipsing most of the three hundred applicants, but during the summer he still prefers to paint houses for a living, working independently. Whenever we refer to his new job sorting mail at the main post office, we call it Kafka.

Ivana works long hours as a rehabilitation nurse. Theirs is a happier family than most. Tonko is deeply loved, not spoiled, a top student and a superb soccer player, trained by his father.

Even though he speaks English as a second language, because Fidel is unfailingly observant, his occasionally fractured sentences are full of insights, often heartfelt, and invariably endearing. When he leaves a message on my answering machine at work, it is always "I call you home." Instead of saying "Thank God," he says "Thanks God." He makes the word *crows* rhyme with *cows*. But few people are more sophisticated in making character assessments.

When it comes to concise evaluations, Fidel is one of the most articulate people I know. It was Fidel who decided Bruce's nickname should be Penicillin. Bruce returned the nicknaming favour during our 2–1 victory over the Stingers. After Fidel made the difference, taking a throw-in from Dr. Bruce and turning on a dime, dummying the ball past his astonished defender, dribbling sideways for five metres, then deftly flicking the ball with the outside of his right foot past the helpless keeper, as we reached the centre line after that goal, Bruce said only one word, out of earshot of everyone but me: "Mozart."

If I were the coach of a team opposing us, I would allocate one or two players to neutralize Fidel – brutally, if necessary. Few teams have the wits to identify his skill early and allocate double coverage, but often teams show their frustration when he continually makes their tacklers look foolish. After we easily went ahead 3–nil in the first half against the Langley Aces, they tried to get physical. Tempers flared and words were said. The usual nonsense. The poor sportsmanship of the Aces gave us licence to drub them.

Before that game ended 7–nil, with our striker scoring six times, Fidel's temperament got the best of him. Having been dangerously fouled twice, he laughed aloud as he dribbled past another hapless defender. This act of revenge on his part naturally infuriated the already humiliated opposition. I knew then that Fidel has a Zidane-like pride that will surface whenever he feels his dignity has been attacked.

In the first half of that game against the Stingers, when we failed to score the first goal, our self-confidence as a team was put to the test. On several occasions during that period, Fidel felt himself surrounded by the opposition, without any of us coming near enough to give him someone to pass to, so he complained to all of us at once, angrily venting his frustration. On that occasion I told him to cool it, which only made him angrier. Bubbling over with fury, he shouted, "Sub!" and promptly removed himself from the game. It was hard to know whether he was feeling bad about his outburst or if he felt it was time to punish the rest of us with his absence.

Fidel knows the game best. But I'm the manager, and I'm responsible for the team's attitudes. Whether you are playing in the Premiership or playing over-fifties soccer in Vancouver, the paradigm is the same. Whether you're Thierry Henry or Fidel, the star players must listen, or at least agree to pretend to listen, so they can appear to be equal members of a team.

In order to perform as special talents, almost all special talents need special confidence. The list of exceptional professional athletes who are consistently humble, such as hockey's Bobby Orr or basketball's Steve Nash, is very short compared to the list of star athletes who are full of themselves.

The mercurial nature of stars – whether it's Fidel or Thierry Henry (they have similar body types, although Fidel can't abide Henry's habit of wearing his socks above his knees) – must be integrated for any team to be successful. Occasionally problems can arise when the mercurial star decides to pull rank, to give himself licence to misbehave, thereby forcing the manager or one of his fellow players to confront him with his selfishness or risk exhibiting weakness in front of the rest of the team by indulging the star. But that's rarely Fidel's style.

Off the field, over time, we became like brothers. I went with him when he bought his new car. Before that, I was glad to lend him one of our cars. He's the only one I go with to the Wolf and Hound for a Guinness. He and I drafted Tony Arimare to play with us, then we both pursued the two Scottish players, Alex and Arthur. I know he has deciphered my character more accurately than almost anyone.

On the field, we are both midfielders. He is the offensive twin; I am the defensive twin. His skills are much superior to mine, but I have the never-say-die pluck of English soccer in the rain. Whereas he is magical, I am relentless. If he were a film star, I would be the director. Whereas he is a chain-smoker who plays in sudden bursts, I am referred to in team emails as the Energizer bunny. There is no competition between us. But he is the better player. If you were picking teams, you'd choose him first.

When he has the ball, Fidel is like the con artist who puts a pea under one of three upside-down bowls, switching the placements of those three bowls so swiftly that it's impossible to know where the pea is hidden. Fidel can glide sideways like a ballet dancer, rolling the ball underneath his cleats, tempting his opponents to lunge. His quickness is like a circus feat, a conjurer's trick achieved only after countless hours of practice in the gym and on the street. It is the best kind of intimidation, this poetry in motion. This is how Fidel creates space for himself, by displaying his masterful control of the ball. In doing so, he is never a show-off, never a selfish player. He is looking to pass at all times, and conversely this makes him always a threat to score. Defenders never know when he will suddenly decide against the pass. Nine times out of ten, he will deliver the ball to an open man, rather than dribble his way forward, but with a sudden burst of acceleration, he can break through on his tenth opportunity.

With feet as sensitive as a pickpocket's hands, his control of the ball under the most violent pressure was hypnotic. The bewildering repertoire of feints and swerves, sudden stops and demoralising turns, exploited a freakish elasticity of limb and torso, tremendous physical strength and resilience for so slight a figure, and balance that would have made Isaac Newton decide he might as well have eaten the apple.

That description of George Best by *Observer* sportswriter Hugh McIlvanney makes me think of Fidel at his shiftiest, when he glides past opponents like a dancer through a field of wheat.

In terms of both physique and style of play, Fidel and George Best are superficially similar on a football field, but Fidel is much more serious off it. Although he might have shared some of Best's self-destructiveness and reckless charm in his youth, Fidel is more reflective now, worrying about raising the down payment for a house, worrying about getting a job with a pension, worrying about somehow quitting smoking.

He teaches Tonko to be fastidious about his homework and his soccer. In our league, he is our Zico. When the great Brazilian midfielder Zico came out of retirement in the early 1990s, forsaking his job as Brazil's first minister of sports, choosing instead to play for a Second Division team in Japan, he demanded that his teammates clean their own boots after each match. In Brazil, Zico used borrowed boots until he gained his tryout for the Flamengo team. He went on to score sixty-eight goals for Brazil in eighty-nine games, a tally bettered only by Pelé. Determined to raise the calibre of play in Japan, even if his rough manners upset the Japanese, "Zico-san" demanded others take the game as seriously as he did. He taught pride. Fidel is less didactic, but after each game he lovingly makes a ritual of cleaning his boots. He says he looks forward to it. It's a habit he wants to pass along to Tonko.

That is a responsibility of every player: to ensure the right attitudes prevail. To the Fidels and Zicos of this world, it is a principle as fundamental as housekeeping or gravity. To see others play in a lackadaisical fashion, or cynically, is deeply distressing, as if someone is insulting their religion.

The year Fidel and Ivana were in that bomb shelter, 1991, was the year that Zico agreed to join the Japanese Sumitomo Metals football team. This was a team that didn't even have its own practice pitch, a team that averaged 540 spectators per game. Having played as a member of the "golden quartet" in Brazil's 1982 midfield, Zico was accepting the challenge of transforming a team that painted the sidelines on the field themselves and showered in the nearby Sumitomo Metals plant. To do so, he had to have the same passion for teaching as he had displayed playing the game.

Zico learned some basic words of Japanese so he could shout directions on the field. To prevent any teammates from drinking the night before a game, he stayed in the team's dormitory before each game. By 1993, when Zico's team had changed its name to the Kashima Antlers, attendance was up to fourteen thousand per game. He played his last seven games in 1994 but remained associated with the club until they won their Japanese league championship, the Emperor's Cup, and the Nabisco League Cup in 2000. A bronze statue of Zico was erected outside the Antlers stadium. As coach of Japan's national team, Zico led Japan into the 2006 World Cup.

In his own way, Fidel wishes he could bring the dedication of Zico to us. Although he is deeply aware of character strengths and weaknesses, he keeps his critical comments to a minimum. As an immigrant with an accent, he doesn't feel entirely comfortable in any overt leadership role, so in some respects I have become his interpreter, his translator.

There has been a bond of loyalty in our desire to play together ever since we went to France in 2005. I still remember the summer evening at Prince of Wales field when I took Fidel aside and said he must make the trip. I had a mickey of Scotch in my equipment bag. We walked up the sideline, out of earshot, taking sips. I told him our whole team wanted him there. I also said I would be run ragged in the midfield without him. Hans had airline points to spare. The details were secondary. We only needed mutual dedication to an idea.

There was a furtive intimacy to that conversation. As Fidel listened carefully to every word, I knew how much he wanted to go. I asked him to go for my sake, not his. As a team, in order to succeed, I explained we had to pool our resources. Money was only one of the many resources we would require to beat the French. We needed his skill and leadership on the field. Like Zico, Fidel could not resist going where he was needed.

In France I ended up coaching, sidelined with a muscle tear. During our final game, in the final minutes, the referee called for a penalty shot inside the opposition area. The game was tied. If we scored, we could win the tournament. Everyone in the stadium knew what was at stake, including the referee. There was no hesitation in my voice as I shouted with a combination of vehemence and confidence. I wanted Fidel to hear that I had absolute faith in him.

"Fidel, Fidel, you take it!"

I kept repeating Fidel's name aloud, even after the team appeared to consent to my selection. It took more than a minute for the referee to settle all the players. Eventually Fidel stepped forward and adjusted the ball slightly on the penalty mark. He took three steps back. He didn't look over at the referee. The ball was struck cleanly, to the goalkeeper's left, along the ground.

The net rippled.

THE WHISTLE BLOWER (L'ÁRBITRO)

No referee is born by pure chance, it's a conscious decision that involves passion and martyrdom and a belief in the rules. – Darwin Pastorin, "Lettera a mio figlio sul calico" ("A Letter to My Son about Football")

The following day I set up my computer on a cement patio overlooking the Sierra Nevada. To see the screen, I constructed a shelter from the sun by hanging my bedspread over a portable clothes hanger. I typed merrily for hours, telling everyone that I was reminding myself I was a writer, not a soccer player. "I'm actually good at this," I said. It was one thing for everyone else to forgive me for missing the penalty; it was quite another to forgive myself.

While most of our regiment buggered off to see the over-hyped Alhambra, I tried to soberly assess our soccer performances. Most of us were privately going through the same process. "We were set up for failure," said young Rob. "This is more humiliation than I wanted," quipped Ed. Alan Cook's viewpoint was refreshing. "Character is revealed by adversity, not success," he said.

As a bunch of old guys facing insurmountable odds, we were remarkably resilient, mentally fit. We didn't collectively crack under the strain. Even some of the Spaniards told us we had *corazón*, or heart.

We all knew, of course, that nobody back home was going to understand our resilience. They would only want to know the score. But we were becoming increasingly proud that collectively, with our strongest possible lineup, we had succeeded in undermining the confidence of the sort of players we had all just watched on the television the night before. We didn't realize it at the time, but holding a team of ex–First and –Second Division professionals to a scoreless draw for the first twenty-five minutes, when their median age was probably under forty, and ours was close to sixty, was a phenomenal achievement.

We were untrained, grey-haired amateurs. And yet we had somehow succeeded in making those supremely talented former pros feel grateful for a lucky break. The stealthy way they retreated back to the centre line after their disputed goal was a small victory in itself.

As for me, I was no longer distraught about my personal failure. Telling the story of our expedition, in the long run, might be better, more useful, than scoring a goal or organizing lineups.

Let the games continue.

❖

On Monday evening, as I had hoped and imagined, Fidel was waiting for everyone at a café near the field at La Chana. It was to be our second game at La Chana, and we were beginning to loathe the place. The combination of cement and artificial turf made La Chana into a hot box. Worst of all, the playing surface and the heat were causing foot problems. And the vending machine for drinks didn't work. It was not a forum for joy; it would be better suited as an exercise yard for a penitentiary.

Monday's opponents, courtesy of Miguel, were players who were training to become coaches. They were mostly in their late twenties and early thirties. Again, our much younger opponents entered the combat area en masse. For social and athletic reasons, we had to disarm them. "We have to go and say hello," I announced. I walked towards them with a smile on my face and extended my hand. Anything was better than remaining strangers. One could argue this was the only successful tactical move I made before relinquishing the task of coaching to Hans. Seeing us face to face like that, close up, our opponents could not depersonalize us as just another team to beat. Instead they had to be saying to themselves, "Good God, these guys are *old*!"

I volunteered to serve as the referee. With my beard, my green tourist shorts, my soccer boots, and my red Canada jersey, I looked fairly unorthodox, even goofy – and that was a good thing. The game proceeded with a more informal style than our previous two encounters had. It helped that we were able to lend them Tonko and seventy-year-old Trevor, our youngest and oldest players.

Playing alongside nine skilled speedsters, Tonko and Trevor had superb games. The Spaniards always had passing options galore. They continually moved into open spaces when they didn't have the ball, and displayed their facility for making diagonal runs in the box. As defenders, our guys never knew whether to stay with our checks or follow the ball.

When the going got tough, Fidel laced up his boots and joined the fray, even though he could have rested. The temptation to play in a game against his talented son was likely too great to ignore, but I didn't ask him about it. He had reverted to private mode. Tony Arimare played only the first half, making numerous remarkable saves. The final score flattered us. Had they played all out, they could have easily beaten us by more than 4–nil.

For my part, I enjoyed refereeing more than I had enjoyed playing. It struck me that I could have a far greater influence on the spirit of the encounter as the *árbitro*, the referee, than as a player. The highlight of the game was subtle. At one point, when Kyle fouled their dangerous striker in our box, I reluctantly blew the whistle for a penalty and looked quizzically at the striker. I was asking him, wordlessly, if he really wanted to proceed with it. Without making any display to the others, we mutually agreed to cancel the penalty.

Nobody seemed to notice the cancelled call, even though I had stopped the play by blowing the whistle. This game had a generous spirit that prevailed above and beyond the competitive level. After the game some of our players took the trouble to thank me for refereeing. It struck me that nobody, with the exception of Bruce, ever thanks the coach or the manager.

My feet were bleeding again. By the time I was ready to leave, I still had the whistle around my neck. We had given our opponents commemorative pins. In return, unintentionally, the Spaniards had given me that whistle. Instead of running after them and returning it, I decided to keep it. It felt like an omen. Maybe there was a future in being the referee.

The older we get, the more we can appreciate law and order, and the more we understand civilization, and the more we are capable of appreciating the loneliness of the long-distance referee. When it comes to understanding his job, the prattle of sportscasters and journalists can seldom be taken seriously, because they generally only notice the referee's contribution to the drama when fault can be found. Meanwhile the referee takes private pride in avoiding controversy. He enters each game knowing that few spectators or players will compliment him for his sublime indifference to a borderline tackle, or his expertly feigned decisiveness for a throw-in after two opposing players have mutually kicked the ball out of bounds.

Referees tend to be measured in accordance with their relative lack of ineptitude, rather than their overall efficiency, so, ironically, the person who administers justice is himself judged unfairly. Any intelligent referee feels this irony acutely. Game after game, he strives to conceal all personal wounds, determined to serve the public good.

The referee, like the priest, must be a complex personality. He must have a strong ego in order to rise to the challenge of his job, and yet he must resist all signs of his egocentricity. This subtle difference between the egoist and the egotist, for the referee, is a precarious and fundamental divide. If he reveals himself too much, he will plunge into the abyss of that divide, losing the respect of the players and coaches and fans. And yet if he remains too austere, too aloof, he will become an object of disdain.

In the eyes of others, the referee can only be a loser, never a winner, and so he enters each match with the private hope that he might walk off the pitch at the end of ninety minutes as a completely unsung hero, rewarding himself or punishing himself with his own objective assessment of his performance.

Beyond a perfunctory handshake or two, the referee's job is mostly joyless and essential, and yet all over the world millions of referees voluntarily rise to the occasion because at every soccer contest, there are two games. There is the game on the field that everyone else sees, and there is another game inside the referee's head, the most complex game of all. The referee's view is the closest and most complete one, embracing both sides together. This is why they take the abuse. The referee has, by far, the most intimate and *superior* view of the game.

All referees have failed at becoming the great player they hoped to be. Therefore refereeing beckons as an opportunity for compensation. Of all the spectators at the game, only the referee is permitted onto the field to join with the players in the dance. As he huffs and puffs, somehow avoiding contact with all the players and the ball, the referee must excel at his own tactics, which require agility, endurance, and creativity. It's not just about legislating right and wrong; the referee's game is played on the razor's edge between personal and impersonal.

The most famous arbitrator of soccer in recent memory has been the completely bald Italian referee Pierluigi Collina, mainly because he officiated the World Cup final between Brazil and Germany in 2002, a game watched by almost 1 billion people. An avid basketball player in his youth, Collina was an unmistakable presence on the field due to his unusual height and his shining dome. Born in Bologna in 1960, he suddenly lost all his hair from total alopecia in 1984.

Collina challenges the sports cliché that the best referee is the one who goes unnoticed. Instead he believes it is often necessary and good for the policeman on the field to assert his presence, his personality, for the good of the game. To this end, he will attempt to insert humour, if he can, to deflate anger. At the end of one famous match, when one of the losing players was lying heartsick on the grass, Collina came along and lifted him up.

As a referee, Collina is an oddity. He does not aspire to be impersonal – only impartial. Collina's willingness to be seen, combined with his inability to be unnoticed, led to the release of a quickie book, *The Rules of the Game*, which mostly reveals him to be a remarkably dull writer. But he does identify the most important character trait for a referee: courage.

Collina maintains that the referee must always have sufficient courage to become a leading character in a football match, "but not *the* leading character." He also cites the importance of concentration and wide-ranging peripheral vision. Just as players can lose their focus towards the end of a match due to fatigue, the referee must never relax and feel a game is going smoothly. Collina aspires to be neither a traffic policeman nor an actor, just a man. Or, as Inter Milan defender Patrick Vieira told *Soccer Three Sixty*, "Being a referee should be like being a player. You should go with your heart, enjoy it and not have to think."

The more respect you have for the rules, the greater respect you have for the game. And there is no better way to learn the rules of a game than to try to fairly enforce them. Instead of having players run laps around the field, coaches should have them learn to blow the offside whistle. Or not.

As a teenager, I liked wearing that striped shirt, transforming myself into a neutral third party. It was a privilege to have control of the game and to step outside the emotionalism of the action. If you can keep your head about you while all those around you are losing theirs, as my father liked to tell me, then you will be a man, my son. I used to dismiss that Kipling quote as stiff upper lip Britishness, but I have grown to understand the referee is like an objective Daniel entering the lion's den of subjectivity. There is unsung heroism in his willingness to do so.

In soccer the referee must run shoulder to shoulder with the players for ninety minutes, but he never receives applause when it's over. On a professional level, he might have two assistants on the sidelines, making decisions about offsides and throw-ins, but otherwise he is the lone sheriff in a Wild West town where two opposing factions of eleven men are having a shoot-out. No matter how well he conducts himself, he is poignantly and courageously alone.

In the late 1940s, George Orwell, a former policeman in Burma, recalled his horrid football experiences at St. Cyprian's, a preparatory school in Sussex that he attended between the ages of eight and thirteen. In an autobiographical essay entitled "Such, Such Were the Joys," published posthumously in 1952, Orwell wrote, "I loathed the game, and since I could see no pleasure or usefulness in it, it was very difficult for me to show courage at it. Football, it seemed to me, is not really played for the pleasure of kicking a ball about, but is a species of fighting."

It is the good referee, more than any other personality on the pitch, who strives to consistently elevate soccer beyond a species of fighting, but, almost always, the respect he receives from the players is paltry. And, of course, the girls *never* fall for the referee. They don't even see him.

REDEMPTION SONG

If you make football too important, you deprive it of its beauty. – Kanu

We should have known better than to feel optimistic about our game against Las Gabias. This was going to be our fourth game in four days, but we told ourselves Las Gabias might be a relatively small town, like Montefrío, and therefore we would have a chance to get a respectable result. Also, the game was scheduled for a 9 p.m. kickoff. Cooler temperatures could help. And we would have a new coach.

During game three, Hans had taken over the job of handling substitutions. When he approached me and asked if he could be the coach for game four, I was delighted. As long as my various injuries didn't make me into a scratch, I much preferred to concentrate on playing.

On Tuesday morning, when Hans and I went for a coffee in La Zubia, he outlined his fresh approach. Hans's theory was that three men scrambling for the ball up front would be more likely to produce at least one goal. Consequently he would play three men up front – Fidel, Kyle, and Tonko – and three of us – me, Ed, and Randey – would serve as defensive midfielders.

Hans would be starting an eleven-year-old. It sounded crazy, but Tonko understood how to play the game better than most of us. Possibly his intelligent decision-making with the ball might produce a vital pass to liberate either Kyle's speed or his father's skill. While I knew other players would likely resent Hans's bold decision to start Tonko, I also knew Hans was earnestly trying to shake things up. We had to inject some optimism. Playing alongside his son on a beautiful evening in Spain, under the lights, might be the catalyst to stir Fidel's smothered ingenuity, and possibly the presence of a talented eleven-year-old might play some tricks in the minds of our opponents.

Even more radical, Hans wanted to refrain from making substitutions until they were necessary. We had erred on the side of fairness for three games, so he felt we had earned the right to experiment. I couldn't disagree, because I knew we had held the Granada Veterans scoreless in the first game, using our best possible lineup, until I made substitutions around the twenty-five-minute mark.

It helped to know this match had serendipitous origins. After Miguel had failed to make appropriate arrangements, Myles had been forced to make eleventh-hour calls to various town halls, searching for opponents. The person who answered the phone at the Las Gabias town hall happened to be the manager of the local soccer team.

The mayor of Las Gabias would be in attendance. Because Mayor Sam Sullivan of Vancouver had already provided an official letter for Miguel, Myles asked if we could provide a similar document for the Spanish mayor. There wasn't enough time to approach Vancouver City Hall for a second letter, so I prepared a second proclamation, forging Mayor Sullivan's signature. I knew Mayor Sullivan personally, and I decided he would agree that international relations were more important than legalistic propriety.

I placed the proclamation in my car in the morning to ensure I would not forget it, but in our haste to make an early departure, Christian and I used his car. We were halfway through the town of La Zubia before I realized we had to go back and get the proclamation.

I was as pumped up as anyone, hoping for redemption. Before leaving, I had taken it upon myself to write an inspirational song that I sang for a few people, using a borrowed guitar, adapting the melody line from Ed's favourite Bob Dylan song, "Positively Fourth Street." The lyrics were inspired by that wonderfully sneering first line, "You've got a lotta nerve . . ."

You've got a lotta nerve / showing up in Spain
Thinkin' you can play the game like we do.

You're from a land of snow / and hockey is your game
Why don't you go home and build an igloo?

You say you play for fun / but that's not where it's at
You have no chance to win and you know it.

You had a penalty / up in the olive trees
And we knew that writer guy would blow it.

I wish that for just one time / you could stand inside our boots
You'd see what a drag it is to see you.

Fidel, Alan, Spain, Defeat, 2007.

Cuz when all is said and done / you're really pretty good.
And we don't have a team of over-fifties in all of Spain that
could beat you.

You played ex-professionals / forty years of age
And held them to a draw for half an hour.

You should be really proud. / You really pissed them.
Maybe that is why they were so sour.

Everyone drove off in high spirits. We remained upbeat
until the kickoff. The eleven of us fortunate enough to start
the game were keen on Hans's win-at-all-costs bravado,
but it was soon apparent that Las Gabias was really a city,
not a town, and they took their football seriously. Whereas

Montefrío had had a dirt pitch, Las Gabias had a floodlit stadium with artificial turf and a concession stand.

The impressive venue with its large covered grandstand made us feel as if we had come all the way to Spain just for this one potentially memorable encounter. When gifts were exchanged at the centre of the pitch, Serge read aloud the proclamation in Spanish. Everyone was pleased by the formalities, which included one minute of silence to mark the death of the mother of one of their players.

For once our opponents didn't look much younger than us. Possibly the average difference in age this time would be fifteen years, if we excluded Tonko. We were keen to forget our previous losses. Hans was prone to be less diplomatic than me, and that could only be a good thing. He was determined to have us score. Unfortunately, we were missing our defender, Ken Falk, who was sitting out as an Orange, and fullbacks Hans and Nick were injured. Moving Kyle to the front looked good on paper, but in practice his speed was crucial for defence. After three games as our stopper, Dave Naphtali had to be exhausted.

At first we exuded confidence, but we soon realized the Las Gabias guys were quick, very quick. We held our own, barely, for about five minutes, when they scored on a deflection. It caromed off two players, more like a fluky hockey goal. Top-notch keepers are supposed to get angry, and Tony Arimare was steamed. He could be expected to make the difficult saves for us, but those lucky goals were soul-destroyers.

We didn't deserve that beginning. We were making some decent forays into their zone. But gradually their level of organization, skill, and determination was apparent. In addition, they were the most physical side we faced. I liked that.

It gave me some licence to play more assertively. It wasn't long before both my knees were bleeding. I took some blood from my knees and wiped it onto my face. But even war paint didn't help.

These guys had played together for years. We were a ragtag outfit by comparison. After they scored two more goals, Hans had to drop his "no substitution" theory and give everyone their run. By halftime, we were disconsolate, speechless. Our best was simply not good enough. And it would never be good enough.

I tried replacing Fidel as striker in the second half. Of course, on a narrow personal level, I knew that if I could score our only goal, I might eradicate some of the stigma of missing that penalty in Montefrío. At one point, when Fidel and I were both up front, we had some chemistry. We were threatening. Then I was fouled outside the box.

I have always liked to be fouled. It gives me energy. I like the opportunity to appear invincible. It gives me fresh enthusiasm to fight back. We were close enough for an attempt on goal. Fidel and I quickly conferred. This time it was different. This time I wanted to take it. There wasn't any confusion in my mind, no lack of confidence. I knew from the distance of about thirty-five metres that I was going to be our best bet.

I thought about a low-screamer. It was only a two-man wall. The distance was so great that our opponents didn't realize I could sometimes convert from there. But lately I had been failing to keep my head down. I didn't want a repeat of the penalty, where I blew the ball harmlessly off-target. To ensure accuracy over power, I decided I should try swinging it around the wall, curling it towards the far corner, as I'd imagined, practising in the schoolyard back home.

I felt completely calm. I wanted to give us at least one decent shot on net. Scoring would be almost secondary to threatening to score. We needed to show that we had some skill, some finesse. I had failed miserably to inspire us at Montefrío, crippling our chances with my ineptitude, with my fatigue. So, privately, I knew I had to take this free kick.

Had I possessed the same inner calm in Montefrío, I would have scored on that penalty. But I was a long way from goal in Las Gabias. Their defence expected me to cross the ball, hoping for a header, but I knew there was nobody on our team who was gifted in that department. So I opted to combine accuracy and velocity, rather than depend on one or the other.

The shot curled around the wall. It sailed in a perfect arc. It was perfectly executed, heading for the net. The keeper in Montefrío would never have saved that shot in a month of Sundays, but the Las Gabias keeper was good, and was quick enough to leap and just barely nudge the ball over the bar before it dropped into the far, top corner.

Uplifted, I took the corner. Kyle came up from our back line. I saw him waiting at the top of their box. We made eye contact. I liked his sense of determination. He had to be the target. "Kyle," I shouted. Again, he acknowledged me with his expression.

I drilled the corner towards his incoming run. If I had to take that corner one hundred times in succession, I could not execute such an ideal delivery. The ball had just enough mustard to generate a powerful header, but it also had a flight path that made it impossible to intercept.

Kyle raced onto it, running directly towards the net, so that his point of interception was just slightly beyond the penalty spot. It was poetic in its choreography, unstoppable. But the ball only grazed his forehead, glancing sideways, just missing the net. We had narrowly missed scoring twice in one minute. There was to be no fairy-tale ending. No redemption.

We were unlucky. Or so I wanted to tell myself when we heard the final whistle. But the truth was more complicated and darker than I wanted to admit at the time. Even though the Granada Veterans had beaten us 8–nil, losing 6–nil to Las Gabias was the clincher, by far our most crushing defeat. It opened the door for regret: how many of us, had we known beforehand that a level playing field wasn't possible in Spain, would have decided *not* to make the trip?

The collective disappointment we felt in Granada after the fourth game was palpable. Fidel changed out of his uniform as quickly as possible. He reluctantly consented to have his photo taken with me on the field at Las Gabias, wearing his street clothes. It was as if we had both tumbled into a trap and we could not extricate ourselves. And inside that trap most of us had become splintered, alienated, ashamed.

At the end of that fourth game, we faltered off the pitch and failed to live up to Jürgen Klinsmann's comments about team spirit: "To any young kid who wants to be a footballer, I would simply say: Have fun playing football and enjoy the team spirit. That's the right attitude; that will bring you pleasure and fulfilment in football. A baker cannot live on bread he made yesterday, and a footballer cannot live on his last game. It's about the here and now."

⚽

As I stood atop the grandstand at Las Gabias, surveying the empty playing field before leaving, I realized there was something fundamentally wrong about the way I had approached all the games in Spain. I had invested too much emotion in these games, too much pride. And I paid a price for it: I failed to have fun.

As a child, you watch sports at a stadium or on television and you quickly invest your emotions in the suspense of the contest. Will my team win? Will my favourite player score? But as an adult, you watch sports and wonder and worry if civility will triumph, if the contest will go off the rails and be marred by violence. Or will the train stay on the track for ninety glorious minutes of inventive action? In Spain, due to mounting frustration, I felt as if I had reverted to childishness.

When the game gets reduced to a proving ground, you have to struggle to rethink the game, to coach yourself, to rescue yourself. Initially, as a boy, I could sense how much sport was a training ground for cruelty. Those who could not excel on the field of combat were to be pitied, or even denigrated, as sissies. Sport was never about learning mercy or forgiveness. It was about beating on your chest like an ape. In the process, if sport taught you any humility, that awareness only arose by default. It was a booby prize.

It had only taken me four or five decades to figure out how much I loathed barbarianism, on the field or off. The Devil is always lurking, trying to do his dirty work, encouraging us to cheat, to convince us that an elbow in the back is justified under some circumstances, to plant the seed of violence. But if you only play the game in order to vanquish the opposition, you are losing out even when you win, because you will eventually discover you are playing on the Devil's team.

Four losses in almost as many days blurred my vision; I temporarily lost sight of the beauty of the game. I needed to remind myself – from the position of spectator – that if a man goes down during a game, you can often feel a twinge of pleasure when the opposing team deliberately kicks the ball out of play in order to allow the wounded player to receive attention. When the play resumes, and the throw-in is taken, and the ball is purposely returned to the team that kicked it out, there is another twinge of relief.

Similarly, when a forward narrowly misses scoring a goal, and he lies on the turf, disconsolate, mystified by his failure, the goalkeeper will sometimes walk past him and tap him on the shoulder, as if to say, "Better luck next time." Or, when a player has been injured, often the rival player who was involved in the altercation will wait nearby, within a respectful distance, indicating that he did not intend to wound his opponent. This diplomatic show of concern can be feigned, a pretence of blamelessness in order to avoid the outright scorn of the referee, but just as often it can be genuine – a recognition that everybody on the field is actually on the same team, one that has been arbitrarily split in two.

These are the civilizing moments that vanquish barbarity. Much of the appeal of soccer is that it is largely self-regulated. That is, if you count the number of whistles during a ninety-minute match, and compare that to the amount of whistles during an American football game, or basketball game, or hockey game, there is hardly any comparison to be made. When the ball goes out of bounds, it is retrieved and thrown back into play without a whistle. When a goal-kick needs to be taken, there is no whistle required.

Most of the time, the players are expected to respect the

limitations of the rules themselves. At some level, all soccer players know this, especially if they have learned the game in the street, or in the backyard, as I did, playing with my older brother, John, and his friends. "Street football," says Rinus Michels, "was and is the best natural way of training you can find. It gives a better feeling for the game." Conversely, the more that boys and girls learn the game strictly within the confines of a formal playing field with lines on it, the less joyous the game will become.

Jürgen Klinsmann is right. It's not about whether you win or lose. It's about whether or not you love your team. If you show up for a game and you aren't glad to see your team-mates, you might as well go home. You don't want to play soccer to return to the jungle, you want to ascend to the heavens. Football must have its moments of generosity and grandeur, glimpses of compassion, respites of humour. I have played over one thousand soccer games in my life, and I can barely remember the scorelines of any of them. If the game cannot be played affectionately, with reverence, it should not be played at all.

OUTGROWING SOCCER

Even though I had to convince Miguel on a number of occasions that we were all over 50 and not former pros, he was guarded and kept a mild suspicion that I was sandbaggin' him. – Myles Ellis, in a letter

For our return match with the Granada Veterans at La Chana, we suggested to Miguel that we should change our lineups,

All's well that ends well, sort of. We played a friendly game with Granada Veterans, mixing our teams. They dressed numerous older players for this encounter and Alan Cook (right) presented a pennant to their side. We also gave them our jerseys.

merging the two teams. Only in this way could we enjoy a relatively even contest.

My bleeding toes were sore, and my knees were burning from the cuts I had accumulated from the artificial fields. I decided it would be better to go and take photographs or volunteer to referee. Fidel and Tony Arimare also decided not to play. We were soccer-sated.

At six in the evening, La Chana was still stifling hot. We were merely seeking a convivial run together, not a memorable battle. We mixed the blue and white jerseys, then started the game. As visitors, we could no longer hope to snatch victory from the proverbial jaws of defeat, but we could re-invent the parameters and salvage our dignity, teaching both teams a lesson.

Everyone on the sidelines immediately noted how pleasing it was to watch the ebb and flow, as with a tennis match. Instead of playing in constant panic, always under siege, our players were able to integrate themselves into the game, enjoying three times more touches on the ball than in the preceding contests.

Hans made a ceremonial appearance, just to tell himself he had played in the final game. When he hobbled after one ball and failed to reach it before it went out of bounds, we all winced to witness his pain. After about one minute on the field, he had to remove himself, but Kyle had been able to take a few photos of his dad in action. When he returned to the bench, Hans quipped, "Now I have the best plus–minus on the team." Having been victimized by an own goal in an earlier game, Ken Falk was already boasting that he was our team's top scorer.

We were all coming back down to earth, and it was a good place to be. Kyle asked me to toss him a water bottle, and I obliged, noting, "I started off as the coach, and I've ended up as the waterboy."

The tone of this scrimmage was markedly different. While we didn't expect Miguel to feel contrite about having taken advantage of us, we were pleased to note that this time he had managed to recruit some older players to his roster. Only a few of the young bucks from that first encounter had returned. By the time one of the Spaniards finally scored for the blue team prior to halftime, everybody understood there was no reason to keep score. The Spanish guys, their expectations now realigned, seemed to enjoy the novelty of the encounter too.

Among the participants in the first half was a much older man wearing a red bandana. He hadn't played in the first game – we would have noticed. Even though he was not able to run fast and now avoided physical contact, obviously this man had once possessed great talent. He played much like Bill Allen, our eldest player in the Sunday-morning kick-arounds at Trafalgar School. He had an uncanny ability to find open spaces, and he seldom failed to make a constructive pass. The wisdom of his touches on the ball obviously rose from many years of confidence.

This, it turned out, was Pedro Fernández. He had played seventeen years in La Liga, the Spanish First Division, primarily for Barcelona. Born in Paraguay, he had played for Paraguay's national team and later served as Paraguay's national coach. He had played soccer around the globe, including a joint exhibition tour of North America with Juventus and Barcelona.

At halftime, as Fernández was packing his gear to leave, I approached him with Tony Arimare. Sure enough, Pedro remembered playing soccer in Medellín, the hometown of Tony's wife. Although he looked stern, he obviously liked to joke and grin. I gave him my blood-stained Canadian jersey, and he was pleased. "No vino," he laughed, pointing at the red smudges, "sangre."

We hastily took one photo of the white-skinned Canadian alongside the dark-skinned Granada Veteran, holding up the Canadian jersey. We asked his age. He was seventy. I called over Trevor Heaver, and I took a photo of the two most senior players together. Tony explained that I was an escritor, a

After I gave my blood-stained Canada jersey to former Barcelona star Pablo Fernández, he gave me his jersey for his last professional team, Granada.

writer, and I was writing a book about our adventure. When I promised to send Pedro a copy, he gladly wrote down his address. He told us he was currently living in Granada and working as a talent scout who helped groom younger players.

At that point Pedro looked across the field at eleven-year-old Tonko, who was having a run for the team wearing the Granada jerseys. Who was that boy? After only a few touches on the ball, Tonko had revealed himself as someone with potential. Tony explained that Tonko was a Canadian with Croatian-born parents. The old player put his index finger up to the side of his eye and nodded, telling us that he believed Tonko was special.

Having seen our first encounter from the sidelines, Pedro had presumed Tony must have played professionally, and

Tony was flattered, delighted to tell Pedro that, no, he was only an amateur. My reward at the end of our tribulations was equally unexpected. Whereas only a few of the Granada Veterans would offer to trade their jerseys after the game, Pedro invited me to follow him to his bag, where he pulled out a red-and-white-striped Granada jersey, with his name and the number 35 on the back. He pointed to the crest sewn onto the front, indicating it was not a store-bought copy. This was not a blue Granada Veterans jersey; it was his personal jersey for his last professional team, Granada. The pale-skinned *escritor* and the genuine soccer star posed for another ceremonial photo. As much as I was moved by his generosity, I was equally pleased to reidentify myself as a writer.

I took a hurried photo of Tonko and Pedro Fernández, when the older man made a point of going over to Tonko to encourage him and to assess his character. Separated by fifty-nine years, but united by their equal passion for soccer, they stood side by side, with similar expressions, like stoic warriors. For the Bacelics, it would be a keepsake for the ages. Pedro might like to have a copy too. And I had his address. Somewhere in middle age, I had been transformed into a playmaker, not a scorer, and I could see a play developing, an important off-the-field play, and I would make the appropriate passes.

Their referee left at halftime, so I took over. I shook hands with Pedro Fernández and blew the whistle to commence the second half. The Blues scored several times, and I didn't have to call a single foul. The game was uneventful in a comforting way. As I ran about the field, I had my cellphone in my pocket. With about ten minutes to go before full-time, I heard the phone ring. I ignored the game and stood in the centre of the pitch, dazed.

It was Tara calling from Canada. It was a girl.

I was hoping for a girl. I got a girl instead of a goal. We were grandparents.

I could have blown the whistle and let everyone know. It would have made for a merry moment. But I kept it to myself until the game was over. Mysteriously, by the time I walked off the pitch, tears were streaming down my cheeks. Missing that penalty kick in Montefrío meant next to nothing.

We came, we saw, we were conquered, but our resiliency had brought rewards that were as good as any victory. We had used our maturity as a shield against extreme adversity. I had gained enhanced respect for my teammates. I had traded jerseys with a real legend, one of the most enduring Barcelona players, a Paraguayan international. And over the course of a complicated year, I had learned how to outgrow soccer.

If Indigo Taylor Twigg never wants to kick a soccer ball, that will be okay by me.